BILLY WILDER

INTERVIEWS

CONVERSATIONS WITH FILMMAKERS SERIES
PETER BRUNETTE, GENERAL EDITOR

Courtesy of Photofest

BILLY
WILDER
INTERVIEWS

EDITED BY ROBERT HORTON

UNIVERSITY PRESS OF MISSISSIPPI / JACKSON

www.upress.state.ms.us

Library of Congress Cataloging-in-Publication Data

Wilder, Billy, 1906–
    Billy Wilder : interviews / edited by Robert Horton.
        p.   cm.— (Conversations with filmmakers series)
    Includes index.
    ISBN 1-57806-443-0 (cloth : alk. paper)—ISBN 1-57806-444-9 (pbk. : alk. paper)
    1. Wilder, Billy, 1906—Interviews.   2. Motion picture producers and
directors—United States—Interviews.   I. Horton, Robert.   II. Title.   III.
Series.

PN1998.3.W56 A5   2001
791.43'0233'092—dc21   2001046665

British Library Cataloging-in-Publication Data available

CONTENTS

INTRODUCTION

IN THE BEGINNING was the Word, and the Word was sacred to Billy Wilder. The reason Wilder, a successful screenwriter, became a director in the first place was his fury at someone else playing around with his words. Take, for example, the ultra-suave actor Charles Boyer's refusal to play a scene in the Wilder-scripted 1941 film *Hold Back the Dawn,* in which Boyer's character conversed with a cockroach. Despite the scene's importance to character development and structural unity, it was simply dropped when the actor balked at such an undignified idea. (Wilder had a screenwriter's revenge: he rewrote the rest of the picture to favor Boyer's co-star, Olivia de Havilland, who ended up with an Oscar nomination for her performance.) Never again, vowed Billy Wilder, and one of the greatest directing careers in the history of Hollywood was launched.

With Wilder renowned as a director who insisted his scripts be spoken *exactly as written*—no on-the-spot improvisations or Method actor mumbling—it should come as no surprise that the man emerges in interviews as a fountain of penetrating, droll, well-chosen words. During (and after) his half-century-long career, Wilder became known as a surefire interview subject, a wit who could be counted on to say something blunt, learned, or simply naughty. After having directed just his fourth picture, he mischievously told the *New York Times* that if *To Have and Have Not* had established Lauren Bacall as "The Look," then Wilder's new film—the somber, daringly adult alcoholism drama *The Lost Weekend*—would surely bring Ray Milland acclaim as "The Kidney." The *Times* reporter delightedly noted the pained expression on the face of the studio publicist sitting nearby.

In the interviews collected here, the reader will find the celebrated Billy Wilder one-liners. France, Wilder opined, is a country where "the money falls apart in your hands and you can't tear the toilet paper." Ernst Lubitsch, Wilder's great model for moviemaking, "could do more with a closed door than most of today's directors can do with an open fly." On the set of *Sunset Boulevard*, when his cinematographer asked how they were planning to shoot the morbid scene in which faded movie queen Norma Desmond buries her deceased chimpanzee, Wilder replied, "Oh, the usual monkey funeral sequence." As for the value of winning Oscars—and he has personally won six—Wilder suggested the practical benefits: "The dentist looks down. 'That's an Oscar-winner in the chair,' he says to himself. Maybe he's a little more careful with the drill."

Aside from the parade of bon mots, and Wilder's talent as an entertaining raconteur, these interviews provide a surfeit of filmmaking know-how and a delicious whiff of old-Hollywood atmosphere. Unlike his reticent American contemporaries from the golden age of Hollywood, John Ford and Howard Hawks (who could be induced into serious examination of their films only by dragging them kicking and screaming—if then), Wilder loves to talk. He clearly uses anecdotes to entertain and to deflect pretentious oratory about The Meaning of His Films, but he's happy to reveal the origins of his ideas, his methods with writing partners and actors, and the importance of structure in screenwriting.

The reader will learn about Wilder's life in the various profiles collected here. (Some information, and some of Wilder's anecdotes, are repeated, but it is the policy of this series of books to retain the original integrity of the articles as they first appeared—and the way Wilder's best stories change shape over the years can be revealing.) After fleeing Europe and the onslaught of the Nazis in the early 1930s, Wilder became one of Hollywood's top screenwriters within a decade. He taught himself English by listening to the radio (thus the appetite for slang in Wilder's films), and always worked with a screenwriting partner, alleging his insecurity as a nonnative English speaker.

Billy Wilder's personality is clearly in full bloom in Lincoln Barnett's 1944 *Life* magazine profile, "The Happiest Couple in Hollywood." It may be difficult to believe, in this age of Hydra-headed media, but there was a time when a single article in a major magazine could define a cultural moment (for instance, *Life*'s 1949 photo spread on Jackson Pollock). "The Happiest Couple in Hollywood" defined Wilder for years thereafter as a feisty, wisecracking, cane-brandishing imp.

Aside from its pleasures as a prime example of a particular era in journalism, "The Happiest Couple" also gives voice to one of the key people in Wilder's career. Charles Brackett (1892–1969), who played the classy blueblood to Wilder's self-made immigrant, was Wilder's writing partner from 1938 to 1950; when Wilder began to direct their films, Brackett produced them. The phrase "Brackettandwilder" became a Hollywood brand before people started talking about brands, a synonym for bold, witty, and invariably popular American films.

The relationship was volatile (Brackett recoiled from producing the sordid subject matter of *Double Indemnity*), and was ended by Wilder after the partners tussled over *Sunset Boulevard*. Only later in his life would Wilder openly describe the break-up, likening it to a worn-out matchbook that can no longer strike a spark. (Considering the intense significance of striking matches and lighting cigarettes in *Double Indemnity*, especially in Fred MacMurray and Edward G. Robinson's "love story between two men," this is an interesting image for Wilder to use.) In a 1950 interview with the *Los Angeles Times*, however, Wilder claims that Paramount Pictures separated the "happiest couple," in order to squeeze more films from each of them. "I sure miss him," Wilder sighs of his erstwhile partner, and perhaps he did; but the story is a fabrication worthy of Paramount's Public Relations office.

It is fitting that Wilder's other major writing collaborator also has a voice in these pages. I. A. L. Diamond, Europe-born like Wilder, began writing with Wilder on *Love in the Afternoon* in 1957, and with *Some Like It Hot* two years later became his permanent coauthor. They were still meeting and hashing through script ideas (Diamond at the typewriter, Wilder pacing the room) until Diamond's death in 1988. In a 1976 "Dialogue on Film" staged by the American Film Institute, Diamond speaks up, and shows that his voice was every bit as observant and sardonic as the more famous director's.

The Billy Wilder voice—filtered through his thick Germanic accent—is barbed and restless. It can be heard at the peak of its powers in Richard Gehman's 1960 profile, "Charming Billy," from *Playboy*. Early in the article an L.A. crony suggests that Wilder is "the most unusual and amusing man in Hollywood," and the remainder of the piece provides ample evidence for the charge. The caustic observations fly, and a portrait of Wilder and his good-humored wife Audrey emerges; the Wilder apartment is seen as a civilized oasis amidst garish Beverly Hills mansions, and Wilder's extensive art collection hovers around him, silent evidence of the director's obsession with collecting beautiful moments. Within this profile of Wilder riding high, the director imparts his filmmaking savvy. As a screenwriter, Billy Wilder's career provides the snappiest wordplay heard on screen between the golden era of Preston Sturges and the emergence of the Coen brothers, and yet his greatest strength is his grasp of structure (and its paramount importance in storytelling). It may come as a surprise, then, to hear his assertion that his screenplays were rarely completed when shooting had begun. Both *Sabrina* and *The Apartment,* he reveals, were finished by writing the dialogue for the next day's scenes the night before.

Here and elsewhere, Wilder speaks about the visual approach to his films, his abhorrence of "style" for its own sake. Describing an assistant who suggested an overhead shot in *Sunset Boulevard,* Wilder explains why he killed the idea. "It is very nice, very artistic, but who sees the scene from this angle? . . . It does not push the story along. We shoot only from the angles that help us tell the story. When somebody turns to his neighbor and says, 'My, that was beautifully directed,' we have proof it was not."

Another topic Wilder returns to in various interviews is his economy on the set. Many films are assembled by shooting each scene from as many different angles as possible and then choosing the best moments in the editing room, but Wilder shot exactly what he knew he needed. He also kept his longtime editor, Doane Harrison, on the set with him during shooting (a very unusual practice in Hollywood), the better to decide how it would all fit together. His credo in the editing room was "When I am finished, there is nothing left on the cutting-room floor but cigarette butts, chewing gum wrappers, and tears." His approach had less to do with a mania for saving the studio money ("Nobody is going to go and see a picture because it came in under budget") than with Wilder's ability to see the finished film in his mind before shooting.

For more on Wilder's methods on the set, we have interviews from far-flung locations. (Wilder loved his adopted country, but he certainly found reasons for returning to shoot in Europe on a regular basis. "It might come from a deep desire to come back here from time to time," he tells Michel Ciment in Rome, "a change of diet, to see the place I came from.") A 1956 *Newsweek* piece finds him in Paris with Audrey Hepburn and Gary Cooper, for the filming of *Love in the Afternoon,* a luscious movie that has all the bright romance of the Lubitsch tradition—yet is laced with the acidic tang of pure distilled Wilder. (The romance is between a detective's daughter and an aging gigolo.) The shooting of a simple sequence between the two stars provides evidence of Wilder's close attention to every detail of a scene.

The *New York Times* trails along to Berlin in 1961, where Wilder is shooting *One, Two, Three*, a topical comedy of the Cold War so frenetic it drove leading man James Cagney out of acting for twenty years. Typically for Wilder, he cheekily shot his satire of East-West anxieties in the shadow of the Berlin Wall. The city had special meaning for him, having been the cradle of his early experiences in journalism and screenwriting. Wilder's charged feelings for the city (and his sweet-sour attitude in general) would find no more exact expression than the montages from *A Foreign Affair* in which bombed-out Berlin cityscapes are accompanied by the pretty tune, "Isn't it Romantic?"

Mark Shivas visited the set of *The Private Life of Sherlock Holmes* outside London in 1969, where Wilder was mounting his most ambitious (and probably most deeply romantic) production. Sixty-three years old at the time, Wilder is obviously reveling in the realization of a long-cherished project; earlier in the decade, he envisioned the film with Peter O'Toole and Peter Sellers as Holmes and Watson, although *Private Life* ended up starring the lesser-known but letter-perfect Robert Stephens and Colin Blakely. "This film isn't camp," says Wilder from the set. "It's a valentine to Sherlock." That attitude results in the film's wonderful blend of comedy and melancholy, but this may be precisely why it flopped with audiences. Unfortunately, Wilder was ahead of the curve; a full-scale revival of all things Holmesian would commence in the nostalgia-crazed 1970s, too late to save the movie.

During those nostalgic seventies, hot on the heels of the smash hit *The Sting*, Wilder indulged in a bit of nostalgia himself: a remake of the stage classic *The Front Page*, heavy with period kitsch. From the set of *The Front Page*, Joseph McBride provides another portrait of the director overseeing the tiniest details of production. Working with Jack Lemmon and Walter Matthau (as he had earlier in *The Fortune Cookie* and would later in *Buddy Buddy*), Wilder gives the veteran performers close instruction in the proper deployment of farce—including a primer for Matthau on how to tear out a telephone cord in two specific motions.

By that time, Wilder was clearly looking for a box office success, having passed through a dry spell—which probably accounts for *The Front Page's* packaged, calculated quality. ("That was a big mistake," he tells interviewer

Burt Prelutsky. ("Never do a remake.") Until the late 1960s, he displayed an
uncanny knack for knowing what audiences wanted—and for knowing how
far he could push them. In more than one interview collected here, Wilder
tells the stories behind his efforts to bring adulthood to movies in the 1940s.
John Allyn does an entire interview devoted to *Double Indemnity*, a film that
originally ended with what must have been a shocking sequence inside a
death row gas chamber. Wilder explains why he eventually cut the scene, as
it was no longer necessary in the film's resolution.

The Lost Weekend, which shoved the horror of alcoholism (complete with
surrealistic d.t.s) into the audience's face, was laughed off the screen at early
previews, until Wilder tinkered with his final cut. *Sunset Boulevard*, a movie
narrated by a corpse, originally began with a sequence inside the L.A. County
morgue; Wilder clearly relishes describing the macabre scene, in which William Holden's recently deceased character sits up amongst the other stiffs
and begins sharing his woeful tale. (Giggling preview audiences nixed this
idea, too.) All of these films were hits, but Wilder pushed his luck with *Ace in
the Hole* (quickly re-titled *The Big Carnival*), a movie so corrosive that the
word "cynical" became permanently attached to Wilder's name. It should
have come as no surprise. *Sunset Boulevard* is an American movie masterpiece,
but despite the official-classic status it now enjoys (and its mutation into an
Andrew Lloyd Webber stage extravaganza), it is no less rancid in its bones
than *Ace in the Hole*.

The reader will find an interesting tendency in Wilder's discussions of
these hits and flops. He is refreshingly honest about some of his lesser
achievements, even if they found box office success. Of *The Seven Year Itch*, a
moneymaker that contributed the image of Marilyn Monroe's blown-up skirt
to popular iconography, Wilder grouses to the American Film Institute that
censorship problems constricted his vision: "It was a nothing picture. . . . It
just didn't come off one bit, and there's nothing I can say about it except I
wish I hadn't made it." As for *Irma La Douce,* an enormous smash in 1963
(and oddly forgotten today), Wilder tells Prelutsky, "Yes, it was a huge hit.
But I'm not sure why. . . . It's nothing to be ashamed of, but it's not a movie
I think about too much." "If I had my way, I'd re-shoot ninety-five percent
of that thing," he says elsewhere.

As for the flops, Wilder treats them with a blend of amnesia and defiance.
"We in Hollywood do not bury our dead," he says in a *Saturday Evening Post*
interview. "They continue to stink. They will stink next week in Cincinnati

and in London and in Paris, and two years from now they will stink on television." Having said that, the director insists he can simply put the past behind. "I have the capacity for erasing it from my mind," he says of failure. "I just don't think about it anymore. It's down the drain, across the river, and into the trees." Although he forcefully disowns the box office failures in his career, Wilder can be cornered by a dogged interviewer into admitting that some of them are among his favorite children. Reading carefully through the interviews, one eventually realizes that once-dismissed titles such as *Ace in the Hole* and *The Private Life of Sherlock Holmes* and *Kiss Me, Stupid* have a special spot in their maker's sweet-and-sour heart.

The debacle of *Kiss Me, Stupid* is described in Richard Lemon's lengthy *Post* profile from 1966, when Wilder was still licking his wounds from the trashing the film received from critics and custodians of public decency. *Kiss Me, Stupid* is actually one of the more interesting American films of the 1960s, and ripe for re-appreciation, but Wilder's sex comedy was slightly ahead of its zeitgeist. The production itself was unlucky: star Peter Sellers was felled by a heart attack a few weeks into shooting, and his role hastily re-cast with Ray Walston, a far cry from Sellers's wild comic genius. "The movie was a dog," Wilder briskly tells Burt Prelutsky. "With Sellers it would have been five percent better. So it would only have been 95% of a bomb." When Joseph McBride and Todd McCarthy express admiration for *Kiss Me, Stupid,* Wilder rises to the occasion, insisting he "thought it was very romantic. I'd like to do it again to show them what the thing was all about."

Avanti! is another Wilder "flop" that has aged beautifully, but Wilder is clearly nagged by its failure to reach audiences. "Too mild, too soft, too gentle," he tells the AFI. "The picture was fifteen years too late, if it should have been done at all." But Wilder's gruff reassessment of the film contrasts with his comments on *Avanti!* to Michel Ciment, conducted before the film's release. In 1972, Wilder still seems to be basking in the romantic glow of the film, singing the praises of the little-known leading lady he found for the picture (Juliet Mills, who is pronounced "miraculous" and "perfect") and being unusually honest about his identity as an artist. In many interviews over the years Wilder tweaks the powerful critics of the era (including Pauline Kael and Andrew Sarris), often with justification. To Ciment, in discussing the roles of director and critic, he says, "That's the role of the serious critic, the analyst, to find in the artist's work things about which he is not conscious. Because if I was, I could no longer work the same way. I can't analyze, that's your job! Mine is to make. I'm there with my palette and brush, or piano or camera. I do my best, how I feel about things and how I think things ought to be. But if I become analytical at that point, I would only produce a dead thing. If one motif reappears, if a theme recurs here and there, I'm not aware of it, believe me. . . . you have the style you're born with, more or less."

Wilder touches on the artist-entertainer split in a 1970 interview published in *Action* magazine. (Since the title of this piece, "Broadcast to Kuala Lumpur," sounds vaguely like a joke from a Preston Sturges movie, some explanation is in order: the interview was originally a Voice of America radio broadcast, conducted for a film festival in Kuala Lumpur, Malaysia. As far as I can tell, interviewer Vanessa Brown is also the actress who originated, on Broadway, the role later played by Marilyn Monroe in Wilder's film of *The Seven Year Itch*.) "I have never made a picture which was a lecture," he tells the Malaysian Wilder fans. "I try to make pictures for entertainment. . . . On the other hand, I don't want to make pictures absolutely flat and without any meaning. Whatever meaning you will find in my pictures, it's all put in kind of contraband, you know—sort of smuggled in a kind of message of, I hope, decency, of liberal thinking, whatever you want to call it, or something biting, something satirical, something poking fun at our way of life."

Clearly, this is an approach that clicked with audiences for many years. In 1961, Kael could write the sentence, "In Hollywood it is now common to hear Billy Wilder called the world's greatest director." Kael herself did not concur with this opinion, nor did her critical rival Andrew Sarris, who relegated Wilder to the "Less Than Meets the Eye" category in his epochal book *The American Cinema*. To his everlasting credit, Sarris eventually came to champion Wilder, recognizing that the romanticist in Wilder was inextricably intertwined with the cynic. (In his delightful book-length interview with Wilder, the director Cameron Crowe coins the term "happy-sad" to convey Wilder's tangy blend of irony and beauty.)

After hitting that high-water mark in the early 1960s, the rockiness of Wilder's later career increased the amount of kvetching in his interviews. Because it's Wilder, of course, the quality of the kvetching is twenty-four carat. A scintillating example is Jon Bradshaw's zesty 1975 interview for *New York* magazine. Bradshaw finds the sixty-nine-year-old director in his office at Universal, cracking the air with a swagger stick as he paces the room: "What did you expect to find when you came out here. . . . A wizened, myopic boob in his dotage? . . . I guess you thought you'd find me playing with my old Oscars?" Wilder doesn't let up from there, blistering the walls with his opinions of audiences, critics, and studio executives. "It's no wonder they say Wilder is out of touch with the times," the embattled director declares. "Who the hell wants to be in touch with *these* times?"

The bumpy saga of Wilder's penultimate film, *Fedora*, is told in the McBride-McCarthy interview for *Film Comment*. That interview quickly turns into a wide-ranging exploration of his career, and also a keen assessment of what happened to the audience during the previous decades of moviegoing. While acknowledging that a layer of educated film buffs has emerged, Wilder also sees the other end: a "big mass of people that have been spoiled by, wrecked by, television. . . . They've seen every plot, they know every plot. . . . the mezzo-brow audience is falling away. It's the high-brow or it's the low-est." That dilemma continues to vex ambitious filmmakers today.

Reluctantly, Wilder made the transition from an active participant in Hollywood to a revered elder statesman. The industry began draping its various lifetime achievement awards around his brow, sometimes to the irritation of the honoree, who clearly would've preferred making movies. Still, the fin-de-siècle Wilder has had an impressive run for a man who has not made movies in twenty years. He remained a fine interview subject, four of his films made the AFI's list of 100 greatest American films, and he sold much of his art collection for over $30 million in 1989—and that was when $30 million was a lot of money. The musical of *Sunset Boulevard* kept him in view, as did the Harrison Ford–Sydney Pollack remake of *Sabrina* in 1994.

He had an especially good run at the Oscars. Voted the Irving G. Thalberg award winner in 1987, Wilder gave a beguiling speech consisting almost entirely of a long anecdote about being detained in Mexico while trying to reestablish residency in the U.S. in the 1930s. At the 1993 ceremony, best Foreign Language Film winner Fernando Trueba got to the podium and declared, "I would like to believe in God in order to thank Him. But I just believe in Billy Wilder, so thank you, Mr. Wilder." As Wilder tells Saul Bass in a *Sight and Sound* interview included here, "I was just mixing myself a Martini and I heard it on the television. The bottle of gin falls out of my hand. . . . Put me in the class of D. W. Griffith or Murnau, but God?"

Wilder may have been mixing himself another drink when Sam Mendes won the directing Oscar for 1999's *American Beauty*. Mendes, too, invoked Billy Wilder in his acceptance speech, and he had even better reason than

Trueba: *American Beauty* is a close spiritual cousin of Wilder's *The Apartment,* a connection made explicit by Kevin Spacey, who acknowledged basing his performance on Jack Lemmon's work in the Wilder film. In March 2001 Cameron Crowe won the best original screenplay award for *Almost Famous,* and ended his speech with a tribute to Wilder as "the master."

Wilder's voice in interviews is finally the same as his voice in his films. Gin and vermouth, side by side, are what make a Martini; although, as Wilder adds in these pages, "I like to mix a little vinegar in the cocktail." His war movies are comedies, his romances contain suicide attempts, his crowning achievement in comedy (possibly the American sound film's crowning achievement in comedy) begins with the St. Valentine's Day Massacre. He has made film classics narrated by the dead *(Sunset Boulevard)* and the dying *(Double Indemnity).* The closest he has come to even obliquely referring to the Holocaust—which claimed his mother—in a film was in the insipid comedy of *The Emperor Waltz,* the plot of which concerns the mating of dogs in the Austro-Hungarian empire. He showers satirical darts on conventional heroes, but prostitutes bring out his gallant sympathy. And his endings are masterpieces. They sometimes connect love and death *(Five Graves to Cairo, The Private Life of Sherlock Holmes,* and *Double Indemnity),* or confront the audience with utter dementia and failure *(Sunset Boulevard* and *Ace in the Hole).* When *Some Like it Hot* decides that "Nobody's perfect," it is the consummate rounding-off of an elaborate scenario, but as David Thomson has observed, it also kicks the movie into some new realm of imagined, delirious offscreen reality. What other movie leaves us so curious about "what happens next"?

The ending, then, we leave to Billy Wilder. In a 1963 *"Playboy* Interview," unavailable for anthologizing, Wilder tells of living in a Berlin rooming house while trying to break into the movies. His room was next to the communal bathroom, and the broken toilet dripped all through the night. To relieve the miserable monotony, the young Wilder would imagine the sound of this leaky toilet as a beautiful waterfall. Twenty-five years later, he found himself taking the cure at a ritzy Austrian spa, the location of a magnificent waterfall. "There I am in bed," says Wilder, "listening to the waterfall. And after all I have been through, all the trouble and all the money I've made, all the awards and everything else, there I am in that resort, and all I can think of is that goddamned toilet. That, like the man says, is the story of my life."

The author would like to thank a few people who gave assistance above and beyond the call of duty in assembling this book. A free treatment of the Re-Vigora System to: Rosanne Conroy, Bridgett Chandler for translating the *Positif* interview, Carolyn Pfeiffer and Joseph McBride and Burt Prelutsky for their particularly gracious generosity, Nancy Locke, David Gaynes, Jim Emerson, the Directors Guild of America, Peter Brunette for extending the invitation, and as always to Kathleen Murphy and Richard T. Jameson. Permesso? Avanti!

CHRONOLOGY

1906   Born Samuel Wilder on June 22, in Sucha Beskidzka, Galicia (part of the Austro-Hungarian empire, now Poland), to Max and Eugenia Wilder.

1925   Begins career as a reporter in Vienna.

1929   First screen credit for "Billie Wilder": as screenwriter on *Die Teufelsreporter: Im Nebel der Grossstadt*. Collaborates on script for landmark Berlin film *Menschen am Sonntag*.

1933   Leaves Berlin and successful screenwriting career in the face of Nazi rise. In Paris, makes directing debut as co-director of *Mauvaise Graine*.

1934   Leaves Paris for Hollywood.

1938   Teamed at Paramount Pictures with screenwriting partner Charles Brackett. They write *Bluebeard's Eighth Wife* for director Ernst Lubitsch.

1939   Oscar nomination for co-writing *Ninotchka*, directed by Lubitsch.

1941   Oscar nominations for co-writing *Hold Back the Dawn*, directed by Mitchell Leisen, and for co-story on *Ball of Fire*, directed by Howard Hawks.

1942   Hollywood directing debut with *The Major and the Minor*.

1943   Release of *Five Graves to Cairo*.

1944   *Double Indemnity*. Oscar nomination for directing, screenplay.

1945 *The Lost Weekend.* Oscars for director and screenplay. The film wins best picture and actor (Ray Milland).

1948 *The Emperor Waltz* and *A Foreign Affair* (Oscar nomination for screenplay) released.

1950 *Sunset Boulevard.* Oscar for screenplay, nomination for director. Wilder and Brackett end partnership.

1951 *Ace in the Hole (The Big Carnival),* Wilder's first flop. Oscar nomination for screenplay.

1953 *Stalag 17.* Oscar nomination for director. William Holden wins for best actor.

1954 *Sabrina.* Oscar nominations for director, screenplay.

1955 *The Seven Year Itch.*

1957 *The Spirit of St. Louis, Love in the Afternoon* (first writing collaboration with I. A. L. Diamond), *Witness for the Prosecution* (Oscar nomination for directing).

1959 *Some Like it Hot.* Oscar nominations for director, screenplay.

1960 *The Apartment.* Oscars for picture, director, screenplay (Wilder becomes first person to win three Oscars in a single night).

1961 *One, Two, Three.*

1963 *Irma La Douce,* Wilder's biggest financial success.

1964 *Kiss Me, Stupid* attacked by critics and Catholic Legion of Decency.

1966 *The Fortune Cookie,* first teaming of Jack Lemmon and Walter Matthau (Oscar to Matthau). Oscar nomination for screenplay.

1970 *The Private Life of Sherlock Holmes* is drastically cut before release, fails to find an audience.

1972 *Avanti!*

1974 *The Front Page.*

1978 *Fedora.*

1981   *Buddy Buddy,* final film of Wilder's directing career.

1983   Film Society of Lincoln Center tribute.

1987   American Film Institute Lifetime Achievement Award.

1988   Presented Irving G. Thalberg award at Academy Awards ceremony.

1989   Sells part of large art collection; revenues exceed $32 million.

1990   Kennedy Center honors.

1996   As a ninetieth birthday tribute, Wilder's home town in Poland creates Ulica Billy Wildera (Billy Wilder Street) in honor of its native son.

1998   Four Wilder films make the American Film Institute's list of 100 greatest American movies: *Sunset Boulevard* (#12), *Some Like it Hot* (#14), *Double Indemnity* (#38), and *The Apartment* (#93).

FILMOGRAPHY

1933
MAUVAISE GRAINE
Pathé Consortium Cinéma
Producer: Georges Bernier
Director: Alexander Esway, **Billy Wilder**
Screenplay: Max Kolpé, Hans G. Lustig, Claude-André Puget, **Billy Wilder**
Cinematography: Paul Cotteret, Maurice Delattre
Music: Allan Gray, Franz Wachsmann (later Franz Waxman)
Cast: Danielle Darrieux (Jeanette), Pierre Mingand (Henri Pasquier), Raymond Galle (Jean la Cravate), Paul Escoffier (Dr. Pasquier), Michel Duran (The Boss), Jean Wall (Zebra), Marcel Maupi (Man in Panama hat), Paul Velsa (Man with peanuts), Georges Malkine (Secretary), Georges Cahuzac (Sir), Gaby Héritier (Gaby)
35 mm, black and white
77 minutes

1942
THE MAJOR AND THE MINOR
Paramount Pictures
Producer: Arthur Hornblow, Jr.
Director: **Billy Wilder**
Screenplay: Charles Brackett and **Billy Wilder**, based on the story "Sunny Goes Home," by Fanny Kilbourne, and the play *Connie Goes Home* by Edward Childs Carpenter

Cinematography: Leo Tover
Production Design: Roland Anderson and Hans Dreier
Music: Robert Emmett Dolan
Editing: Doane Harrison
Cast: Ginger Rogers (Susan Applegate), Ray Milland (Major Philip Kirby), Rita Johnson (Pamela Hill), Robert Benchley (Mr. Osborne), Diana Lynn (Lucy Hill), Edward Fielding (Colonel Hill), Frankie Thomas (Cadet Osborne), Raymond Roe (Cadet Wigton), Charles Smith (Cadet Korner), Larry Nunn (Cadet Babcock), Billy Dawson (Cadet Miller), Lela E. Rogers (Mrs. Applegate), Aldrich Bowker (Reverend Doyle), Boyd Irwin (Major Griscom), Byron Shores (Captain Durand), Richard Fiske (Will Duffy), Norma Varden (Mrs. Osborne), Gretl Dupont (Miss Shackleford), Roland Kibbee (Station Agent), Ken Lundy (elevator boy)
35 mm, black and white
100 minutes

1943
FIVE GRAVES TO CAIRO
Paramount Pictures
Producer: Charles Brackett
Director: **Billy Wilder**
Screenplay: Charles Brackett and **Billy Wilder**, based on the play *Hotel Imperial* by Lajos Biró
Cinematography: John F. Seitz
Production Design: Hans Dreier and Ernst Fegté
Editing: Doane Harrison
Music: Miklós Rózsa
Cast: Franchot Tone (Corporal John J. Bramble), Anne Baxter (Mouche), Erich von Stroheim (Field Marshal Erwin Rommel), Akim Tamiroff (Farid), Fortunio Bonanova (General Sebastiano), Peter van Eyck (Lieutenant Schwegler), Konstantin Shayne (Major von Buelow), Fred Nurney (Major Lamprecht), Miles Mander (Colonel Fitzhume), Ian Keith (Captain St. Bride)
35 mm, black and white
96 minutes

1944
DOUBLE INDEMNITY
Paramount Pictures

Producer: Joseph Sistrom (associate), B. G. DeSylva (executive)
Director: **Billy Wilder**
Screenplay: Raymond Chandler and **Billy Wilder**, based on the novel by
James M. Cain
Cinematography: John F. Seitz
Production Design: Hans Dreier and Hal Periera
Editing: Doane Harrison
Music: Miklós Rózsa
Cast: Fred MacMurray (Walter Neff), Barbara Stanwyck (Phyllis Dietrichson),
Edward G. Robinson (Barton Keyes), Porter Hall (Mr. Jackson), Jean Heather
(Lola Dietrichson), Tom Powers (Mr. Dietrichson), Byron Barr (Nino
Zachetti), Richard Gaines (Edward S. Norton), Fortunio Bonanova (Sam Gar-
lopis), John Philliber (Joe Peters), Bess Flowers (Norton's secretary), Betty Far-
rington (Nettie, the maid), Sam McDaniel (Charlie)
35 mm, black and white
107 minutes

1945
THE LOST WEEKEND
Paramount Pictures
Producer: Charles Brackett
Director: **Billy Wilder**
Screenplay: Charles Brackett and **Billy Wilder**, based on the novel by Charles
R. Jackson
Cinematography: John F. Seitz
Production Design: Hans Dreier and A. Earl Hedrick
Editing: Doane Harrison
Music: Miklós Rózsa
Cast: Ray Milland (Don Birnam), Jane Wyman (Helen St. James), Phillip
Terry (Wick Birnam), Howard Da Silva (Nat the bartender), Doris Dowling
(Gloria), Frank Faylen ('Bim' Nolan, the nurse), Mary Young (Mrs. Dever-
idge), Anita Sharp-Bolster (Mrs. Foley, cleaning lady), Lillian Fontaine (Mrs.
St. James), Frank Orth (opera attendant), Lewis L. Russell (Mr. St. James),
Clarence Muse, Fred Toones (washroom attendants)
35 mm, black and white
101 minutes

1948
THE EMPEROR WALTZ
Paramount Pictures
Producer: Charles Brackett
Director: **Billy Wilder**
Screenplay: Charles Brackett and **Billy Wilder**
Cinematography: George Barnes
Production Design: Hans Dreier and Franz Bachelin
Editing: Doane Harrison
Music: Johnny Burke and Victor Young
Cast: Bing Crosby (Virgil Smith), Joan Fontaine (Johanna Augusta Franziska von Stoltzenberg-Stoltzenberg), Roland Culver (Baron Holenia), Lucile Watson (Princess Bitotska), Richard Haydn (Emperor Franz-Josef), Harold Vermilyea (Chamberlain), Sig Ruman (Dr. Zwieback), Julia Dean (Archduchess Stephanie), Bert Prival (chauffeur), Alma Macrorie (inn owner), Roberta Jonay (chambermaid), John Goldsworthy (Obersthofmeister), Doris Dowling (Tyrolean girl)
35 mm, Technicolor
106 minutes

A FOREIGN AFFAIR
Paramount Pictures
Producer: Charles Brackett
Director: **Billy Wilder**
Screenplay: Charles Brackett, **Billy Wilder,** and Richard L. Breen, from a story by David Shaw and Robert Harari
Cinematography: Charles Lang
Production Design: Hans Dreier and Walter H. Tyler
Editing: Doane Harrison
Music: Frederick Hollander
Cast: Jean Arthur (Phoebe Frost), Marlene Dietrich (Erika von Schluetow), John Lund (Captain John Pringle), Millard Mitchell (Colonel Rufus J. Plummer), Peter von Zerneck (Hans Otto Birgel), Stanley Prager (Mike), William Murphy (Joe), Raymond Bond (Pennecot), Boyd Davis (Giffin), Robert Malcolm (Kramer), Charles Meredith (Yandell), Michael Raffetto (Salvatore), Damian O'Flynn (Lieutenant Colonel), Frank Fenton (Major Mathews), James Larmore (Lieutenant Hornby), Harland Tucker (General McAndrew),

William Neff (Lieutenant Lee Thompson), George M. Carleton (General Fin-
ney), Gordon Jones (first M.P.), Freddie Steele (second M.P.), Bobby Watson
(Hitler)
35 mm, black and white
116 minutes

1950
SUNSET BOULEVARD
Paramount Pictures
Producer: Charles Brackett
Director: **Billy Wilder**
Screenplay: Charles Brackett, **Billy Wilder,** and D. M. Marshman, Jr.
Cinematography: John F. Seitz
Production Design: Hans Dreier
Editing: Doane Harrison and Arthur P. Schmidt
Music: Franz Waxman
Cast: William Holden (Joe Gillis), Gloria Swanson (Norma Desmond), Erich
von Stroheim (Max von Mayerling), Nancy Olson (Betty Schaefer), Cecil B.
DeMille (himself), Fred Clark (Sheldrake), Lloyd Gough (Morino), Jack Webb
(Artie Green), Franklyn Farnum (undertaker), Larry J. Blake (first finance
man), Charles Dayton (second finance man), Hedda Hopper (herself), Buster
Keaton (himself), Anna Q. Nilsson (herself), H. B. Warner (himself), Ray
Evans (himself), Jay Livingston (himself)
35 mm, black and white
110 minutes

1951
ACE IN THE HOLE (THE BIG CARNIVAL)
Paramount Pictures
Producer: **Billy Wilder**
Director: **Billy Wilder**
Screenplay: Walter Newman, Lesser Samuels, and **Billy Wilder**
Cinematography: Charles Lang
Production Design: Hal Pereira and A. Earl Hedrick
Editing: Doane Harrison and Arthur P. Schmidt
Music: Hugo Friedhofer
Cast: Kirk Douglas (Charles Tatum), Jan Sterling (Lorraine), Robert Arthur

(Herbie Cook), Porter Hall (Jacob Q. Boot), Richard Benedict (Leo Minosa), Ray Teal (Sheriff), Gene Evans (Deputy), Frank Cady (Mr. Federber), Frank Jaquet (Smollett), Iron Eyes Cody (copy boy)
35 mm, black and white
III minutes

1953
STALAG 17
Paramount Pictures
Producer: **Billy Wilder**
Director: **Billy Wilder**
Screenplay: **Billy Wilder** and Edwin Blum, based on the play by Donald Bevan and Edmund Trzcinski
Cinematography: Ernest Laszlo
Production Design: Franz Bachelin and Hal Pereira
Editing: Doane Harrison and George Tomasini
Music: Franz Waxman
Cast: William Holden (Sefton), Don Taylor (Lieutenant Dunbar), Otto Preminger (Oberst Von Scherbach), Robert Strauss, (Stosh "Animal" Krusawa), Harvey Lembeck (Harry Shapiro), Richard Erdman (Hoffy), Peter Graves (Price), Neville Brand (Duke), Sig Ruman (Schulz), Michael Moore (Manfredi), Peter Baldwin (Jonson), Robinson Stone (Joey), Robert Shawley (Blondie), William Pierson (Marko), Gil Stratton (Cookie), Jay Lawrence (Bagradian), Erwin Kalser (Geneva Man), Edmund Trzcinski (Triz), Tommy Cook (prisoner)
35 mm, black and white
120 minutes

1954
SABRINA
Paramount Pictures
Producer: **Billy Wilder**
Director: **Billy Wilder**
Screenplay: **Billy Wilder**, Samuel A. Taylor, Ernest Lehman, based on the play *Sabrina Fair* by Samuel A. Taylor
Cinematography: Charles Lang
Production Design: Hal Pereira and Walter H. Tyler

Editing: Arthur P. Schmidt
Music: Frederick Hollander
Cast: Audrey Hepburn (Sabrina Fairchild), Humphrey Bogart (Linus Larrabee), William Holden (David Larrabee), Walter Hampden (Oliver Larrabee), John Williams (Thomas Fairchild), Martha Hyer (Elizabeth Tyson), Joan Vohs (Gretchen Van Horn), Marcel Dalio (Baron St. Fontanel), Marcel Hillaire (the professor), Nella Walker (Maude Larrabee), Francis X. Bushman (Tyson), Ellen Corby (Miss McCardle), Marjorie Bennett (Margaret, the cook), Emory Parnell (Charles, the butler), Nancy Kulp (Jenny, the maid), Paul Harvey (doctor)
35 mm, black and white
114 minutes

1955
THE SEVEN YEAR ITCH
Twentieth Century Fox
Producer: Charles K. Feldman and **Billy Wilder**
Director: **Billy Wilder**
Screenplay: **Billy Wilder** and George Axelrod, based on the play by George Axelrod
Cinematography: Milton Krasner
Production Design: Lyle Wheeler and George W. Davis
Editing: Hugh S. Fowler
Music: Alfred Newman
Cast: Marilyn Monroe (The Girl), Tom Ewell (Richard Sherman), Evelyn Keyes (Helen Sherman), Sonny Tufts (Tom MacKenzie), Robert Strauss (Kruhulik), Oskar Homolka (Dr. Brubaker), Marguerite Chapman (Miss Morris), Victor Moore (plumber), Roxanne (Elaine), Donald MacBride (Mr. Brady), Carolyn Jones (Miss Finch), Butch Bernard (Ricky)
35 mm, color, CinemaScope
105 minutes

1957
THE SPIRIT OF ST. LOUIS
Warner Brothers
Producer: Leland Hayward
Director: **Billy Wilder**

Screenplay: **Billy Wilder**, Wendell Mayes, and Charles Lederer, based on the book by Charles A. Lindbergh
Cinematography: Robert Burks and J. Peverell Marley
Production Design: Art Loel
Editing: Arthur P. Schmidt
Music: Franz Waxman
Cast: James Stewart (Charles Augustus Lindbergh), Murray Hamilton (Bud Gurney), Patricia Smith (Mirror Girl), Bartlett Robinson (B. F. Mahoney), Marc Connelly (Father Hussman), Arthur Space (Donald Hall), Charles Watts (O. W. Schultz), Dabbs Greer (Goldsborough), Robert Cornthwaite (Knight), Robert Burton (Major Lambert), Richard Deacon (Levine)
35 mm, color, CinemaScope
138 minutes

LOVE IN THE AFTERNOON
Allied Artists
Producer: **Billy Wilder**
Director: **Billy Wilder**
Screenplay: **Billy Wilder** and I. A. L. Diamond, based on the novel *Ariane* by Claude Anet
Cinematography: William C. Mellor
Production Design: Alexander Trauner
Editing: Leonide Azar
Music: Franz Waxman
Cast: Gary Cooper (Frank Flannagan), Audrey Hepburn (Ariane Chavasse), Maurice Chevalier (Claude Chavasse), Van Doude (Michel), John McGiver (Monsieur X), Lise Bourdin (Madame X), Bonifas (Commissioner of Police), Alexander Trauner (artist), Audrey Wilder (Brunette)
35 mm, black and white
130 minutes

WITNESS FOR THE PROSECUTION
United Artists
Producer: Arthur Hornblow Jr. and Edward Small
Director: **Billy Wilder**
Screenplay: **Billy Wilder** and Harry Kurnitz, based on the play by Agatha Christie

Cinematography: Russell Harlan
Production Design: Alexander Trauner
Editing: Daniel Mandell
Music: Matty Malneck
Cast: Tyrone Power (Leonard Vole), Marlene Dietrich (Christine Vole), Charles Laughton (Sir Wilfrid Robarts), Elsa Lanchester (Miss Plimsoll), John Williams (Brogan-Moore), Henry Daniell (Mayhew), Ian Wolfe (Carter), Torin Thatcher (Mr. Myers), Norma Varden (Mrs. French), Una O'Connor (Janet McKenzie), Francis Compton (Judge), Philip Tonge (Inspector Hearne), Ruta Lee (Diana), Marjorie Eaton (Miss O'Brien), Ottola Nesmith (Miss Johnson), J. Pat O'Malley (shorts salesman), Molly Roden (Miss McHugh)
35 mm, black and white
116 minutes

1959
SOME LIKE IT HOT
United Artists
Producer: **Billy Wilder**
Director: **Billy Wilder**
Screenplay: **Billy Wilder** and I. A. L. Diamond, based on the film *Fanfaren des Liebe* by M. Logan and Robert Thoeren
Cinematography: Charles Lang
Production Design: Ted Haworth
Editing: Arthur P. Schmidt
Music: Adolph Deutsch
Cast: Marilyn Monroe (Sugar Kane, nee Kowalczyk), Tony Curtis (Joe/Josephine), Jack Lemmon (Jerry/Daphne), Joe E. Brown (Osgood Fielding III), George Raft (Spats Colombo), Pat O'Brien (Mulligan), Nehemiah Persoff (Bonaparte), Joan Shawlee (Sweet Sue), Billy Gray (Sig Poliakoff), George E. Stone (Toothpick Charlie), Dave Barry (Beinstock), Mike Mazurki (Spats's henchman), Harry Wilson (Spats's henchman), Beverly Wills (Dolores), Barbara Drew (Nellie), Edward G. Robinson, Jr. (Paradise), Marian Collier (Olga)
35 mm, black and white
119 minutes

1960
THE APARTMENT
United Artists

Producer: **Billy Wilder**
Director: **Billy Wilder**
Screenplay: **Billy Wilder** and I. A. L. Diamond
Cinematography: Joseph LaShelle
Production Design: Alexander Trauner
Editing: Daniel Mandell
Music: Adolph Deutsch
Cast: Jack Lemmon (C. C. "Bud" Baxter), Shirley MacLaine (Fran Kubelik),
Fred MacMurray (Jeff D. Sheldrake), Ray Walston (Joe Dobisch), Jack
Kruschen (Doctor Dreyfuss), David Lewis (Al Kirkeby), Hope Holiday (Margie
MacDougall), Joan Shawlee (Sylvia), Naomi Stevens (Mrs. Mildred Dreyfuss),
Johnny Seven (Karl Matuschka), Joyce Jameson (The Blonde), Willard Water-
man (Mr. Vanderhof), David White (Mr. Eichelberger), Edie Adams (Miss
Olsen), Benny Burt (bartender), Frances Weintraub Lax (Mrs. Lieberman),
Hal Smith (Santa Claus)
35 mm, black and white
125 minutes

1961
ONE, TWO, THREE
United Artists
Producer: **Billy Wilder**
Director: **Billy Wilder**
Screenplay: **Billy Wilder** and I. A. L. Diamond, based on the play by Ferenc
Molnar
Cinematography: Daniel Fapp
Production Design: Alexander Trauner
Editing: Daniel Mandell
Music: André Previn
Cast: James Cagney (C. R. MacNamara), Horst Buchholz (Otto Ludwig Piffl),
Pamela Tiffin (Scarlett Hazeltine), Arlene Francis (Phyllis MacNamara), How-
ard St. John (Hazeltine), Hanns Lothar (Schlemmer), Leon Askin (Peripetchi-
koff), Ralf Wolter (Borodenko), Karl Lieffen (Fritz), Hubert von Meyerinck
(Count von Droste Schattenburg), Loïs Bolton (Melanie Hazeltine), Peter
Capell (Mishkin), Til Kiwe (reporter), Henning Schlüter (Doctor Bauer), Karl
Ludwig Lindt (Zeidlitz), Liselotte Pulver (Ingeborg), Red Buttons (M.P.),
Christine Allen (Cindy MacNamara), John Allen (Tommy MacNamara)

35 mm, black and white, Panavision
115 minutes

1963
IRMA LA DOUCE
United Artists
Producer: **Billy Wilder**
Director: **Billy Wilder**
Screenplay: **Billy Wilder** and I. A. L. Diamond, from the musical play by
Alexandre Breffort and Marguerite Monnot
Cinematography: Joseph LaShelle
Production Design: Alexander Trauner
Editing: Daniel Mandell
Music: André Previn
Cast: Jack Lemmon (Nestor Patou), Shirley MacLaine (Irma), Lou Jacobi
(Moustache), Bruce Yarnell (Hippolyte), Herschel Bernardi (Inspector Lefe-
vre), Hope Holiday (Lolita), Joan Shawlee (Amazon Annie), Grace Lee Whit-
ney (Kiki the Cossack), Paul Dubov (Andre), Howard McNear (concierge),
Cliff Osmond (police sergeant), Diki Lerner (Jojo), Herb Jones (Casablanca
Charlie), Ruth Earl and Jane Earl (Zebra Twins), Tura Satana (Suzette Wong),
Lou Krugman (first customer), James Brown (customer from Texas), Bill
Bixby (tattooed sailor), James Caan (soldier with radio)
35 mm, color, Panavision
142 minutes

1964
KISS ME, STUPID
Lopert Pictures (United Artists)
Producer: **Billy Wilder**
Director: **Billy Wilder**
Screenplay: **Billy Wilder** and I. A. L. Diamond, based on the play *L'Ora della
Fantasia* by Anna Bonacci
Cinematography: Joseph LaShelle
Production Design: Alexander Trauner
Editing: Daniel Mandell
Music: André Previn (songs by George and Ira Gershwin)
Cast: Dean Martin (Dino), Kim Novak (Polly the Pistol), Ray Walston (Orville

J. Spooner), Felicia Farr (Zelda Spooner), Cliff Osmond (Barney Milsap), Bar-
bara Pepper (Big Bertha), James Ward (milkman), Howard McNear (Mr. Petti-
bone), Doro Merande (Mrs. Pettibone), Bobo Lewis (waitress), Tommy Nolan
(Johnnie Mulligan), Alice Pearce (Mrs. Mulligan), John Fiedler (Reverend
Carruthers), Arlen Stuart (Rosalie Schultz), Cliff Norton (Mack Gray), Mel
Blanc (Dr. Sheldrake), Eileen O'Neal (Showgirl), Susan Wedell (showgirl),
Bernd Hoffmann (barkeeper), Henry Gibson (Smith), Alan Dexter (Wesson),
Henry Beckman (truck driver)
35 mm, black and white, Panavision
124 minutes

1966
THE FORTUNE COOKIE
United Artists
Producer: **Billy Wilder**
Director: **Billy Wilder**
Screenplay: **Billy Wilder** and I. A. L. Diamond
Cinematography: Joseph LaShelle
Production Design: Robert Luthardt
Editing: Daniel Mandell
Music: André Previn
Cast: Jack Lemmon (Harry Hinkle), Walter Matthau (Willie Gingrich), Ron
Rich (Luther "Boom Boom" Jackson), Judi West (Sandy Hinkle), Cliff
Osmond (Purkey), Lurene Tuttle (Mother Hinkle), Harry Holcombe
(O'Brien), Les Tremayne (Thompson), Lauren Gilbert (Kincaid), Marge Red-
mond (Charlotte Gingrich), Noam Pitlik (Max), Harry Davis (Dr. Krugman),
Ann Shoemaker (Sister Veronica), Maryesther Denver (Nurse), Ned Glass
(Doc Schindler), Sig Ruman (Professor Winterhalter), Archie Moore (Mr.
Jackson), Howard McNear (Mr. Cimoli), William Christopher (intern), Dodie
Heath (nun), Herbie Faye (Maury, the equipment man), Billy Beck (Maury's
assistant), Judy Pace (Elvira), Helen Kleeb (receptionist), Keith Jackson (football announcer), Don Reed (newscaster), Robert DoQui (man in bar)
35 mm, black and white, Panavision
125 minutes

1970
THE PRIVATE LIFE OF SHERLOCK HOLMES
United Artists

Producer: **Billy Wilder**
Director: **Billy Wilder**
Screenplay: **Billy Wilder** and I. A. L. Diamond, based on characters by Arthur
Conan Doyle
Cinematography: Christopher Challis
Production Design: Alexander Trauner
Editing: Ernest Walter
Music: Miklós Rózsa
Cast: Robert Stephens (Sherlock Holmes), Colin Blakely (Dr. John Watson),
Genevieve Page (Gabrielle Valladon), Christopher Lee (Mycroft Holmes),
Tamara Toumanova (Patrova), Clive Revill (Rogozhin), Irene Handl (Mrs.
Hudson), Mollie Maureen (Queen Victoria), Stanley Holloway (first gravedig-
ger), Catherine Lacey (old lady), Peter Madden (Von Tirpitz), Michael Balfour
(cabbie), James Copeland (guide), John Garrie (first Carter), Godfrey James
(second Carter), Robert Cawdron (hotel manager), Alex McCrindle (baggage-
man), Frank Thornton (Porter), Paul Hansard (monk), George Benson
(Inspector Lestrade), Miklós Rózsa (conductor)
35 mm, color, Panavision
125 minutes

1972
AVANTI!
United Artists
Producer: **Billy Wilder**
Director: **Billy Wilder**
Screenplay: **Billy Wilder** and I. A. L. Diamond, with Luciano Vincenzoni,
based on the play by Samuel A. Taylor
Cinematography: Luigi Kuveiller
Production Design: Ferdinando Scarfiotti
Editing: Ralph E. Winters
Music: Carlo Rustichelli
Cast: Jack Lemmon (Wendell Armbruster), Juliet Mills (Pamela Piggott), Clive
Revill (Carlo Carlucci), Edward Andrews (J. J. Blodgett), Gianfranco Barra
(Bruno), Francesco Angrisano (Arnoldo Trotta), Pippo Franco (Mattarazzo),
Franco Acampora (Armado Trotta), Giselda Castrini (Anna), Raffaele Mottola
(passport officer), Lino Coletta (Cipriani), Harry Ray (Dr. Fleischmann),

Guidarino Guidi (maitre d'), Giacomo Rizzo (barman), Antonino Di Bruno
(concierge), Yanti Somer (nurse), Janet Agren (nurse), Aldo Rendine (Rossi)
35 mm, color
144 minutes

1974
THE FRONT PAGE
Universal International
Producer: Jennings Lang and Paul Monash
Director: **Billy Wilder**
Screenplay: **Billy Wilder** and I. A. L. Diamond, from the play by Ben Hecht
and Charles MacArthur
Cinematography: Jordan Cronenweth
Production Design: Henry Bumstead
Editing: Ralph E. Winters
Music: Billy May
Cast: Jack Lemmon (Hildy Johnson), Walter Matthau (Walter Burns), Susan
Sarandon (Peggy Grant), Carol Burnett (Mollie Malloy), Vincent Gardenia
("Honest Pete" Hartman), David Wayne (Roy Bensinger), Allen Garfield (Kru-
ger), Austin Pendleton (Earl Williams), Charles Durning (Murphy), Herb Ede-
lman (Schwartz), Martin Gabel (Dr. Max J. Eggelhofer), Harold Gould
(mayor), Cliff Osmond (Officer Jacobi), Dick O'Neill (McHugh), Jon Korkes
(Rudy Keppler), Lou Frizzell (Endicott), Paul Benedict (Plunkett), Doro Merande (Jennie the janitor), Noam Pitlik (Wilson), Joshua Shelley (cab driver),
Allen Jenkins (telegrapher), John Furlong (Duffy), Biff Elliot (police dis-
patcher), Barbara Davis (Myrtle), Leonard Bremen (Butch)
35 mm, color, Panavision
105 minutes

1978
FEDORA
Geria-Bavaria
Producer: **Billy Wilder**
Director: **Billy Wilder**
Screenplay: **Billy Wilder** and I. A. L. Diamond, from the story by Tom Tryon
Cinematography: Gerry Fisher
Production Design: Alexander Trauner

Editing: Stefan Arsten and Fredric Steinkamp
Music: Miklós Rózsa
Cast: William Holden (Barry "Dutch" Detweiler), Marthe Keller (Fedora), Hildegard Knef (Countess Sobryanski), José Ferrer (Doctor Vando), Frances Sternhagen (Miss Balfour), Mario Adorf (hotel manager), Stephen Collins (Young Barry), Henry Fonda (President of the Academy), Michael York (himself), Hans Jaray (Count Sobryanski), Gottfried John (Kritos), Arlene Francis (newscaster), Jacques Maury (usher), Christine Mueller (young Antonia)
35 mm, color, Panavision
113 minutes

1981
BUDDY BUDDY
MGM
Producer: Jay Weston
Director: **Billy Wilder**
Screenplay: **Billy Wilder** and I. A. L. Diamond, based on the film *L'Emmerdeur (A Pain in the A—),* by Francis Veber
Cinematography: Harry Stradling, Jr.
Production Design: Daniel A. Lomino
Editing: Argyle Nelson
Music: Lalo Schifrin
Cast: Jack Lemmon (Victor Clooney), Walter Matthau (Trabucco), Paula Prentiss (Celia Clooney), Klaus Kinski (Dr. Hugo Zuckerbrot), Dana Elcar (Captain Hubris), Miles Chapin (Eddie, the bellhop), Michael Ensign (assistant manager), Joan Shawlee (receptionist), Fil Formicola (Rudy "Disco" Gambola), C. J. Hunt (Kowalski), Bette Raya (Mexican maid), Ronnie Sperling (hippie husband), Suzie Galler (pregnant wife), John Schubeck (newscaster), Ed Begley Jr. (lieutenant #1), Frank Farmer (lieutenant #2), Neile McQueen (saleswoman)
35 mm, color, Panavision
96 minutes

BILLY WILDER

INTERVIEWS

The Happiest Couple in Hollywood

LINCOLN BARNETT / 1944

IT IS A HOLLYWOOD AXIOM that all screen writers nurse an inferiority complex. Though their salaries range up to $3,000 a week, they envy the eminence of less affluent Broadway playwrights. The public seldom notes their names as they flicker subordinately across the screen. Most fans, indeed, like to think that bright dialog is invented extemporaneously by the performers who utter it. And even the stars sometimes tend to credit themselves with authorship of their favorite lines.

Under such circumstances many a Hollywood writer becomes morbid and tries to attract attention to himself by wearing loud suits and neckties. Some go around muttering, "In the beginning was the word." The ultimate tragedy that can befall a screen writer is exemplified by an incident that makes members of the brotherhood shudder when they think of it. Not long ago a writer named Cyril lay dying. On his deathbed he composed some lines of verse which he asked his best friend to read at his funeral. When he passed away, his friend, who happened to be a director, telephoned another director and said, "Cyril's funeral is tomorrow noon. Could you meet me a couple of hours beforehand?" The other asked why. "Cyril gave me a poem to read at his grave," the friend replied. "And frankly it stinks. I want you to help me fix it up." So the two directors got together and rewrote the departed's last words.

This episode, which has haunted every screen playwright in Hollywood, made its most profound impression on the consciousness of Charles Brackett

From *Life*, 11 December 1944. © 1944 by Time-Life. Reprinted by permission.

and Billy Wilder. To prevent such an indignity from being visited on them has been their obsession. They have been successful thus far. They are currently regarded as the ablest and most versatile writing team in Hollywood. Between them they earn $4,500 a week. And they boast a kind of prestige and independence no other writers in any major studio have attained. Their happy lot is attributable in part to eight years of felicitous association during which they have never hatched a flop or even a mediocre effort. All their pictures have been hits both from the standpoint of the box office and in the eyes of the critics. Their impressive list of credits includes such varied films as *Ninotchka, Ball of Fire, The Major and the Minor, Hold Back the Dawn* and *Five Graves to Cairo*. All in all Brackett & Wilder movies have grossed $19,000,000.

More important than their undeniable talent in maintaining the dignity of their position in Hollywood are their healthy aggressive egos. Several years ago Paramount, their alma mater, lent them to M-G-M for a special project. They were summoned into conference with Sidney Franklin, M-G-M's top executive producer, whose customary relationship with screen writers is somewhat less personal than that of a zoo curator with inmates of the small-mammal house. Outlining the work at hand, Franklin would recurrently turn to Charlie Brackett and say, "Jack, would you lower that window," or addressing Billy Wilder he would command, "Steve, take your foot off that chair." After a half hour of this treatment, Brackett rose to his feet. "Mr. Franklin," he said haughtily, "my name is Charles Brackett. I'm too old and too rich to put up with this sort of nonsense. If you call us once again by any other names than our own, we'll walk out that door and never come back." The fact that M-G-M dispensed with their services three days later did not dim the luster of the moment.

In battles to uphold his professional dignity, Brackett is armored by his stout antecedents as a well-born easterner and alumnus of Williams '15 and Harvard Law School '20 and by his successful career in New York as a drama critic and novelist. Wilder, though he is younger and has lived in this country less than a decade, outbraves his partner for he knows he is a genius—a conviction by no means exclusively his own. Truculence and talent combined have thus elevated Brackett & Wilder to a position where they can translate their energies into finished films without intrusive collaboration.

To preserve the integrity of their product Wilder now directs all their pictures and Brackett produces them. They are known on the Paramount lot as "executive writers." As such they have freedom to evolve their own ideas and try experiments that run-of-the-mill $1,000-a-week writers could not attempt. Their current undertaking is an adaptation of *The Lost Weekend,* Charles Jackson's psychological novel about alcoholism. While it was perhaps the most talked-of book in Hollywood last spring, Brackett & Wilder alone believed it held the makings of a movie. Its tense and horrifying story revolved around a single major character; it presented few situations and almost no dialog. But its challenge was so compelling Brackett & Wilder lay awake nights pondering how to translate its stream-of-consciousness drama into animate scenes. Ultimately they bought the book, dropped another project which they had been incubating for several months, and started work. Production is well under way and the picture will probably be released early next spring. "If they bring it off," a friend remarked, "I bet they'll try next to make a musical out of *Finnegans Wake.*"

In a community famed for the vigor of its intramural animosities, the partnership of Brackett & Wilder has become a monument of professional friendship comparable in its way to that of Beaumont & Fletcher. So indivisible is their collaboration that a producer once suggested their screen credit should read, "Story by Brackettandwilder." And a gossip columnist reported that at a merry party not long ago Brackett, who is a one-champagne-cocktail man, warned Wilder, "Better stop drinking now or they will say all over town tomorrow that Brackett & Wilder got drunk." The anomaly of their relationship is that two more antithetic personalities would be hard to find. Brackett is a courtly, somewhat rumpled, affable gentleman of 52 who looks as though he might be vice president of a bank in Saratoga Springs, N.Y.—which he is. Wilder is a loquacious, elegant, sardonic young man of 38 who moves with the lithe grace of a professional dancer—which he once was. Brackett is something of a blue blood, whose family is respectably distributed through upstate New York and Rhode Island and whose father was a prominent lawyer and New York State senator. Wilder is a naturalized citizen whose Austrian father owned a watch factory outside Vienna until he swapped it one day for a trout hatchery. Brackett is a congenital Republican with liberal instincts, Wilder is a fervid New Dealer with leftish leanings. Brackett is an agoraphobe who jitters if the office door is left open. Wilder is a claustrophobe who can't stand closed doors.

They exercise their creative talents in a big suite on the ground floor of the Paramount writers' building. Since much of their work consists of thinking aloud, which they can do while eating, shaving or lying down, Brackett & Wilder never appear busy. Their office has a kind of convivial coffeehouse atmosphere. Idling actors and writers drop in every few minutes to grouse or gossip. After lunch every day Brackett & Wilder enter the larger of their two offices, which they call the Bedroom, and nap for an inviolate hour. For another hour each morning and afternoon they repair to their smaller office, The Game Room, for a round of cribbage with any available colleagues. Brackett generally wins. Wilder, who much prefers gin rummy (for hair-raising stakes), complained one day recently, "Charlie won't play my game. He's bought a house, married off his daughters and had two grandchildren—all on my money. Oh well, what do you expect from a man who voted for Dewey?" "Good cribbage," growled Brackett.

Not until the final phase of composition do Brackett & Wilder begin to act like authors. They never write any "story line" or preliminary "treatment," for experience has taught them that uninvited collaborators move in as soon as anything is put on paper. Many a writer, happily completing the dialog of his screen play, has suddenly found several competitors at work on the same project, using the "treatment" he had innocently submitted to his producer weeks before. The practice of secretly assigning one or more writers to write "behind" another has been somewhat curtailed recently through the Screen Writers Guild. Now producers must notify any writer who *asks* if someone is writing behind him. If he doesn't ask, the producer needn't tell him. Brackett & Wilder successfully avoided such pitfalls before they became executive writers by evolving stories in their heads and keeping them there despite badgering by studio executives. Their motto was, "He who writes last gets the credit." Now secrecy has become a habit with them. Situations, scenes, gags are carried for weeks in Wilder's extraordinary flypaper memory, along with old football scores, the dates of championship fights and themes from most of the major symphonies from Haydn through Sibelius. They generally dole out their first few pages of dialog a day or so before shooting is scheduled to begin. Then, scene by scene, they unveil the rest of their script, keeping 24 to 48 hours ahead of the camera. This technique naturally makes a head producer, however confident of their talents, feel somewhat like a newspaper editor whose star reporter has submitted copy on a lead story so close to deadline that no editing can be done.

Brackett & Wilder consider four months about par for the composition of a screen play. For the first three months they orally resolve such problems as

"Who are we rooting for?" "Why do they fall in love?" and "How do we get the dame out of the room?" When they are ready for "paper work" (a generic term commonly understood in Hollywood to mean writing as opposed to talking), they go into The Bedroom and warn their secretary, Helen Hernandez, to exclude all but their best friends. Brackett takes off his shoes, lies down on the sofa with a gross of sharp pencils at his side and props a tablet of legal foolscap on his knees. Wilder paces the floor swinging a cane—a light one when inspiration flows freely, a bludgeon when the going is slow. Every syllable of every line of dialog is exhaustively discussed. No word or bit of business, no fade-in, camera angle or dissolve is recorded until both partners agree fully on its dramatic value.

The homogeneity of Brackett & Wilder's product is such that curious colleagues long ago despaired of distinguishing the craftsmanship of one from the other's. Brackett & Wilder jointly share their laurels, never pout at criticism and, most extraordinary of all, go out of their way to give generous credit for whatever borrowed ideas they may have used. Since their scripts are dually conceived, the individual elements in their work can only be deduced from their temperamental differences. Wilder is galvanic, facile, prolific with ideas, endowed with visual imagination. Brackett is critical, contemplative, gifted with a graceful literary style and cultivated taste. When Wilder sparks off a salvo of suggestions, Brackett sorts good from bad and imparts to the best of them adroit turns of action and phrase. The exquisite, lambent dialog that is the hallmark of all their pictures is generally ascribed to Brackett although Wilder, despite his accent, has a keen ear for the American idiom and an acute sense of the flexibility of words. They complement each other in other ways. Wilder is cynical, taut, acidulous, a realist. Brackett is urbane, gentle, fanciful. Wilder is an instinctive dramatist who envisages story ideas through the camera's mobile eye: "I'm a celluloid maniac," he says. Brackett is primarily a novelist, attuned to niceties of continuity and construction.

Asked once, during negotiations for a Screen Writers Guild contract, to define a team, Brackett replied, "Whom God hath joined together." Terrestrially Brackett & Wilder were joined together by a Paramount story editor named Manny Wolf. Neither had made any dent in Hollywood up to that time. Wilder had come to this country in 1935 in the wake of his brother Willy. (His mother, who had once lived in the U. S., wanted her sons to have good American names, so she named them Willy and Billy.) Willy is now a

businessman in New York. Billy Wilder, who had briefly studied law at the
University of Vienna and had worked on a newspaper in Berlin, became
screen-struck during the late '20s and ultimately made a reputation as a
screen writer and director in Germany and France. But Hollywood, he found,
was glutted with European geniuses. He earned his first $50 there by jumping
fully clad into a swimming pool at a producer's garden party. Jobless, almost
penniless, handicapped by inadequate English, he lived for a while in the
ladies' lavatory of an apartment hotel. Since it was rarely used, the manage-
ment rented it to him cheaply on condition he keep the door locked. Wilder
at first protested he did not wish to inconvenience its regular patronesses,
but when the hotel insisted he maintain privacy, he made himself at home
and hung the walls with modern French canvases he had brought with him
from Paris. Meanwhile he wrote assiduously, grinding out stories and scripts
which the studios unanimously turned down at the time, but which he sold
for fat sums in later years when his name became known.

Brackett's advent in Hollywood, which antedated Wilder's by three years,
was equally unspectacular but rather less painful since he arrived with an
eastern reputation and ample funds. He had peddled his first short story
while serving overseas during the last war, and had crashed the pages of *The
Saturday Evening Post* with a three-part serial during his last year at Harvard
Law School. He continued to turn out fiction during six years of practice
with his father's law firm, Brackett & Eddy, in Saratoga Springs. (He is now
senior partner of the firm.) Impressed by his work, Editor Harold Ross offered
him a job as drama critic for *The New Yorker* in 1926. Though he had no previous experience in the theater, Brackett's reviews soon came to be highly
regarded as models of good writing and critical perception. After three years
with *The New Yorker* Brackett resigned and wrote his third novel. Then Hollywood called him.

The summons was imperative. RKO had a story which required dialog.
Brackett, it appeared, was the man to write it. A New York agent shoved him
aboard a plane. A Hollywood agent met him at Burbank airport and rushed
him to the studio, baggage and all. Impressed by a sense of urgency, Brackett
expected to find RKO's executive hierarchy lined up to welcome him with
tongues hanging out. Instead he was kept waiting an hour, then introduced
into the presence of David Selznick, who greeted him vaguely with, "Oh yes,
that story of Adela Rogers St. Johns'. I guess you'd better talk to her." Next
Brackett discovered that the "story" was simply an article in *Liberty* about

the heart problems of Jack Dempsey and Estelle Taylor, that no story line had been discussed and that no one had any ideas at all. Feeling very much at sea, he nevertheless went to work and outlined a treatment. When it was finished he was called into story conference. "I didn't then appreciate the dreadful significance of a story conference," Brackett recalls. "So I simply got up and stammered out my story. When I got through there was a deadly silence. Then Adela said quietly, 'I don't see it that way at all. The boy loved that girl. That girl loved that boy. They loved each other.' And on that note I was wafted out of Hollywood."

Back home Brackett found himself inexplicably bored. Hence when Hollywood bid for his services a second time he again responded, though with misgivings. One day, after several months of performing sundry literary jobs for various studios, he was called to the office of Paramount's Manny Wolf. "Charlie Brackett meet Billy Wilder," Wolf said. "From now on you're a team." Wolf immediately assigned them to collaborate with Ernst Lubitsch on *Bluebeard's Eighth Wife* (starring Gary Cooper and Claudette Colbert). The trio clicked immediately. At their first session Lubitsch posed the question: how do the boy and girl get together? Wilder promptly suggested that the opening scene should be the men's shop of a department store. "The boy is trying to buy a pajama," he extemporized glibly. "But he sleeps only in the tops. He is thrifty so he insists on buying only the tops. The clerk says he must buy the pants too. It looks like a catastrophe. Then the girl comes into the shop and buys the pants because she sleeps only in the pants." Brackett and Lubitsch were enchanted. It wasn't till months later they discovered that Wilder himself is a tops-only sleeper and that he had been nursing the idea for months waiting for a chance to use it.

Catalyzed by this beginning, Brackett, Wilder and Lubitsch erupted bright ideas. When they reached the dialog phase their spirits were dampened by a pretty but deadpan secretary named Iva who had been assigned to them by the personnel office. All Hollywood writers rely heavily on secretarial reactions. Although Brackett, Wilder and Lubitsch repeatedly produced lines that convulsed them, Iva never changed expression. One day, exasperated, Lubitsch turned on her and asked, "Don't you think that's a funny line?" Iva said, "I think it's hilarious. This is the funniest script I've ever worked on." "But you've never laughed," said Lubitsch. Obviously distressed, Iva said, "Please excuse me if I don't laugh. Please." That night the three writers decided Iva was the victim of an unhappy love affair or some other profound misfortune.

Four weeks later they uncorked an especially funny line and Iva burst out laughing. They stared at her. "Iva, you laughed," they shouted. "Yes, I know," she gasped, tears in her eyes. "Yesterday the dentist removed the bands from my teeth."

After *Bluebeard's Eighth Wife*, Brackett & Wilder wrote *Midnight*. On this job they worked for a producer who adhered to the old theory that too many writers improve the script. Hence when they had completed their script, the producer turned it over to a third writer named Ken Englund. "What do you want me to do with it?" Englund asked. "It looks fine to me." The producer said, "Rewrite it." Englund rewrote it. When he had read the new script, the producer said, "Well the trouble with this is it doesn't sound like Brackett & Wilder. You've lost the flavor of the original. Now who can we get who writes like Brackett & Wilder?" Tentatively Englund pointed out that Brackett & Wilder were at that moment sitting in their office with nothing to do. "Why don't you get them to rewrite it?" he asked. "That's a good idea," the producer said. So he called them in and told them to rewrite Englund's script. After several days of feverish cribbage, they turned in their original manuscript with a few minor revisions and it was a great success. Their sparkling dialog even impressed John Barrymore, who at that time had lost his memory and had to read his lines from slates held up by stagehands outside camera range. One day his wife came into the Brackett & Wilder office and asked for a copy of *Midnight*. "I've never known John to be so amused by a picture," she said. "He's actually asked if he could read the script."

Their next picture, *Ninotchka*, which they wrote in collaboration with their friend Writer Walter Reisch, is generally regarded by critics as one of the finest and most sophisticated films Hollywood ever produced. It gave Greta Garbo her most engaging role. Of this picture Writer-Producer Nunnally Johnson wrote, "There hasn't been a stage comedy in 15 years as good as *Ninotchka*." Today Brackett & Wilder disagree on the place *Ninotchka* holds in their hearts. Brackett recalls it fondly because he confesses to a crush on Garbo. He used to haunt the set during the filming, despite Garbo's distaste for visitors. One day, noticing Brackett goggling from the sidelines, she ordered a stagehand to place a black screen in front of him. He promptly found a crack near the bottom of the screen, knelt down on all fours and peeked through. While he was in this ignominious position, his partner arrived on the set. "You a family father!" Wilder sneered. "And vice president of a bank! What would the directors of the Adirondack Trust Company say if they could see you now!" Wilder has mixed feelings about *Ninotchka* because as a Russophile he fears it offended the U. S. S. R. "I've always wanted to see Odessa," he mused recently, "and now I'm afraid we never will." "I can last a long time," said Brackett, "without seeing Odessa."

Next came *Arise My Love* and *Hold Back the Dawn.* The former, a daringly interventionist film, was released a few weeks after the fall of France and evoked storms of protest from isolationist fans. Its inception was curious. Producer Arthur Hornblow had handed Brackett & Wilder a story manuscript and, after explaining that it concerned an American flier with the Loyalists in Spain, advised them not to trammel their imaginations by reading it. So, laying source material aside, they proceeded to compose their script around Hornblow's one-sentence digest. In the same way *Hold Back the Dawn,* a thoughtful parable on the plight of immigrants seeking admission to the U.S., was based on a novel which Brackett & Wilder never read. They occasionally joke about the flights of invention which lead them off on narrative tangents far removed from their point of departure. Often as not their finished screen plays are 99.99% original. Their working formula for adaptations is, "In the novel it's a bunch of roses; in the screen play it's a torpedo boat."

After *Hold Back the Dawn* Paramount lent Brackett & Wilder to Goldwyn to write *Ball of Fire.* This screwball comedy, dealing with the compilation of an encyclopedia, derived from an original story written by Wilder during his first threadbare days in Hollywood. At that period he would have sold it for $100. Goldwyn gave him $7,500 with promise of another $2,500 if it should be a success. When it proved a huge success, Wilder demanded his bonus. Goldwyn had apparently forgotten this small matter and at first refused, saying (according to Wilder), "If I make a promise I make it in writing." Eventually, however, he not only surrendered the bonus but told Brackett & Wilder to order suits from the best tailor in Hollywood and to send him the bill. Their suits cost $175 each. Today Brackett's aristocratic conscience recoils from the recollection that he once accepted a suit of clothes as a gratuity. "Taking that suit was the most humiliating thing I ever did," he remarked not long ago. "I still wear mine," Wilder said. "So do I," said Brackett.

Back with Paramount again, they wrote *The Major and the Minor* as a vehicle for Ginger Rogers. They had hoped to persuade Ginger to accept the lead in *Ball of Fire,* but she had declined the role—that of a burlesque dancer—because she wanted to play "ladies." When this explanation was conveyed to Goldwyn he lost his temper and yelled at her agent. "You tell Ginger

Rogers ladies stink up the place." Ginger was delighted, however, with her part in *The Major and the Minor,* which enabled her to appear not only as a young lady, but as an old lady and a demure schoolgirl as well. As a critical success *The Major and the Minor* was second only to *Ninotchka* and at the box office it was a smash. After that, as a change of pace Brackett & Wilder wrote *Five Graves to Cairo.*

Since they spend most of their daylight hours together, Brackett & Wilder seldom see each other socially after work. Both men are extremely gregarious and count among their friends all the amiable and intelligent people in Hollywood. Wilder's wife, a California girl whom he married in 1936, once said, "Billy is strictly a coffeehouse guy. He will go to any party. And he would like to live at the corner of Hollywood and Vine"—which is the West Coast equivalent of Broadway and 42nd Street. Actually the Wilders live on the far fringes of Beverly Hills, a half-hour drive from Paramount, in open, rolling country. Mrs. Wilder, who is a competent painter and equestrienne, loves her bucolic surroundings, and the wide view from her veranda. Wilder loathes the country and detests animals and flowers. His domestic interests focus on the interior of his house, which he has lovingly fitted with early American furniture. He has a special passion for fabrics and is forever bringing home bolts of material which Mrs. Wilder stores away in an attic already stuffed with enough cretonne, needle point and glazed chintz to reupholster a hotel.

Wilder is profoundly devoted to his 4-year-old daughter Victoria, who is gifted, like her father, with a superlative memory, social graces and highly competitive instincts. "Billy and Victoria are happiest," Mrs. Wilder says, "when they are surrounded by crowds of people, doing something better than anyone else." Wilder excels at intellectual parlor games. He also plays a first-rate game of tennis and occasionally competes in chess tournaments with local masters. A restless man who rarely stays seated for more than ten minutes at any dinner table, Wilder sleeps badly and like most movie people is a hypochondriac. "You don't dare mention a new disease in front of Billy," his wife says, "or he has it the next day. Right now he's toying with spinal meningitis."

Brackett less frequently suffers from imaginary ills. He sometimes exhibits a tendency to deafness, although his friends insist he feigns it in order to exclude unpleasant sounds like directorial objections or symphonic music. He explains his musical insensitivity on the grounds that he is tone deaf, and he once talked of acquiring a "hearing-ear dog" trained to nudge him at the first strains of *The Star-Spangled Banner*. Like Wilder, Brackett feels that his all-round efficiency is abetted by a weekly injection of Vitamin B-1. He augments his shots with daily doses of B-1 pills and cod liver oil, regarding these measures as adequate substitutes for sunshine and fresh air, which he disdains. His only form of exercise is moving the pegs up and down a cribbage board. In general Brackett conveys an impression of sound metabolism and repose which his friends find downright soothing. Lubitsch relates that on one occasion when he, Lubitsch, lay seriously ill in a hospital, his pulse rate, which had jumped to 125 following a visit from Miriam Hopkins, eased down to 68 when Brackett dropped in. Although inwardly Brackett suffers the gestative pangs chronic with all writers, they are lulled each evening when he gazes on the Victorian tranquility of his home. He has bedizened his modern stone house in Bel-Air with red plush sofas and chairs, tasseled lamps, antimacassars, scrolled mahogany, bric-a-brac and other windfalls from the Brackett family tree that reflect his rather recherché 19th Century taste and temperament. A self-conscious easterner, he continually professes nostalgia for Saratoga Springs. Unlike Wilder, who unashamedly proclaims his love of Hollywood, Brackett feels uneasy about his own perfect adjustment to Lotusland. He expresses wonderment at his painless literary transition "from esoteric novels to exoteric pictures." He keeps his eastern roots alive with streams of correspondence to his law partners, to the directors of his bank and to the caretaker of his inherited Victorian mansion in Providence, R. I., where he insists he wants to die.

Sunday-noon dinners at the Bracketts' are Hollywood's equivalent of Mme. de Staël's salons in 18th Century Paris. To them troop the most entertainingly articulate writers, actors, actresses and assorted geniuses in the craft. Brackett, who is an appreciative listener as well as an excellent raconteur, presides over them with solicitude and grace. In this function he is ably assisted by his wife, a kindly but witty lady whose occasionally corrosive remarks have from time to time been attributed to Dorothy Parker. A Fletcher of Indiana, Mrs. Brackett met her husband at a Williams prom 25 years ago and took an instant dislike to him. "He was the rich young man of his fraternity," she recalls, "literary and very sure of himself." But she married him soon afterward. Their two daughters, Alexandra and Elizabeth, are both extremely pretty, both competent fliers and both married. "Xani," the eldest, eloped in accordance with Hollywood convention. When Brackett discovered her flight, he talked of putting a ladder under her window so she could climb back in. But when she returned next day with her husband, a young actor, he greeted them with champagne. When "Bean" became engaged to an Army pilot, the Bracketts gave her a formal church wedding. Lubitsch recalls that "when father and daughter came down the aisle, no one looked at the bride, no one looked at the bridegroom or the best man or the bridesmaids. Everybody looked at Charlie. He was the perfect father."

There comes a time in the careers of all collaborators when they begin to wonder whether their talents are inextricably entwined or whether their separate wings can still sustain them independently and alone. Such a time came to Brackett & Wilder last year. To fortify their individual egos they temporarily dissolved their partnership. Wilder wrote and directed *Double Indemnity*, a murder story. Brackett produced *The Uninvited*, a ghost story. Then, invigorated and with renewed confidence each in his own abilities, they moved back into their old clubrooms to collaborate on *The Lost Weekend*. "So now we're together again," Wilder told a friend a few weeks ago, "and we're the happiest couple in Hollywood."

Wilder Seeks Films "With Bite" to Satisfy "Nation of Hecklers"

PHILIP K. SCHEUER/1950

"WE ARE A NATION OF HECKLERS," said Billy Wilder, discussing movie audiences today and apparently including himself in—"the most hard-boiled, undisciplined people in the world. First our heroes smack their girls' faces with grapefruit, then they kick mothers in wheel chairs downstairs and now they slap their lady loves with wet towels. How much farther can we go?

"Class in pictures nowadays has to be smuggled in like contraband, and artistry is a nasty word. One doesn't want to make every film the greatest ever turned out. But if movie-goers would just walk to the nearest drugstore and talk about the last one they've seen for 15 minutes, it would be very gratifying. That's all we (of Hollywood) ask."

Wilder, who is likely to have his wish come true now that *Sunset Boulevard,* which he co-wrote and directed, is in general circulation, thinks of himself as a writer who is lucky enough to be able to follow through on his own yarns.

That was why he got out behind the camera in 1942, with *The Major and the Minor,* and has stayed there ever since—on *Five Graves to Cairo, Double Indemnity, The Lost Weekend, The Emperor Waltz, A Foreign Affair* and *Sunset Boulevard.*

"The question about a picture is not whether it is good or bad, but whether it is alive or dead," he said. "*Madame Curie* was produced like perfection itself, but what came out in the theaters was dead weight. *Casablanca* was full of holes as a story, but it was alive as a film and the public loved it.

"All I try to do is get myself a story, splash it on the screen and get it over with. And I try, for God's sake, to have news in every picture I make! To open up, to unroll a problem is interesting enough. We don't have to know the answer, too!"

In *Ace in the Hole*, which Billy Wilder was shooting the day I visited the set at Paramount, he is opening up and unrolling the problem of the "quick buck" and the American mania for making it, even if it has to be made on somebody's personal tragedy.

Possibly suggested by the notable plights of Floyd Collins and Kathy Fiscus, it details the trapping of an obscure trading post proprietor in a cave-in and the repercussions of the occurrence on the world above.

The trader has entered an abandoned Indian cliff dwelling in search of funeral urns when the cave-in occurs. Up to his waist in sand and shale, the trader is located by Kirk Douglas, playing a discredited quick-buck reporter who immediately senses the possibilities in exploiting the event.

"White man half buried by angry spirits," he gloats, visualizing the headlines—"King Tut in New Mexico!"

Meanwhile, the curious have gathered outside—by tens, hundreds, then thousands. A tent city goes up and the hawkers arrive, selling everything from a helicopter ride over the cave to hot wieners. The reporter has not only his story—and his readers—but also the trader's pretty wife (Jan Sterling) to keep him company above ground. It is almost too good to be true.

"He's a hungry guy who bites off more than he can swallow," Wilder explained, with gusto. "What we have is an indictment against cheesy tabloids and the people who are buying them who need 'em for breakfast. On the other side we have a publisher, an old-time newspaperman like William Allen White, who makes some telling points about honor in his profession."

Long associated with Charles Brackett, Wilder admits to having two writing collaborators on *Ace in the Hole*, Lesser Samuels and Walter Newman, as well as an associate producer, William Schorr. After *Sunset Boulevard* he and Brackett separated, he said, because "the studio wanted to get two pictures a year out of us instead of one. So they split us up.

"He gets another director and I get other writers to work with," Billy added, "but I sure miss him."

They were first together, he and Charlie, on *Bluebeard's Eighth Wife,* in

1938. *Ninotchka* was one felicitous product of this partnership. In 1943 they set up their own writing-directing-producing unit with *Five Graves to Cairo,* continuing it (with the exception of *Double Indemnity,* produced by Joseph Sistrom) up to the present time.

With or without Brackett, Wilder said, it takes about eight months to concoct a story.

"I always make things very tough on myself," he grinned, "by not going out and buying a successful stage play or novel but starting, instead, from scratch. The wonder is that *Sunset Boulevard* ever got made, for that reason alone: usually a studio prefers to bank on a sure-fire property.

"We weren't particularly interested in doing a Hollywood story," he continued, explaining what inspired *Sunset Boulevard.* "What appealed to us was the comeback story—which is much more moving than the success story—plus the tragedy of an aging woman. This was the part we gave to Gloria Swanson—and for added values we had directors Erich von Stroheim and Cecil DeMille.

"*Ace in the Hole,* I think, is equally unorthodox."

Billy Wilder is not to be confused—although people always are doing it—with William Wyler, no slouch as a director himself and on the same lot. Billy came to America and Hollywood in 1934 from Germany and France, where he had written and/or directed several films. Born in Austria, he sums up his life to date as "from Adolph Hitler to Adolph Zukor (chairman of the Paramount board)."

Now 44, he has a brother Willy, so named by his mother—as she named Billy Billy—because she had once been to America and thought the combination very American. (Willy, an independent producer, presently calls himself W. Lee Wilder.)

For the future, Billy intends to stick to his belief that audiences want "anything with bite." Because of the troubled state of the world he has all but dropped the Berlin comedy he was planning, in which Marlene Dietrich would have played a one-legged prostitute. He's looking for "another comedy with significance—like *Ninotchka*"—but adds that humor is a risky commodity these days.

"A whole year and a half would elapse between planning and release," he observes—"and God only knows what the world will be like then! It would be like commenting on the day before yesterday."

Why Not Be in Paris?

NEWSWEEK/1956

ON A SMALL COUCH IN PARIS one day last week, Gary Cooper lay asleep, the lower third of him hanging off the couch's end.

"Somebody wake up Coop," requested the director, Billy Wilder.

Awakened, Cooper got to his feet, blinking. He wore a dressing gown over a shirt and slacks. He slowly tucked in the shirt. A few feet away stood Audrey Hepburn, fully dressed but wearing only one shoe.

"Now, Coop," said the director, "this time we'll take it from 'Where's my other shoe,' and I want you to try getting down on the floor *after* you say, 'You sure you had them both on when you came?' " The director walked to a point between Cooper and a small desk. "You drop down about here," he said. He walked to a chair and sat down. "OK," he said.

Miss Hepburn got down on all fours and scrambled rapidly toward the desk. "Where's my other shoe?" she said. "This is ridiculous . . ."

Cooper frowned and looked at the script girl. "What was that line?" he said.

" 'Relax . . .' "

"Oh, yes. 'Relax. It'll turn up sooner or later'." Audrey, on all fours, spoke a line, and Cooper spoke his—"You sure you had them both on when you came?"—and got down on his hands and knees. He crawled a couple of feet, spoke his next line, and crawled again.

Some hours later that day, Cooper was lying asleep on the couch. The little scene was finally almost ready to be shot. "Somebody wake up Coop,"

From *Newsweek*, 26 November, 1956. Reprinted by permission.

said the director. He walked to a window near the desk, fluffed out the curtains, went to his chair, and sat down. Cooper was now standing up, looking thoughtfully toward the desk, tucking in his shirt, waking up. Miss Hepburn was on all fours some distance away.

"Go!" said the director. Miss Hepburn rapidly crawled and spoke her lines. Cooper, frowning, looked toward the script girl. " 'Relax,' " she prompted. "Relax," said Cooper. "It'll turn up sooner or later."

An hour more of going through these actions, and the director was ready to shoot. Miss Hepburn now played the scene as if for the first time, with the utmost inner tension, Cooper was now letter-perfect in his lines, and completely at home in all his actions.

As director Billy Wilder watched the two perform, he began to smile gently. His eyes brimmed with a kind of loving tenderness. His head tipped from side to side as if to sentimental music. His expression became that of a proud father setting eyes on his newborn child for the first time.

At the end of the scene, he lay back in his chair, threw up his hands, and laughed wildly as if he had never watched the scene before. It had taken hours to make, and in the final rendition it lasted perhaps five minutes. Cooper and Miss Hepburn had been going through such repetitions on the picture ever since last July.

The most probable result of this interminable hauling and straining, improbable as it might seem, would be a tripping, buoyant, and unusually engaging comedy, a light love lyric, perfectly balanced, and full of style. The movie, to be titled *Love in the Afternoon,* concerned a romance in the Paris Ritz between a well-seasoned international wolf and the tremulous young daughter of a French private detective.

It was almost bound to be a success. For one thing, it had Gary Cooper and Audrey Hepburn. For another, the third principal in the cast (a very small one) was Maurice Chevalier, playing a straight dramatic role for the first time in his American movie career—and for a change not a dashing, romantic rascal. (He sings not a note, tilts not a hat, ogles not a leg.) Finally, the man running the show was Billy Wilder, who has participated in the making of such movies as *Double Indemnity, Sunset Boulevard, Ninotchka,* and *The Lost Weekend.*

The shooting on *Love in the Afternoon* was to come to an end next week. The actors' job was over, but Wilder, as the picture's producer, director, and writer (with I. A. L. Diamond), would have his hands full for another two months, scoring the film, dubbing, editing, flicking away the last speck of flaw. He was happy enough to linger in Paris. "We could have made this picture just as well in Hollywood," he says. "But why not be in Paris? Besides, it's a picture about life here, and I think that living here in Paris all this time is good for the picture." Good in its psychological effect on the players, that is, rather than in any visual background gains.

Virtually the entire movie has been shot inside the studio, and Wilder points out the distinction which this gives the movie, for one made in Paris. So many Americans have been making movies in the streets of Paris that, at one point, the mayor of Paris took the embattled attitude that he would not stand idly by while his city was turned into a Hollywood set. "What WE are making is a real movie," says Wilder, "not a travelogue."

He feels that he is also making current history of another sort. "There isn't a sweat shirt in the picture," he points out. "In this one, everybody sits on chairs instead of on the floor." In talking about the picture, he tends to recall the late director Ernst Lubitsch, who specialized in similarly elegant amatory trifles back in the '20s, and whom Wilder knew. Why has Wilder himself not tried to make this sort of thing in recent years? He answers simply: "Because it's too —— hard to do."

Among the surprising difficulties Wilder encountered on the picture was that of teaching Gary Cooper to dance—just some routine ballroom dancing with Audrey, as the script requires. Cooper has not been playing roles which require this talent, and Wilder, who likes to dance and personally took Cooper in hand, had a struggle. He shakes his head, incredulously. "Old Hopalong Nijinsky."

A nearsighted man of 50 with a face rather like a kewpie's, and a comedy German accent, Wilder is one of the gentlest, most patient, and most respected directors in the business. A fugitive from Adolf Hitler in 1933, he directed his first movie (starring Danielle Darrieux) in a garage in Paris. Not long after he arrived in Hollywood he took up the study of English (largely by listening intently to radio commercials twelve hours a day) and became a movie writer. After a memorable period of collaboration with Charles Brackett he left the team six years ago, and has since been a writer-producer-director.

He is a simple man who wears old flannels, a sweater, scarf, and cap on the set. He gets around Paris these days in a new, chocolate-colored Rolls-Royce chauffeured by a Hungarian.

Charming Billy

RICHARD GEHMAN/1960

ONE NIGHT JACK LEMMON was sitting in Dominick's, a Hollywood restaurant, when he was approached by a man with a face like a per-
simmon ripening in the sun.

"I have an idea for a picture I would like you to play in," the man said.

"Sit down," the actor said.

"I haven't got time now," the man said, "but I will tell you what it is
about. It is about two men on the lam from gangsters, running for their lives,
and they dress up in girls' clothes and join an all-girl orchestra."

Later, Lemmon said, "If anybody else had said that, I would have run like
a jack rabbit. Go in *drag?* Since it was Billy Wilder, I said, 'Fine, I'll do it if I'm
free to do it, and if I'm not free I'll get free.' " The film was *Some Like It Hot,*
conceived by Billy Wilder, written by Billy Wilder, produced by Billy Wilder,
directed by Billy Wilder, promoted by Billy Wilder, and forgotten by Billy
Wilder as soon as it was finished, for by then Billy Wilder was thinking about
a new film with Lemmon to be called *The Apartment,* which appears in fair
shape to break the box-office record of *Hot,* the biggest-grossing comedy of
all time. In September the figures on *Hot* showed that it had pulled in fourteen million clameroos, as they say there in that land of vodka and honey.

Marilyn Monroe, the Number One box-office attraction in the world, had
never gone into a project until she had read the script and had it redone to
her own special measurements. But she too agreed to go into *Hot* after hear-

Originally appeared in *Playboy,* December 1960. Reprinted by permission of the author's
estate.

ing a couple of sentences from Wilder. So did Tony Curtis, another high-priced property. So did Shirley MacLaine agree to go into *The Apartment* when she heard Wilder's one-line summary, which was, "This is about a young fellow who gets ahead in a big company by lending his apartment to executives for that grand old American folk ritual, the afternoon shack-up."

These people—even Miss Monroe, who has had numerous volcanic clashes with Wilder—are all attracted to this man perhaps in large measure because he makes films that reflect our time in all its floundering comedy and pain, and he makes them with a wry and tough-minded attitude that cuts into the heart of all pretense and posturing. When Citizen Mike Romanoff, ex-prince, ex-impostor, den father to Those Who Count in the Industry, says, "Billy Wilder is the most unusual and amusing man in Hollywood," he is not saying enough. He could go further. Billy Wilder is the most versatile and perhaps the most brilliant writer-director-producer alive, as well as a *bon vivant*, a generous gentleman and cautious gambler ($100 a night and quit). He is one of those rare human beings who, by washing his glum cynicism with streaks of light and hopefulness, and by annealing himself to principle when nearly everybody else seems determined to abandon it, makes an increasingly important contribution to our filmic entertainment.

Wilder also is known for his ability to toss off sharp, perceptive lines that are, in their own way, as funny and cynical as his movies. He sputters them forth in an accent revelatory of his early days in Germany; he is a poor man's Rilke who seems to stumble upon his observations as the poet discovered images. Many of them begin slowly, almost solemnly, and wind up quickly and devastatingly. Speaking of *Suddenly, Last Summer,* the first American picture to deal with contemporary cannibalism, he once assured me that it was bound to be a financial failure.

"The first thing you learn in Hollywood," Wilder said, his eyes glinting with a wicked luminosity behind his spectacles, "is that you must not offend pressure groups. Don't offend the Catholics, the Jews, the Protestants, the Seventh-Day Adventists, the dentists, the Rotarians, or any other group. That picture will flop because it offends the vegetarians."

Tony Curtis told me, "Billy Wilder is something else again." This is a remarkable statement for an actor to make, for all actors are a little nuts, all actors have monstrous egos, and all actors are convinced that they do not really need directors. Curtis is all actor. His *shtick* (an old burlesque word for a personal idiosyncrasy or bit of business) is wearing tight, Continental-style clothes, some of which he designs himself. ("Tony's pants look as though someone dipped him in India ink up to his waist," Wilder once said.)

One day on the set of *Some,* there arose a question of billing which involved Curtis' not having his name in the big type size called for by his contract. He went to Wilder and squawked. Wilder listened to him patiently, then said, "The trouble with you, Tony, is that you're only interested in little pants and big billing."

Curtis, telling this, roars and says, "I *kvel* when I think of that. Do you know what *kvel* is? It's a Yiddish word meaning I like flipped. I feel about that man the way I feel about my poor dead father, rest his soul."

Everybody in Hollywood *kvels* when Wilder's name is mentioned. People on all levels love him—the high-spirited Sinatra Clan, of which he is a part-time member; the 'upper-register' industry social crowd, such as the William Goetzes, the Gary Coopers and the Ira Gershwins; and the prop men, the electricians and the wardrobe ladies. This is all the more significant when one considers that Wilder has taken Hollywood only on his own terms. His tongue can be sulfuric and he has never failed to use it on those needing a burning. He has invariably clung to what he believes is right. "He's always been the way he is today," says Walter Reisch, the writer, who knew Wilder more than thirty-five years ago in Vienna.

"He was never sentimental, he was always fearless, even when he had nothing. He was sassy and aggressive—he would rather have lost a job than compromise or say yes. And he did lose jobs. He made himself unpopular in the early days—he was overbearing and arrogant, and still is today, in some ways—but even when he told them to go to hell, they always came back to him."

Wilder still strikes some people as being a "mean" man, among them George Axelrod, who wrote *The Seven Year Itch* as a play and then worked on the movie version with Wilder. When Axelrod reported to Wilder he had the original playscript under his arm.

"I thought we might use this as a guide," he said. "Fine ," said Wilder, dropping it to the floor. "We'll use it as a doorstop."

Axelrod was not too offended by this acerb dismissal because he admires Wilder's ability to cross-cut the bole of any situation and extract the meaningful sap within. (He can also hack up a whole country in one slash, as he did when he told columnist Art Buchwald, "France is a place where the money falls apart in your hand and you can't tear the toilet paper.")

Wilder doesn't spare friends. One of his closest is Otto Preminger, who is Jewish but resembles a Central Casting Nazi (in fact, he played a Nazi for Wilder in *Stalag 17*). Preminger has an explosive temper: once he tried to get an actor to calm down by pasting his face against the man's and shouting at the top of his lungs, "RELAX!" Sometimes, when Preminger is embroiled with a studio mogul, Wilder is called in as referee. This happened one day when Preminger was quarreling with Sam Goldwyn and yelling like a bull.

"Calm down, Otto," said Wilder, "I'm not going to fight with you—I've still got relatives in Germany." (Actually, Billy's father died in Berlin in 1927. His mother, it was believed, was one of the millions of Jewish victims of the Nazis. Wilder tried unsuccessfully to find some trace of her after World War II. His total lack of banal sentimentality may be seen in his ability to joke about the Nazis with Preminger.) Some time later, after Preminger had left Hollywood temporarily, Wilder was asked where he had gone. "His summer home—in Belsen," Wilder said.

Not even Wilder's wife escapes his satiric quips. Mrs. Wilder, the former Audrey Young, lived in the Pico La Brea district when he was courting her. That is not the best section in the Los Angeles area, but she gamely referred to it as "East Beverly Hills." When Wilder first learned where she was living, he said to her, "I'd worship the ground you walk on, if you lived in a better neighborhood."

On their first wedding anniversary, Mrs. Wilder, who is fifteen years younger than Billy, got up in the morning and found him reading *The Hollywood Reporter* at breakfast. He did not look up as she came dewy-eyed into the room.

"Do you know what day this is, dear?" she asked.

"June thirtieth," Wilder said.

"It's our first anniversary," she said, pouting.

"Please," Wilder said, grimacing, "not while I'm eating."

Wilder travels a good deal when he is exploiting a new film, and Mrs. Wilder, as many wives do, usually gives him a list of gifts to bring back. When he was going to Paris last year, she said she wanted some Charvet ties for a friend of hers to give to her husband for his birthday. "And," she added, "ever since I first went to Paris, I've wanted a bidet of my own." Wilder frowned and said he might have trouble getting a bidet without wrenching it out of a Paris hotel bathroom. Nevertheless, he would try.

A few days later a cable came back. CHARVET TIES ON WAY, it said. BUT BIDET IMPOSSIBLE OBTAIN. SUGGEST HANDSTAND IN SHOWER.

Many of Wilder's one-line nifties are directed at women and some critics have noted a strong anti-female undercurrent in many of Wilder's films. He denies that this is so, but his cracks about women are repeated over and over. Hal Wallis, the producer, is married to Louise Fazenda, the silent-film actress. Wilder one night referred to Wallis as "The Prisoner of Fazenda."

Some of Wilder's most anti-female comments were directed against Marilyn Monroe during the shooting of *Some Like It Hot* and just afterward. As is M.M.'s wont, she kept Tony Curtis and the other stars in a state of nerves—by failing to show up, by showing up late, and by being high-handed when she did show up.

Asked if he would ever make a picture with Monroe again, Wilder said, "In the United States, I'd hate it. In Paris, it might not be so bad—while we were waiting, we could all take painting lessons on the side."

Monroe, hearing this, became furious and began retorting in interviews. In New York, a friend tried to get her to call Wilder and make peace. When they put the call through, Mrs. Wilder answered. "Marilyn wants to make up with Billy," the friend said. "Billy isn't here," Mrs. Wilder said. "Marilyn will talk to you, Audrey," the buddy said, single-mindedly.

The famous breathy voice came on the wire. It began sweetly: "Hello, Audrey? I just want to tell you [pause] that I think [pause] your husband [pause]" And then those slowly-grinding brainwheels went into reverse: "is the worst son of a bitch who ever lived, and he can go and——." She ended with a phrase familiar to us all but unprintable on these pages. Then, abruptly, the wheels shifted into politeness and gentility again. "And [pause] my very best to you, Audrey," Marilyn finished.

Wilder was philosophical when he heard about it. "She is a very great actress," he said. "Better Marilyn late than most of the others on time."

After the picture was released to critical raves, including some comments that it was Marilyn's best performance, tempers cooled somewhat. Both have said publicly that they would be more than delighted to make a film together again.

Conceivably, only someone as temperamental as Monroe could have caused any commotion at all on a Wilder set, for despite his bluntness and his unfettered language (he uses four-letter words the way most of us use prepositions), and despite what seems to be a snarling contempt for the human race, he is a kind and patient director. Shirley MacLaine has said that she learned more from him than from anybody else in Hollywood.

In a sense this is odd, for although Wilder always knows where he is going in every script, he is not always sure how he is going to get there. Ordinarily he improvises the dialog on a day-to-day basis. When he and Ernest Lehman wrote *Sabrina*, they conceived one part originally for Cary Grant, who, after agreeing to play it, changed his mind. The only other actor of stature available was Humphrey Bogart.

At once, Lehman and Wilder began rewriting in an frenzy, fixing Grant's scenes for Bogart. They would stay up most of each night getting a few pages together for the next day.

One afternoon, midway in the shooting, Wilder went to Doane Harrison, his favorite film cutter and right-hand man, and said, "Please get the electricians to invent some complicated lighting effects for the next scene. Get them to do something that will take some time."

Wilder is known for his economy, and the remark puzzled Harrison. "What for?"

"We haven't got the dialog written yet," Wilder said.

A similar situation developed on the set of *The Apartment*. "We wrote the last four scenes in the last four days and nights before shooting," says I. A. L. Diamond, Wilder's collaborator on the film.

Wilder believes that last-minute work on the script affords him a flexibility that helps the actors develop truer interpretations of their parts. He is also convinced that he can only work effectively with a collaborator, for although he has been in this country for twenty-six years, he still believes his English is not as good as it should be. One can only wonder what epigrams he would coin if his language measured up to his standards, for many of his ad-libs are classics: it was he, not Robert Benchley, who said, "Let me get out of these wet clothes and into a dry martini." This has been in print many times, always attributed to Benchley. Other Wilderisms are too typical of his unique humor to be attributed to anyone else, such as one uttered during the filming of *Sunset Boulevard*. Wilder came to a scene in which there was to be a funeral for Gloria Swanson's pet monkey. "How do you see this scene?" asked the assistant director. "Oh," Wilder said, shrugging, "the usual monkey funeral."

Wilder's impatience with trivia—and his combination of corrosive wit and wry amusement at human foibles—stem to a very real degree from his experiences as a young man in post–World War I Berlin. That was a city of dreary disillusionment and cynicism which produced the savage art of George Grosz and the savagely angry poetry and plays of Bertolt Brecht. Berlin was a place of disenchantment in which the majority of intellectuals could only reflect bitterly upon man's essential, constitutional foolishness. It took a tough-minded, resilient spirit to merely survive.

Into this atmosphere arrived young Billy Wilder, born in Galicia, on June 22, 1906, son of Max Wilder, who flitted from business to business: owner of a trout hatchery, proprietor of a watch factory, operator of restaurants, exporter of leather handbags—in short, says Wilder, "A dreamer, never very successful at any one thing, always going into something else." The boy, christened Samuel, was called "Billy" because his mother wanted him to have an American name.

Wilder's father, hoping Billy would be a lawyer, sent him for eight years to the *Real Gymnasium,* where he absorbed Latin and Greek and chafed to get out into the world. At his father's insistence he went next to the University of Vienna, but lasted there less than a year. He got a job as a reporter on a newspaper where he was paid space rates, that is, according to the amount of material he was able to get into print.

Soon, he was doing fairly well. Part of his success was due to the fact that there were so many famous and talented people in Vienna at the time. "One year they were preparing a Christmas edition of the paper, and my job was to get messages from well known people," Wilder recalls. "In a single morning I interviewed Sigmund Freud, his colleague Alfred Adler, the playwright and novelist Arthur Schnitzler, and the composer Richard Strauss. In *one* morning."

Paul Whiteman was responsible for Wilder's deserting Vienna for Berlin. Whiteman went to Vienna with his huge "symphonic jazz" orchestra, and Wilder reviewed the concert for his newspaper. Whiteman was so pleased with the review that he called Wilder and asked him to go to Berlin to write another review of Whiteman's forthcoming appearance there. When Wilder's editor refused to pay his expenses, Whiteman said he would sponsor him. Wilder went along to Berlin, became enchanted with the city, and never went back to Vienna.

In Berlin he got another newspaper space-rates job and augmented his income by hiring out as a tea-time dancing partner for unescorted women in hotels and restaurants. One day he ran into Robert Siodmak, the director, who knew a man who had five thousand reichsmarks floating around and wanted to make a film. Wilder was hired to write it. The film, *People on Sunday*, became a minor classic, and Wilder today is pleased to recollect that it is in the permanent film collection of the Museum of Modern Art in New York. He had another reason to be pleased with it then, for it plunged him into the German film industry, at that time the second largest in the world. During the next few years he wrote fifty-odd films of his own and worked on at least as many more. He made money and spent it all. In 1933, when he was twenty-seven, fairly well-known, but inconveniently Jewish, he moved to Paris. He got off the train carrying one suitcase and a rolled-up bunch of canvases, for he already had begun to collect paintings. He checked them in the station and rushed to the tennis matches to watch the great Fred Perry and Bunny Austin wrest the Davis Cup from the French. (By then he was mad about sports, too. Today, apart from making films, fine art and sports are still Wilder's principal delights. His apartment is full of Picassos, Rouaults, Dufys, and other famous modernists, and his head is full of such statistics as how many bases Lou Gehrig stole, a collection which affords him nearly as much pleasure as his paintings and sculpture do.)

Paris proved to be not as hospitable as Berlin. Wilder scrounged, living off German expatriates who had money to lend, enduring the days in a sour little hotel. Presently he got a job as director on the first film to star Danielle Darrieux, *Mauvaise Graine*—another small classic—and that brought him to the attention of an American film executive then in Paris, Joe May, who liked an original screen treatment Wilder had written, *Pam-Pam*. May took it to Hollywood, where it was bought by Paramount. The money transported Wilder himself to Hollywood, but things were even tougher there than in Paris. He was reduced to living in a lavatory in a fleabag actors' hotel on Sunset Strip until he bumped into Peter Lorre, an old friend from his Berlin days, and moved in with him. Lorre's room was not especially good either—it cost around five dollars a week—but it was a distinct improvement over his previous abode.

Meanwhile, he was learning English, mostly from the radio and American girls. Once able to communicate, his luck changed. His first break in Hollywood came in 1934, when Sam Briskin at Columbia hired him as a junior writer at $125 a week. He lasted six weeks. Then, in order to get his immigration status straightened out, he had to go to Mexico and re-enter the U.S. By the time he got back, Paramount was ready to take him on.

Manny Wolf, an executive there, called him in one day and introduced him to another writer, Charles Brackett. Brackett, who came from a blooded East Coast family, had been a lawyer in Saratoga Springs, New York, a part-time novelist, and drama critic of *The New Yorker* before he had been called to Hollywood. Now, acting on a hunch, Brackett paired with Wilder to do the screenplay for *Bluebeard's Eighth Wife,* to star Gary Cooper and Claudette Colbert, and to be directed by the fabulous Ernst Lubitsch. It was a great hit and the writing team was made as a result of it. By 1945, they were rocketing toward legendary status: that year, their *Lost Weekend* made an all-but-clean sweep of the Academy Awards. (Wilder alone has been nominated for Oscars eighteen times, and has won three. "I was robbed fifteen times," he says. He was not robbed of approximately seventy other citations handed out by various foreign film festivals for his U.S. films. The walls of his office are covered with plaques, certificates and scrolls.)

Wilder and Brackett became legends in other ways. They were known for their ability to work anywhere—in barber chairs, while playing The Word Game or cribbage, or at parties. They were known for their no-nonsense atti-tude toward the industrialists who were in charge of the industry: where other writers acted like serfs, they stood up for their rights. Brackett, a most articulate and persuasive man, presently got them into the position where they not only wrote but also produced and directed their films, he doing the former and Wilder the latter. Eventually, they were regarded as a pair who could do no wrong. In addition to those films already mentioned, they made *Midnight, What a Life, Rhythm on the River, Arise, My Love, Hold Back the Dawn, Ball of Fire, The Major and the Minor, Five Graves to Cairo, The Emperor Waltz,* and others, the last named the only bomb they had. Their pictures had already grossed more than fifteen million dollars. Then they made *Sunset Boulevard,* one of their best. In 1950, at the peak of their partnership, they split up. The Happiest Couple in Hollywood, as writer Lincoln Barnett once called them, got a divorce. Neither will say exactly why.

Since the separation, Wilder has done much better than Brackett, but at first it did not look as though he would. His first film as a single was *Ace in the Hole,* in which Kirk Douglas played a hard-bitten, opportunistic newspa-perman covering a mine disaster that attracted tremendous crowds hoping to be in on an authentic tragedy. It was panned in the U.S. on its first screen-ing and was then tried with a new title (*The Big Carnival*), but not even that could save it. The critics said it was full of hatred for the human race, but it remained for Wilder's friend I. A. L. Diamond to make the definitive comment on it, as he did when we were talking: "Sure, they called it cynical," Diamond told me. "And then you see thousands and thousands of people turning up at Idlewild airport in New York to watch a plane coming down with a bad landing gear. People clog the runway waiting for it to crash—and you ask yourself how cynical *Ace in the Hole* really was."

Ace was the only American box-office flop Billy turned out alone, but it did well overseas and won a lot of awards. There followed *Stalag 17, Sabrina, The Seven Year Itch,* and all the rest. Wilder became an independent with a major financial interest in his own productions. On his two most recent films he worked with the Mirisch Brothers, who provided financing and distribution. The Mirisches are former popcorn concessionaires from Chicago who are delighted to let Wilder have his own way about everything.

This is good, for Wilder is in many ways as autocratic and imperious as was his old friend, the late Erich von Stroheim. He will listen to advice but usually reject it. Yet this does not mean that he is a totalitarian martinet. He is, on the surface at any rate, the most amiable and easygoing of men.

This is true on the set and doubly true of his private and social life. His wife, Audrey, finds him a delightful combination of husband and mentor. They were married soon after he finished *The Lost Weekend.* In it, she played a checkroom girl who gave the drunk—Ray Milland—his hat as he was being hurled out of a bar. Wilder cut the scene so that only her forearm appeared and both Wilders agreed that the forearm gave a superb performance. Having achieved that triumph, Miss Young and her forearm retired from the screen for good.

The Wilders are great go-outers. They like to attend parties and they like to go to Las Vegas when Sinatra, Sammy Davis, Jr., Dean Martin and other members of The Clan are appearing there. They do not entertain much at home, but when they do, Wilder's idea of a fine evening is to play some bridge or chess with friends or to sit and stare at the Roller Derby on television. He is enchanted by the savagery exhibited by female roller skaters and wrestlers. Home, to the Wilders, is an apartment on Wilshire Boulevard, consisting of a bedroom, a bath, a kitchen, and one huge room divided by furniture into living, dining and library areas, all lavishly strewn with proof of Wilder's unshakable passion for poking around art galleries and antique shops. The library section is distinguished by its lack of leather-bound copies of The Collected Works of Billy Wilder. Hollywood writers usually have their scripts bound in hand-tooled leather after they are completed, but Wilder says, "I don't believe in that crap."

He is unconcerned about the Hollywood heresy he commits by not maintaining an elaborate house, a swimming pool, a tennis court, and a huge stall of servants (the Wilders have one woman who comes in to help clean up after Audrey has cooked). "I am simplifying my life," he says. "It is important to simplify everything. Everything is too cluttered—everybody owns too many things." As though contradicting this, he goes on buying paintings, sculpture, *objects d'art* and bric-a-brac at a fast clip. The apartment now is one of the showplaces of Hollywood, and people go to great lengths to get invited there. One person who was invited not long ago was Vladimir Nabokov, author of *Lolita;* Wilder loves to tell guests about Nabokov's visit. "Which of my paintings," he asks, "do you think Nabokov liked best?" And then he leads the way to the bedroom to display a painting by Balthus of a nymphet standing in her camisole. "That is the one he liked," he says.

Wilder seldom goes to bed before two A.M., but he is always in his office early the next morning. Often, even before he has finished a film, he starts work on a new one. When he is writing, he puts up a blackboard and scribbles on it key words that he and his collaborator use as guides. While working, he paces. More accurately, he lunges and flings himself back and forth across the room, into the Danish black leather chair behind his desk, out of it, into a nubby red Saarinen chair and out of that, down onto a long cream-colored couch and up from that too, pausing every now and then to stop and stare at the pictures on the wall—a Ben Shahn, a Saul Steinberg—as though seeing them for the first time, all the while absent-mindedly flicking at his legs with one of a large collection of carved walking sticks and canes and umbrellas kept handy in an antique stand.

Wilder carries some supporting baton much of the time because he is subject to back pains—especially when he is shooting a picture. His wife says, "It used to be headaches, then it was stomach trouble—now it's the back." Wilder says he has been to doctors everywhere for years and has decided simply to live with the back as comfortably as he can. "It is *not* psychosomatic," he says, flatly. "It goes back to my days in Vienna, where I got it making love to girls in doorways—and very often there were no girls, only doorways." His wife, who has picked up some of his caustic outlook, adds to that: "*I'm* paying for his youthful indiscretions."

One day recently Wilder invited me to his office for lunch. He told me at the time that he was thinking about doing *Irma La Douce,* the London musical now also on Broadway, and that he hoped to be able to convince the Mirisches to let him do it in black and white. "I hate color," he said, angrily. "Even words sound phony when the picture is in color. Everybody looks blue or red. It's like shooting a jukebox. Some of the colored films that the English and the Japanese have done are subtle, but the way we pour on that multicolored sherbet, it's nauseating." He lighted a cigarette. "I smoke too much," he observed (he pulls four packs a day, and once remarked that he would give it up, except that he might be hit by an automobile and he would hate lying in the gutter bleeding to death and thinking about all the fun he had missed).

He began pacing, as though he had something on his mind, which indeed he did: he always has something on his mind. I told him that I had enjoyed *The Apartment* and that I had been annoyed by critics who thought it something less than moral.

"In my opinion it is a highly moral picture," Wilder said. "I had to show two people who were being emancipated, and in order to do that I had to show what they were emancipated by."

"From," I said.

"With," he said, grinning. "Look here, my friend. I don't want to talk about Art. I am an artist but I am a man who makes motion pictures for a mass audience, I am making pictures on all levels. To be a mechanic working in a back-alley garage, tinkering away for years and coming out with one little automobile, that is one thing, but to work on an assembly line and come out with a Cadillac—that is something else. That is what I am trying to do here."

I asked him how he felt about arty camera angles and he told me about what happened during the shooting of *Sunset Boulevard.* There was a scene in which Gloria Swanson and William Holden danced together in the dusty, deserted ballroom of her crumbling, once-elegant mansion. Willie Shore, Wilder's assistant producer, had gone up on the catwalk, high above the set, and looked down. "He urged me to photograph the scene from that vantage. I told him, 'It is very nice, very artistic, but who sees the scene from this angle?' Shore argued with me: 'What do you care who sees it? It's a great shot.' " As he was relating the incident, Wilder shook his head so violently the cigarette waggled in the corner of his mouth. "No," I told him. "It does not push the story along. We shoot only from the angles that help us tell the story. When somebody turns to his neighbor and says, 'My, that was beautifully directed,' we have proof it was not."

I then brought up the subject of Ingmar Bergman and Wilder jumped to the bait. "Ingmar Bergman to me is very interesting, but only for a limited young audience. For me, his things are *deja vu*, for we used every shot he does back in Berlin. To me, a director who uses phenomenal neck-craning setups, beautiful pictures everywhere, isn't worth a damn. He isn't doing what he should be doing, telling the story." Such strict addiction to storytelling is part of what enables Wilder to shoot economically and to bring his pictures to completion on time and within his budget. "I do not believe in wasting money," Wilder said. "On the other hand, nobody is going to go and see a picture because it came in under its budget."

Wilder brandished a scarlet umbrella he had picked up. "I know what is going into my pictures before I start," he stated. "Once I said, 'When I am finished, there is nothing left on the cutting-room floor but cigarette butts, chewing gum wrappers and tears.' It is true. I could probably win any number of prizes, but prizes are of no interest to me. I could clean up in the film festivals—if I took $25,000 and made a picture about the sex life of fishermen in Sardinia, as long as it had a certain morbid message and was slightly out of focus. This is true, too—but I am not interested in that. I am interested in producing adult entertainment. What seems to make the European pictures more adult than ours is that we don't understand the dialog."

He paused, replaced the umbrella in the stand, then picked up a sword cane he had found in Berlin. "On the other hand, I don't believe that people out here in this factory should pay too much attention to either the critics or the exhibitors. Neither of them knows much about the picture business. These days movies are longer than they used to be. The exhibitors complain about that. But I believe we should ignore them. An exhibitor complaining about length is like a motel manager telling his guests to get out before midnight."

He threw the sword cane into the umbrella stand and took up a cane with a telescoped fishing rod inside it, a present William Holden sent him from Japan. Then he put that down and walked briskly to a niche in his office that contains a refrigerator, a stove and a sink. He mixed us each a martini, handed me mine, set his on his desk, and began to stride about again.

"Out here they are always talking about deals," he said, sighing. "I tell them, 'You spend a whole year making a deal—why don't you spend that time making a picture? No, they are more interested in the deals. And the deals are for pictures in cycles. Western cycles, gangster cycles, all kinds of cycles. Now there is a cycle of Freudian pictures coming up. I would not be surprised if soon they make *Hopalong Oedipus, Frontier Mother Lover*."

As he paused again, putting down the fishing rod cane and picking up a carved stick he had bought in London, I asked him if he had considered working in television. He looked as though he was positive I had lost my reason. "I wouldn't drink the water on television," he said. "No, my dear friend. I am too old, too tired, too rich—but I am delighted with that medium, I must say, because it used to be that we in films were in the eyes of the snobs the lowest art form. Now we have something to look down on. The whole thing is degrading to the performers. Imagine if you were a novelist and every fourteen pages the publisher stuck in a full-page advertisement. I must say some of the performers are not bad.

"No, seriously, I have no interest in television. Not for all the money, all the freedom in the world. Somebody asked me once if I thought any of the television stories would be good on the big screen. I said I didn't think most of them were worth even the small screen."

While he continued to pace, I asked him if there were any of his films that were his special favorites. "There are some I loathe less than others," he said. "The worst was *The Spirit of St. Louis*. Some things I did make were copied in others—*Double Indemnity* set the pattern for a lot of things. I liked *Sunset Boulevard*. Nearly all of them have some pretty fine stretches and some booboos here and there, but I would go crazy if I woke up at night, bathed in sweat and thought, '*This* is what I should have done.' " Now he was going back and forth across the room like a newly caged jaguar. "Don't make me think about the dogs I have committed," he said, setting down his empty martini glass. "Come, we go to lunch."

We walked down to the commissary. On the way, Wilder was stopped and buttonholed by three men who wanted his advice on various problems. He listened patiently to all. At lunch, producers, directors and actors kept stopping by his table, each with something to ask. Wilder was obviously enjoying himself. Yet, on the way back to his office he indicated the full measure of his dedication and his seriousness about his work with one significant remark which belied his relaxed and chatty outward manner. "Sometime," he said with the finality and intensity of the true artist, "I will make a picture a little less imperfect than all the rest."

In Wilder's Wild West

THOMAS WOOD/1961

BILLY WILDER, PRODUCER-DIRECTOR, strode out of his Hilton headquarters here the other day, took a quick look up at the clearing skies and said, in his nervous, impatient way: "Okay. Get your steel helmets everybody. We're going back to the Gate." And with that he jumped into a waiting car and sped to a location site on the Strasse des 17 Juni, near the Brandenburg Gate, followed by the cast and crew of his new comedy, *One, Two, Three,* which he is making here for United Artists release late this year.

While the armament was strictly a figure of speech, it did fit the situation. Ever since Wilder placed the picture before the cameras in early June, he has been engaged in a private war with the East Berlin authorities over permission to shoot a sequence through the gate, which lies entirely within the Soviet sector of "Splitsville," as the divided city is known to the company.

The sequence he wanted to make was a simple one, showing Horst Buchholz—co-starring in the picture with James Cagney, Pamela Tiffin, Arlene Francis, Hanns Lothar and Lilo Pulver—riding a battered motor bike through the gate into East Berlin. When the Communist authorities were first asked about the shot, they readily agreed to let it be made. Everything was set up, Buchholz got on his bike and started down the street toward the gate, with the camera, mounted on a truck, following him. Then Wilder pulled the first of what will be one of many topical notes in the picture. Attached to the

From the *New York Times,* 16 July 1961. © 1961 The New York Times Company. Reprinted by permission.

motor bike was a large yellow balloon on which was printed, in big black letters, "Russki Go Home."

Unfortunately for Wilder, the weather turned bad that first day and he was unable to complete the sequence. "It was Hitler's last revenge," he says now, because, when he went back the next day to finish the shot, he found the Soviet sector out of bounds and the gate bristling with uniformed policemen, equipped with field glasses through which they watched every move he was making. Wilder was able to stage the sequence up to the boundary line, some thirty yards from the gate, but that was all.

However, before withdrawing from the field, Wilder scored a minor victory. He made a dry run of the shot up to the boundary line, and then sent word to the Communists that they were in the picture and, while it was all right with him, he was afraid that it would give audiences the impression that East Berlin was a police state. That cleared the gate fast.

Wilder, who is producer, director and co-author of his pictures, is an incurable optimist. He began to negotiate with the Communists again. On this particular morning, it appeared that positive thinking might pay off. The East Berlin police, he was told, were in a bargaining mood. But, as the camera was being strapped into position on the truck, the war was on again. Before they could grant permission, the East Berlin authorities insisted they be allowed to read the script. Wilder rejected that notion and at the same time, struck a mighty blow for free speech. "Nonsense," he replied. "I wouldn't even show my script to President Kennedy."

Not all of the picture takes place at the Brandenburg Gate, of course. Nor were the Communists the only targets of Wilder's humor. The screen play, written in association with I. A. L. Diamond (with whom Wilder wrote the scripts of *The Apartment, Some Like It Hot,* and *Love in the Afternoon*), pokes fun at everybody. It is, essentially, a topical story set in modern-day Berlin.

The project represents the Viennese-born director's return to his old home grounds. In 1933, carrying a half-filled suitcase, he fled Berlin one step ahead of the Gestapo. Eleven years later, he was back as film chief of the American Information Control Division in Germany. Those experiences inspired the memorable comedy *A Foreign Affair,* with Marlene Dietrich as postwar Berlin's most attractive commodity.

Only the film's exteriors are being shot here. The interiors will be done in Munich. But, though the picture is being made entirely in Europe, it cannot be termed a so-called "runaway" production. All of the key people in the crew, such as camera man, script supervisor, special-effects man, head gaffer and cutter, are from Hollywood, and all have worked with Wilder before.

In many respects, Wilder is a bigger star on his own pictures than any of his actors. Something of an aggressive imp, he achieves his results with a steady barrage of bubbling comments, most of them derogatory, many of them unprintable, but all of them highly quotable. Speaking of one of his associates of some twenty years, for example, he said, "Obviously the man has no talent but I'm used to him." Another time, after one of the rebuffs at the gate, he commented, "I wonder if they'll let us shoot there if I have the musical score written by Irving East Berlin."

Though some of the action of the story, which is an outrageous attempt of American big business to penetrate the Iron Curtain market, takes place in East Berlin, none of the film will be shot there. Thanks to Berlin's sense of history, there are many places here that have been left just as they were when the Third Reich fell. Some of these areas, particularly those centering on Margareten and Victoria Strassen and the Anhalter railway station, are dotted with gutted buildings and piles of debris and look for all the world like most of the Soviet sector.

In contrast to this background of utter desolation, the scenes that take place in West Berlin are being staged in such rebuilt and restored sections as the Kurfuerstendamm, the Siegesalle, the Tiergarten, the Coca-Cola bottling plant and, of course, the West Berlin side of the Brandenburg Gate.

As a matter of fact, the East Berlin side of the gate is also going to appear in the Mirisch Company presentation. Even now a full-size reproduction of the gate is being built on the back lot of the Bavaria studio in Munich. Its construction is adding a few pfennigs to the budget, naturally, but Wilder feels that, whatever it costs, it'll be worth it.

"Those people over there have no sense of humor. That's their trouble," he pointed out. "So now we'll get back at them. Just wait and see what we shoot on the other side."

The Message in Billy Wilder's Fortune Cookie: "Well, Nobody's Perfect..."

RICHARD LEMON/1966

POETS HAVE LONG MAINTAINED that success is an illusion, but much less attention has been paid to the illusory quality of failure. Kipling spoke of the wisdom of meeting with triumph and disaster and treating those two impostors just the same, but then, Kipling is out of style just now. The fact is, however, that throughout history man's epic failures have come about not through ineptness alone but through an ingenious combination of misused talent, bad timing, and sheer rotten luck. First Lord of the Admiralty Winston Churchill was only partly to blame for the British debacle at Gallipoli in World War I, but he resigned in disgrace and was considered finished in politics. Ernest Hemingway's novel *Across the River and Into the Trees* was only a bad book, but it was written in his usual vigorous style; reviewers reacted as though it were some sort of offense against mankind, probably done on purpose. Charlie Chaplin's *Limelight* came out when he was in political disgrace, and Ingrid Bergman and Roberto Rossellini released *Stromboli* after having a baby out of wedlock; almost nobody but pickets went near the two movies, which in turn was taken as proof that Chaplin, Bergman and Rossellini were all washed up.

The most notable recent example of this eminence by catastrophe was a movie by Billy Wilder, a director who, in a 30-year career, has had about as many successes as anybody in American movies. Wilder has won six Academy Awards—two for directing, three for writing, one for producing—which is a record. He has had hits in just about every dramatic form: he co-wrote

From *The Saturday Evening Post,* 17 December 1966. Reprinted by permission.

Ninotchka, Greta Garbo's great sophisticated comedy, and he co-wrote and directed *Double Indemnity,* a classic murder melodrama; *The Lost Weekend,* a film about alcoholism which won four Oscars all told; *Sunset Boulevard,* a tragedy about Hollywood; and *The Apartment,* which brought him three Oscars and was the best movie of the year. His productions have grossed more than $60 million, which puts him up with the top money-making directors, and his reputation inside the movie world is almost mystical. Wilder and his wife, Audrey, are considered the social leaders for a large chunk of the movie-world's elite, and his professional judgment is so respected that he has been able to sign up virtually any actor he wanted even before a script was written. Most striking of all, Wilder's recent comedies, from *Some Like It Hot* to *Irma La Douce,* had made daring use of sex without offending the general public, with the result that Hollywood's censor, Geoffrey Shurlock, had concluded that Wilder could "beat the odds"—meaning that he could get away with material that would be called vulgar if it came from anybody less skillful. It is a good bet that, as of two years ago, a great many movie people would have named Billy Wilder as the most talented and successful man in American movies.

Then, in December of 1964, while a showing of his life's work was running at New York's Museum of Modern Art and one week after U.S. Catholics had pledged to stay away from "indecent, immoral and unwholesome motion pictures," Wilder released *Kiss Me, Stupid.* If one had excerpted the strongest parts of the ensuing reviews, after the custom of movie advertising, the result would have run like this:

REPELLENT! SQUALID!—*The New Yorker*

LOUDMOUTHED! TASTELESS! CHEAP!—*Christian Century*

THE SLIMIEST MOVIE OF THE YEAR!—N. Y. *Herald Tribune*

COARSE! SMUTTY! SNEAKY DOUBLE ENTENDRES!—N. Y. *Daily News*

A TITANIC DIRTY JOKE!—*Life*

THOROUGHLY SORDID! REPULSIVE!—Legion of Decency

ONE WONDERS ABOUT BILLY WILDER—IS SENILITY SETTING IN OR HAS HE ALWAYS BEEN . . . NOT QUITE BRIGHT?—*Films in Review*

Of course there were exceptions. One magazine critic wrote that he liked the picture immensely, then tried to sell Wilder a movie script. European critics praised the movie's "cheery bad taste." But about the only U.S. review that was both favorable and sensible appeared in *Vogue,* whose lady critic promptly got a note:

"I read your piece in the beauty parlor while sitting under the hair drier," it read, "and it sure did the old pornographer's heart good. Cheers. Billy Wilder."

Excluding *The Spirit of St. Louis*, a commercially unsuccessful but respectable movie about Charles Lindbergh, *Kiss Me, Stupid* was Wilder's first taste of big-time failure in 14 years, but it might have been custom-made to undermine his reputation. Some critics had frequently berated Wilder for failures of taste and morality, complaining that his heroes were sinful weaklings, and that he hooked up his satires with happy endings. Wilder and co-writer I. A. L. Diamond had envisioned *Kiss Me, Stupid* as a bawdy comedy, in the manner of the Restoration theater, which would satirize some American preoccupations with sex. Instead they found themselves accused of the same preoccupations, which seemed to prove that Wilder's critics had been right all along. Furthermore, *Kiss Me, Stupid* arrived at a time when many people of stern conscience, frustrated by arguments that sex was permissible in works of art, were on the lookout for a work that seemed plainly dirty without being cluttered up with redeeming artistic qualities. *Kiss Me, Stupid* was ideally suited to a morality backlash.

"Billy was spoiled lately with success, and they really let him have it," says Walter Reisch, a screenwriter who is Wilder's oldest friend. "He asked me not to see the picture. It is the one thing about which he has no sense of humor."

"I was absolutely baffled by the reaction," Wilder said, pacing up and down his office many long months after these events; he then was already far into the writing of his next movie, *The Fortune Cookie*, which opened last October. "I've seen many a picture, believe me, that was far more suggestive and dirty. I don't mind reading a slew of reviews that say it was bad. It probably was bad. But what hurt me was that old pals said I set out deliberately to make a dirty picture. I go out into new territory and dig for oil, and sometimes all that comes up is vinegar. And sometimes the digging operation is so expensive we try to recoup the losses by selling the vinegar. I have the greatest respect for a director like [George] Cukor [director of *My Fair Lady*], but he is in a slightly different business. He buys oil and decants it. It would bore the —— off me to make *The Sound of Music* and *My Fair Lady*. They're very good pictures, but for me there's no challenge to it.

"When I was lying in the gutter," he said briskly, "a number of people came along and administered a kick in the groin. But in that period of depression and self-doubt, there was an element of beauty. My office is a clearing house usually for my chums—maybe they have third-act troubles, maybe they have actor troubles, and I work with them. Well, they stayed away in droves. They don't even put the bite on me right now. It's like the Ford plant after the Edsel was made. And it's wonderful. I have some time for the first time.

"We in Hollywood do not bury our dead," Wilder said suddenly, shifting metaphors; Wilder has the equivalent of a syncro-mesh transmission when it comes to metaphors, and can shift them at very high speeds. "They continue to stink. They will stink next week in Cincinnati and in London and in Paris, and two years from now they will stink on television."

Wilder ticked off a few dozen paces back and forth. "After the picture came out," he said, "I went to Europe and walked through the snow and got it out of my system and came back and sat down with my esteemed colleague, I. A. L. Diamond. For twelve weeks we sat and stared at each other. He said we were like parents who have produced a two-headed child and don't dare to have sexual intercourse.

"But we shall survive," he added, picking up steam. "We shall now come out with the Mustang and sweep the market."

But then it was noted that Wilder had not really given his personal opinion of the picture and he was asked what *he* thought of it. There was a pause, during which Wilder placed himself against a partition and stared at his inquisitor. "I have the capacity for erasing it from my mind," he said, finally. "I just don't think about it anymore. It's down the drain, across the river, and into the trees." Then he abruptly erased himself from the room, returning five minutes later with his coat on, to go out to lunch.

"Well, you can't figure them all, Walter."

—DOUBLE INDEMNITY

Billy Wilder is as at home in Hollywood as if he had invented the place, as, to a small extent, he has. He "invented" The Bistro, which is currently about the most fashionable restaurant in Beverly Hills, and he invented *Sunset Boulevard,* which may be the best movie ever made about Hollywood. Wilder has even become a little proprietary about the movie community, and he takes considerable umbrage at those who disparage or mistreat it. "Billy thinks it's his town," a fellow worker noted recently with hostility.

When Darryl Zanuck took over 20th Century-Fox studios and let go a number of movie veterans, including one of Wilder's former associates, Wilder
told him, in a telegram released to the press, that the firings were callous and
his studio should be razed by bulldozers. When screenwriter Abby Mann
spoke critically of Hollywood while at the Moscow Film Festival, Wilder shot
the trade papers another wire: WHO APPOINTED ABBY MANN AS SPOKES-
MAN FOR THE AMERICAN FILM WORLD IN MOSCOW? PERSONALLY, I'D
RATHER BE REPRESENTED BY ABBEY RENTS [which is a local agency renting
everything from hospital beds to hair dryers].

Nonetheless, Wilder himself at first seems a surprising spokesman for Hollywood to have produced. He lives unostentatiously and does not call people
"baby" or "pussycat." He is more apt to call them "Mr. Green" or "Mr. Watson," in the ironic, formal manner of a college professor. He cares little about
personal publicity, except as it will help a picture, and has no public-relations
man. He also has no agent and, beyond one secretary, who has been with
him 16 years, no employees. Even his commercial success is anachronistic,
because many of his pictures have been exuberantly cynical and bitter. After
Kiss Me, Stupid was attacked for being cheaply commercial, Wilder's co-
writer, I. A. L. Diamond, protested that "Nobody ever made a fast buck by
telling people they're no damned good," but that is just about what Wilder
has been doing for years.

Wilder and his second wife, Audrey, live in an apartment in Westwood,
and they are among the few movie people whose reputations could stand it.
Westwood is fairly elegant, but it isn't at all chic. Furthermore, around Hollywood, almost nobody above the rank of spear carrier lives in an apartment,
if only because it's hard to have a swimming pool there. But there are the
Wilders, living like New Yorkers high above Westwood, with elevator service
and a small terrace, which sports Wilder's collection of Bonsai trees, and a
medium-size living room festooned with art. Wilder began collecting art
before he collected any money, and when he fled Berlin as a young man he
left behind a fine collection of Mies van der Rohe furniture. Today, small
Picassos, Chagalls, Bonnards, Dufys, Roualts, Calder mobiles, Maillol and
Moore statues, and simple $10 obelisks, all sprout from the walls, tables,
floors and ceilings. "You don't have paintings," one dealer told him, "you
have *hors d'oeuvres.*"

For all his prominence in Hollywood, Wilder has no entourage, and many
of his friends are linked to the movies indirectly or not at all. One of his

closest friends is Charles Eames, the architect and designer who created, among other things, a rosewood-and-leather chair which has become a classic and a status symbol and shows up in everything from high-priced doctors' offices to Scotch whisky ads. The chair was originally made as a present for Wilder. The two men have been exchanging furniture for 16 years, and Eames had no thought of marketing this one until Herman Miller, the furniture company, asked to be allowed to manufacture it. Since then, about 12,000 chairs, at roughly $600 each, have been sold.

"You design for someone in particular," Eames notes, with pleasure, "and then you find out that other people have more in common with the object of your affection than you realized."

Wilder is an excellent bridge player, and he is a member of a bridge set that meets every Saturday and Sunday and sometimes in-between. The game is noisy, with lots of jokes. Lew Wasserman, the president of M.C.A., a large, powerful production company, was pressured into joining it one afternoon, although he protested that he was out of practice. "You know, for a fella who hasn't played for a year," Wilder said cheerfully, as the game broke up, "he certainly played badly."

"Billy is a regular winner in that game, and not because he's a great technician," says Alfred Sheinwold, the professional player and columnist, who is another regular. "He can't be bothered with that. He's a *good* technician, but more than anything else, he plays the people. Bridge players would use an expression: 'He always knows where the queen of spades is.' The expert may try all sorts of discovery plays to find that out. Billy just looks at the people and knows."

Speed is probably the dominant element in Billy Wilder's life. He is an avid sports fan and loves to watch baseball and football, particularly at the same time. He keeps two TV sets for the purpose. He is a very good chess player, but he won't play chess because it takes too long.

"Speed is absolutely of the essence to him," Walter Reisch says. "He cannot do anything slowly. If he enters a party, and everybody is talking slowly, he leaves. People who insist on finishing their sentences drive him crazy—he wants to write it himself. That's why he likes paintings—they don't talk back. That's his only fear in life—to be bored. He cannot stand to be with people who bore him.

"Which doesn't mean he doesn't like them or respect them. He just doesn't mingle with them. He loves them and avoids them."

Wilder's speediness is illustrated by his entry into the restaurant business. "My pal Romanoff [of the famous Romanoff's restaurant], you know, closed." Wilder says, "and I wanted there to be a restaurant I would like to go to." Kurt Niklas, a former captain at Romanoff's, who is the manager and principal stockholder in The Bistro, recently recalled its founding.

"When you're a captain, everybody tells you, 'If you ever want to open your own restaurant, come and see me,' " he said. "It's all baloney. It never happens. Billy was the only one I knew would be as good as his word, so when Romanoff's closed, I went to him. Within twenty-four hours Billy had checks in the mail for ninety thousand dollars. We have sixty stockholders, and the people Billy didn't get, his wife got."

Nonetheless, The Bistro did not turn out quite the way Wilder planned. It was conceived as a simple place with sawdust on the floor and red-checked tablecloths. It wound up with red carpets and dark paneling and mirrors for watching other tables. Wives, led by Audrey Wilder, are credited with the change, which doesn't surprise or bother Wilder. As he has noted about writing movies, "The background starts out to be a flower shop and winds up as a PT boat."

"You should be glad I'm not twelve. I was a very straightforward child. I used to spit."

—THE MAJOR AND THE MINOR

"Billy's too elusive, you know," Charles Lederer, the screenwriter, said to a reporter recently. "You won't be able to get him down on paper."

Still and all, the reporter felt he ought to try, so he went home and wrote:

Wilder, Billy, American film director, was born in Galicia, June 22, 1906. His father was in various businesses, including restaurants and trout hatcheries. Wilder briefly attended the University of Vienna and spent three years as a Vienna newspaper reporter, once interviewing Sigmund Freud, Alfred Adler, and Richard Strauss all in one morning. Bandleader Paul Whiteman was so pleased with a Wilder review of one of his concerts that he paid Wilder's way to Berlin to have him review a Whiteman concert there. Wilder stayed on in Berlin, where he wrote about 20 pictures in four years, his first being *People on Sunday,* which is now in the Museum of Modern Art's collection. Wilder fled to Paris when the Nazis came to power, and in a garage there he wrote and directed *Mauvaise Graine,* starring Danielle Darrieux. Before it came out in 1934, he moved on to Hollywood, where he won $15 at a party by jumping into a swimming pool with his clothes on and swimming the length. For some time this was the biggest splash he made in Hollywood. But in 1936 director Ernst Lubitsch was looking for a "cute-meet," which is to say a cute way of having a movie hero and heroine meet each other, for *Bluebeard's Eighth Wife,* starring Gary Cooper and Claudette Colbert. Wilder thought up the idea of having them meet at the pajama counter of a department store, where Cooper wanted to buy just the top from a pair of men's pajamas and Colbert wanted to buy just the pants. After that it was clear sailing. In collaboration with Charles Brackett, Wilder wrote a string of hits, including *Ninotchka, Midnight, What a Life, Arise My Love, Hold Back the Dawn,* and *Ball of Fire.* His first pictures as a director were *The Major and the Minor, Five Graves to Cairo* (both written with Brackett), and *Double Indemnity,* written with Raymond Chandler. Since then, Wilder has co-written and directed *The Lost Weekend, The Emperor Waltz, A Foreign Affair, Sunset Boulevard* (all with Brackett), *Ace in the Hole, Stalag 17, Sabrina, Seven Year Itch, The Spirit of St. Louis, Witness for the Prosecution,* and with Diamond, *Love in the Afternoon, Some Like It Hot, The Apartment, One, Two, Three, Irma La Douce,* and *Kiss Me, Stupid.*

But that didn't seem to get very much of Wilder, so then the reporter wrote:

The hallmarks of the filmic style of Billy Wilder are realism, cynicism, and a convoluted approach to the matter of sex. Although he has amended his filmic style somewhat in recent works in favor of a broader comedic approach, Wilder's greatest cinematic achievements have featured such settings as gas stations, bowling alleys, insurance offices, drive-ins and other commonplaces of the American milieu. They have also been marked by a low view of life and love. Wilder films being populated by insurance cheats, tax dodgers, gawkers, hookers, wife cheaters, low tippers, and other petty malefactors, creating a misanthropic ambience. . . .

But the reporter couldn't keep that up, so then he wrote:

An office in Hollywood. Standing behind a cluttered desk is BILLY WILDER, a short man of 60 who, oddly enough, gives the impression of being too tall for his age. He wears a checked cap and glasses and would be pacing except that he is tethered to a telephone. A few feet away, sprawled in a black

Eames chair, is I. A. L. DIAMOND. He is tall, thin, and bespectacled, and has the owlish look of a man who expects the worst but is content anyway.

WILDER: You still want to do a story on an old, tired, discouraged director?

(Cut to a hotel room where a nondescript reporter sits talking into the phone.)

REPORTER: Oh, yes, unless you've gotten cold feet about it.

WILDER: No cold feet. *(Talking faster.)* When all those people jumped on me, and I was definitively labeled as the pornographer of the West Coast, the Henry Miller of celluloid, everybody wanted me to write the Mad Hatter and Mr. X, the critics, and I just decided not to. But maybe the time has come to talk again. Have you met the Mad Hatter?

REPORTER: I met her just the other night.

WILDER: How many heads did she have?

REPORTER: Just one, Monday night.

WILDER: And even that was too much?

REPORTER: Well—

WILDER: I picture her as looking like Z, only uglier, which is very ugly.

REPORTER: No, in fact she's quite pleasant-looking.

WILDER: Please. Don't destroy my illusions.

But the reporter couldn't continue that long, either, so he gave up. A few days later, at an interview, Wilder handed him a piece of paper. "I thought you might be able to use this for your story," he said. The reporter unfolded it and read:

"I found out that the only way to improve your bridge game is to play with the experts for big stakes. Of course this does not improve your bank account. But who cares? Give me another fifteen years and I shall be runner-up for the Vanderbilt Cup—that's Sam Vanderbilt, who organizes the annual Salvation Army tournament, and the first prize is a cup of lentil soup."

"So now I have Wilder on paper," the reporter thought, and pocketed it.

"He is a tall, loose-jointed man of forty, with a brain full of razor blades and a heart full of chutzpah."

—DESCRIPTION OF A CHARACTER IN THE SCRIPT OF *The Fortune Cookie;* ALSO, REPORTEDLY, A DESCRIPTION BY WILLIAM HOLDEN OF BILLY WILDER.

One warm and pleasant afternoon—the sort of warm and pleasant afternoon that inspired ordinary men to make up Beverly Hills and Bel Air and

Holmby Hills—Walter Reisch served a visitor coffee, white wine, and rich, homemade cookies in his Bel-Air house. Mrs. Reisch, in a hostess gown, and their daughter, a student at U.C.L.A., sat by the fireplace. Reisch is a short, quick, energetic man with a tanned face who, in his 6o's, looks and bears himself a lot like a peppery gentleman who for years coached boxing at Yale.

"Billy and I started together in Berlin in 'Twenty-nine or so," Reisch said. "Berlin was an enormously inspiring city, full of experiments. It had come back to reality after the war, and we came from Austria, a little schnook country, and Billy was received as with open arms. He was a newspaperman from Austria who had developed a fantastic knack for getting interviews. For instance, the richest man in the world was Sir Basil Zaharoff, he sold arms to governments, to the Fascists. Nobody ever saw this man. Billy found out he was going to make a two-hour stopover on the train in Vienna. He walked right onto his train and got the interview. That man was stupefied by such *chutzpah.*

"Between trains he caught them," Reisch said. "How do you like the cookies?"

"Wonderful," the visitor said.

"You have to dunk them," Reisch said, grabbing a cookie and demonstrating. "In Vienna, everybody dunks the cookies in the wine. Did Billy tell you about the time he interviewed Freud? He was supposed to get famous people's opinions on something, and he got into his office and said, 'Dr. Freud, I'm from the paper.' " Reisch, imitating Freud, jumped up, extended his arm straight out, forefinger pointing, and growled " *'Rrrraus!'* ", which means "Get out!"

(Later, Wilder expanded on this. "The deal was very short. 'Herr Wilder?' 'Yes.' 'Dere is the door.' At that time Freud was attacked constantly. He was the funny charlatan who took everybody for a complicated cerebral ride; he felt about newspapermen the way I feel about them now. You know even now, every Strauss in Vienna has a statue, but Freud—nothing.")

"More than anything else it was Wilder's absolute zest for life that made him beloved," Reisch said. "He was the most gregarious sort. Always the fourth for bridge. Not too much work if possible. And a lot of poker games in between. A terrible critic, an absolute cynic. He never missed a poker match, never a tennis match and never a date with a pretty girl.

"In Berlin for a time, Billy was a dancer," Reisch went on. "The Hotel Eden was an international center for movie people, it held tea dances—*thé dansants*—every afternoon. Every famous hotel had a tea dance from five to eight. If a lady came with her husband who was not a dancer, the hotels saw that there was a gentleman who could dance with her. One had to have impeccable manners. That was the way you got your dinner, a few drinks, a cigarette and a little salary too.

"Hitler took over Berlin in January of 'Thirty-three. A few days later Wilder and I left for Paris, and our first stop when we got off the train was not at the producer's office. Our first stop in Paris was at the Stade Roland Garros to see a French-English tennis match. That was the most important event when Hitler came to power.

"Billy enjoys life more than anybody I know," Reisch said, walking his visitor to the door. "He has never gone 'Hollywood.' He makes everybody in his pictures feel important. Of course, he's also cruelly rude. He has very little leniency. But that's not from success. His wife once said, 'Long before Billy Wilder was Billy Wilder, he behaved as though he were Billy Wilder.' "

Wilder arrived in Hollywood in 1934, with little money and less reputation. To buck up his family during the lean days in Berlin, he had written that he had changed his name to 'Thornton' and enclosed clippings about Thornton Wilder's *The Bridge of San Luis Rey*. His mother learned the truth when she bought the book and saw the author's picture, but she took it well. "That other fellow Wilder," she said, "I never really liked his stuff very much." In America, Wilder spent two years carrying two scripts around, making no sales. For a while he was reduced to living—with permission—in the ladies room of an apartment hotel. Then in 1936 Wilder wrote *Bluebeard's Eighth Wife* with Charles Brackett, the urbane and witty former drama critic at *The New Yorker,* in what became the most famous writing team in the movies.

Wilder's father had died in Berlin in 1926, and his mother had remarried. Wilder never saw his family after he came to Hollywood. "My mother, my grandmother and my stepfather died in Auschwitz," he says. "My mother died around Nineteen-forty, 'Forty-one—I could never find out exactly when—but I know through the Red Cross that she was gassed at Auschwitz."

In 1945, near the end of the war, Wilder was appointed by Elmer Davis to head the motion picture section, Psychological Warfare Division of the U.S. Army in Germany, with the rank of colonel and responsibility for all theaters and radio stations in occupied Germany. The nearest he got to action was a time when some requisitioned champagne exploded and, thinking they were under fire, Wilder led all his men under their Jeep.

"After the war," Wilder says, "some Germans wanted to put on a passion play, and a carpenter wrote me asking permission to play Jesus. After we screened them we found out that six of the Apostles were Gestapo men and the carpenter was a stormtrooper. I said, 'Yes, as long as the nails are real.' "

Wilder's directing career got into high gear with *Double Indemnity,* and in 1950 the Wilder-Brackett writing partnership was dissolved. There were rumors of an argument, but the two men have nothing but good to say about each other now.

Wilder's first picture after the breakup was *Ace in the Hole,* since retitled *The Big Carnival.* It was a black and ferocious parable about man's inhumanity to man in which a reporter (Kirk Douglas) prolongs the rescue of a man trapped in a cave in order to make a bigger story out of it; finally, while thousands of curiosity seekers and a carnival and TV cameras are massed outside the cave, the man dies. *Ace* was Wilder's darkest movie and it was a commercial flop, which may have given him a permanent aversion to unhappy endings. The fact that it was his first picture without Brackett boded doubly ill for his future; he was warned that his next had to earn enough profit to cover both movies. His next was *Stalag 17;* it earned enough for both of them, and it also brought its star, William Holden, an Academy Award.

In 1936 Wilder had married the daughter of a prominent California family. They were divorced in 1948, and she now lives near San Francisco with Wilder's only child, a daughter. In 1949 Wilder married Audrey Young, a former singer with the Tommy Dorsey band, whom Reisch describes as "brilliant, beautiful, and as hard as he is." She is also more phlegmatic than he is—he refuses to play bridge with her, and she cheerfully tells people so—and she bears strong responsibility for the Wilders' social eminence. By himself, Wilder tends to scare people.

Wilder loves to talk, and he is a careful listener, but he approaches a conversation somewhat the way a big-game hunter approaches a safari. He doesn't grope for words, he jumps on them. And when he talks, he paces. As soon as he gets the scent of an original notion, Wilder is on his feet, and when he sits, it means that things are getting dull. The knowledge of having bored Wilder is as burdensome as if one had passed on a cold, but keeping him going can be hard work. "Do you like opera?" a floundering interviewer asked recently, trying to sound as though the question had just occurred to him. "An idiotic art form." Wilder said, and meant all four words. He has no small talk.

Wilder's impatience is now legendary, but there are many ways of looking at it. Charles Eames talks about "this constant sense of quality, this impatience with the second-rate." Other friends say he has a passion for avoiding the obvious, and doesn't even like to give Christmas presents because there's no originality in it. Charles Lederer, a friend of Wilder, with a reputation for a sharp tongue, recently tried to put Wilder's acerbity into focus.

"For surgery that takes off three-quarters of a person's hide, I can't compete with Billy," Lederer said, pacing ferociously in the Wilder manner. "But the reason is that Billy doesn't have malice. I don't think he's aware of other people's constant fear that they are the target of malice. I don't believe Billy would open his mouth—and believe me, that would be a deprivation to him—if he thought he would hurt somebody's feelings."

But Wilder's occasional attempts at tact do not work out well. Hope Holiday is an actress who has appeared in two Wilder movies (she was the blonde who picked up Jack Lemmon in a bar in *The Apartment*). A few years ago Miss Holiday decided to take up painting, and after months of hard work she asked Wilder to look at the results.

"He looked at them and didn't say a word, and finally I said, 'Well, what do you *think?*' " she recalls. "He said, 'Don't ask me what I think. Stick to comedy.' I haven't painted since."

Over the years Wilder has been credited by Hollywood with a large number of funny and cutting remarks, many of which he actually said:

"I'd worship the ground you walk on if you lived in a better neighborhood." (Said to his prospective wife, Audrey, when she was a Goldwyn girl.)

"Please, not while I'm eating." (When his wife announced at the breakfast table that it was their first wedding anniversary.)

"The usual monkey funeral." (To an eager assistant director on *Sunset Boulevard,* who asked Wilder how he "saw" an upcoming scene in which a monkey was to be buried.)

"Why don't you get out of that wet coat and into a dry Martini?" (Often credited to Robert Benchley—sometimes Alexander Woollcott—and actually written by Wilder and spoken by Benchley in *The Major and the Minor.*)

"I can't. I still have relatives in Germany." (Supposedly said when Wilder was asked why he didn't put Otto Preminger, an Austrian with a dictatorial reputation, in his place.)

But Wilder denies authorship of this last one. "A certain kind of joke will come along, and they slap it on somebody because they think it fits his personality," he says. "It becomes 'a Dorothy Parker story.' If it's a little bit cynical, it becomes 'a Wilder story.' It fits a sort of fictitious image of me, that I am cynical and rude and crude and bitter."

"All right, Mr. DeMille, I'm ready for my close-up."

—SUNSET BOULEVARD

"I do not have in my cellar prints of my old movies." Wilder says. "I don't read my old screenplays. I don't live in past glories. That was last week—what have we done this week?"

The fact is, Wilder hates looking backward, and he goes to great lengths to avoid his past glories. If somebody springs one of his pictures at a Hollywood party, he gets out of there fast and plays gin with anybody he can find. "I start sweating," he says. "I see all the mistakes. I feel very inferior." After the first public preview of *Irma La Douce*, which eventually grossed $11 million, Wilder was disconsolate. "If I had my way," he said, "I'd reshoot ninety-five percent of that thing." He is more at ease watching other people's movies, and he admires proficiency in everything from Fellini to James Bond, but he is almost as frustrated by other people's mistakes as by his own. "Billy doesn't dislike bad movies." Walter Reisch once said. "He resents bad movies."

Wilder's approach to movie-making is plain and functional. He uses close-ups sparingly ("I think a close-up is such a valuable thing—like playing a trump in a bridge game"), is fond of surprises ("Anyone who enters a room not through a door but through a window already is a center of interest, right?"), and will write a script only with specific actors signed up ("A movie is a star vehicle. What good is it to have a magnificent dramatic concept for which you must have Laurence Olivier and Audrey Hepburn—if they're not available?"). When pressed, he will name the themes of movies ("Peculiarly enough, the theme of *Kiss Me, Stupid* was human dignity. It was also about the sanctity of marriage"), but he considers a theme so basic as to be hardly worth discussing. "The theme is there. You try to dramatize it. You can't just start writing into the blue and say let's see, retroactively, what it's all about. We knew damn well *The Apartment* was a movie about the price of success. That one was called a dirty fairy tale, by the way.

"I did not approach the movies from the theater, the Stanislavsky approach," he says. "I'm just a storyteller."

Wilder has said that 80 percent of the creation of a movie is the writing of it, and he goes at the writing with a kind of wild, headlong care. In his office at the Goldwyn studios he paces back and forth between two rooms, whacking objects with a cane or some reasonable facsimile, such as a shillelagh. In earlier days he whipped darts at a dart board during his walks. His collaborator sits at a typewriter. Brackett, who shared a long and narrow office with Wilder, once complained that working with him was like watching a tennis match, and gave him a stiff neck.

"Both of us sit in the same office, week after week, month after month, five days a week, from nine to six," Diamond says, explaining how he and Wilder work. "Then we start working Saturday and Sunday mornings too. Everything is worked out line by line. In the course of a script there will be one joke he wants to get in, and I'm dead set against, and vice versa. On plot, we've had knock-down, drag-out fights. It's more or less predirected—he knows in the office where he's going to put the camera. We've never started shooting with a completed script. We usually have a third of it to write. We spend three months shooting, three months postproduction—editing and scoring—then a short vacation, and we start again."

"It's such an ordeal to write," Wilder has said, "and such a pleasure to direct." The Wilder-Diamond scripts are models of economy. "They're lean and specific and simple," says Jack Lemmon. "There's not an extra 'if,' 'and,' or 'but.' In four pictures I have never heard of an actor wanting to change a line, which is common on other sets. No, there was one in *Some Like It Hot*— 'Now you're talking.' I wanted to say it twice. Twenty minutes Billy took before he decided to let me do it."

In contrast to the clarity of the writing, the typical Wilder plot is a model of confusion. Wilder loves to think up ways for his characters to fool each other—he has disguised men in women's clothes, women in men's clothes, and women in tot's clothes—and his cruelest deceptions usually involve love and/or sex. In *Double Indemnity*, which he got from the James M. Cain novel, Barbara Stanwyck has her lover, Fred MacMurray, murder her husband, then she shoots MacMurray; in a belated rush of affection, she finds it impossible to finish him off, so he shoots her. In *Sunset Boulevard,* a young screenwriter, William Holden, is kept by a deluded, fading star, Gloria Swanson, who guns him into her swimming pool when he tries to leave her. And in *Some Like It Hot,* poor Joe E. Brown actually gets himself engaged to Jack Lemmon, who isn't unmasked until the last line of the movie.

Like any master of disguise, however, Wilder is a stickler for authenticity. The names of many of his characters have been lifted from real life, usually from a famous and inappropriate person. In *The Apartment,* Shirley MacLaine got her name (Miss Kubelik) from a violinist, and Marilyn Monroe in *Some Like It Hot* was named for a Michigan State halfback. In pursuit of the appearance of reality, he has had many battles with production departments as a result. "They always try to give you 'Lucky Chesters' or 'Camel Strikes,' and I will not stand for that," he says. "Or phony names on newspapers—'The N.Y. Blade.' Once you have that, you know, all believability goes out the window." Once, Wilder even demonstrated that when he sends a character to a good show, he really means for him to see a show he feels is good. In the script of *The Apartment,* Lemmon was given two tickets to *The Sound of Music,* a musical in which Wilder had invested, and arrangements were made to film him outside the theater. Wilder went to see the show, hated it, and switched Lemmon's tickets to *The Music Man.*

The filming of Wilder's movies is relaxed but efficient, and many of his crew members are veterans of other Wilder movies. Doane Harrison, his film editor, has worked with him for more than 25 years and, unlike most editors, is always there during filming to advise Wilder and reduce the excess footage. Other directors have wound up with as much as two hours of extra film. Wilder generally cuts his films by two or three minutes. Moving through the complex machinery of movie-making, overseeing the assembling of his picture, he is intent, observant, calm and detached, like the captain of a well-trained ship who no longer needs to give a lot of orders. Charles Eames, whose own creations run from furniture to a multi-screen movie system, has observed Wilder in action often and with fascination.

"You don't go to watch Billy shoot to learn how to make a picture," he says, "but to learn how to write an editorial, how to make a chair, how to make a piece of architecture."

When a movie is finished, Wilder usually refreshes himself by getting out of Hollywood for a while. "I often think I will go someplace different, but somehow I always find myself in Bahnhofstrasse in Zurich, and Piccadilly, and the Champs Élysées. I go to places where I speak the language. It makes me feel very uncomfortable otherwise." He does not "look for ideas" when he's traveling. "You see," he says, "you don't look. It occurs to you. I love to make pictures from original stories, and maybe they are my best pictures—*Sunset Boulevard, The Apartment*—but there is no such thing as looking. It occurs to you, and the time comes when you have to get it off your chest.

"*The Apartment* occurred to me while I was in New York, where I go twice a year," Wilder said, traveling around his apartment one recent Sunday morning. "On the other hand, maybe that theme would have occurred to me in Oklahoma. Either you have a sense of your time or you don't. A guy can be at the front and write a lousy piece about it, and another guy can write a good piece about it from his desk in Santa Monica.

"The big trick is to find the subject that relates to a human experience. Explain the rules, involve people, and they will do most of the work for you. You say, 'This guy is greedy, this guy is something else'—and you let the clashes of the drama unfold. Then you throw them a few curves, and once in a while you feel you have them by the throat—those conscientious objectors in the audience—and then you let them have it.

"Boston University and the University of Oregon would like my correspondence," Wilder said suddenly. "I blush, and I cringe, and I am going to try to talk them out of it, because I can't stand that sort of thing. My correspondence will be of very little interest to posterity." He took a few paces, smoking. "I am a dedicated man, not after the fast buck," he said. "But if there is one thing I loathe more than not to be taken seriously, it's to be taken too seriously."

The phone rang. Wilder picked it up and said hello and listened for a moment and then started talking. "I'll have lunch with you, but I won't play bridge with you," he said. "You're a marvelous guy, and I'm a great admirer, and I'll be happy to see you any time—but I won't play bridge with you. OK?" He hung up.

"I think the whole idea of making movies is to suck them in and make them do the work for you, make them participate," he went on. "You have to catch them, and they have to be playing with you. It is calculated to look natural. I admire elegant camera work but not fancy stuff. The camera hanging off the chandelier—that's for children, to astonish the middle-class critics. I would like to have them forget there is a camera, a dolly, a crew of one hundred fifty. If it was possible, I'd like to get them up on the screen and working.

"I have been criticized for happy endings. The easiest ending is the unhappy ending—that you can write any time. It's become sort of a bromide now that they don't live happily ever after. . . . The question is whether you have a right to get people into the theater, and they expect a cocktail and they get a shot of acid. People don't want to hear that they stink. It's not like the theater. For seven-seventy you can give a message. For a dollar twenty-five—no message.

"When they go to a play, they are primed what to expect, but in the movies they are not prepared for what they are going to see," Wilder said. "*Some Like It Hot* bombed when it had a preview in Pacific Palisades. Joe Mankiewicz [the director] stood on the sidewalk with me afterward, commiserating. Then we showed it at Westwood, and they loved it. Pacific Palisades loved it later, but they had to be told it was funny. *Lost Weekend* was a disaster until they were told it was serious. Audiences laughed."

Wilder took two quick puffs on his cigarette. "Everybody in that audience is an idiot," he said. "But fifteen hundred of them are geniuses."

"We're coming, we're coming, Leo,
So Leo, don't despair.
While you are in the cave a-hopin',
We are up above you pokin',
We will finally make an openin',
Lee-O."

—ACE IN THE HOLE

On a gray, chilly—or "gloomy bone-chilling," as the script called it—day in Cleveland last fall, during the third period of a professional-football game between the Cleveland Browns and the Minnesota Vikings, the Browns' Leroy Kelly ran a punt back from his own 10 to midfield, and Billy Wilder's latest movie began. The movie was called *The Fortune Cookie,* and it starred Jack Lemmon as a CBS-TV cameraman who gets run over by a Browns' back during a game; Walter Matthau plays his lawyer-brother who persuades Lemmon to fake serious injuries and sue the Browns and CBS for a million dollars. The other two stars are movie newcomers: Ron Rich, a Negro, as the back, and Judi West, as Lemmon's ex-wife, who comes back when she gets wind of his impending fortune. The movie is a sardonic comedy, and its closest relatives among Wilder's pictures are *Ace in the Hole* and *The Apartment*.

Kelly's run was the start of an intricate sequence in which, in a fine piece of directing chicanery, Wilder planned to give reality to the fiction of his story, and it was about the only thing that went right that afternoon. The favored Browns played badly and lost by ten points. Quarterback Frank Ryan passed poorly and was booed off the field in the fourth period. When it was over, Browns' owner Art Modell told Wilder that, as planned, he would have his players in uniform for a walk-through the next day.

"They did the walk-through today," Wilder said. "Tomorrow I want the real thing."

Later, at a press party, Wilder told reporters, "After my last picture, I know how Modell feels. But he shouldn't worry. There'll be further disasters."

The next day, with some of the Browns in their own uniforms and some of them dressed up in Vikings uniforms, Wilder began stitching together his deception. With halfback Ernie Green wearing number 44 in place of Kelly, who was too small to pass for actor Ron Rich at close range, the run was faked out for an extra 20 yards, where Green was knocked out of bounds. Next, Wilder substituted a stuntman for Green, and another stuntman for Jack Lemmon, as the cameraman; the Kelly-Green-Rich stuntman was then filmed smacking into the Lemmon stuntman, who reeled backward against a large, rolled up tarpaulin. Next, the Lemmon stuntman got up onto a small platform, jumped onto a trampoline, and was photographed flying head over heels over the tarpaulin, landing on his back on a pile of mattresses covered with fake grass. Then Lemmon went in for his stuntman and did a tiny but violent fall to simulate the end of his spill. Finally Rich went in for his stuntman and was photographed taking off his helmet and looking with dismay at Lemmon, who was pretending to be out cold.

On the sidelines, Wilder, wearing a tan cap, checked topcoat, and tan sport shirt, smoked and walked back and forth by himself, head down, occasionally pausing to watch Lemmon clowning with reporters and a football. From time to time he gave short directions: "One more, just for security"—"OK, let's go" (clapping his hands and beckoning to the referees)—"Hit him good" (to the Browns-Vikings). "Very concerned" (to Rich as he bent over Lemmon). When a scene was shot, Wilder stood beside the camera in a half crouch, shoulders hunched, his arms held away from his body as though he were carrying two buckets of water, watching intently.

Afterward, a member of the company hailed one of a dozen visiting reporters. "I thought of something for your story," he said. "You know Billy directed Otto Preminger in *Sunset Boulevard,* and somebody wanted to know why Billy didn't make Preminger behave more. 'I can't,' Billy said. . . ."

The next day, election day, the stands were packed as far as the camera's eye could see, which is to say as far as one section on each side of one exit. Some 10,000 fans had been lured into place by an offer of 5,636 prizes, including a sports car worth more than $20,000, and the chance to watch a movie being shot. Under the stands a press agent was phoning *Variety* in Hollywood to report the event as probably the largest extras-call in history. On the sidelines the St. Edward High School band played *Hello, Dolly,* while on the bench the Kent State University freshman football team played the part of some of the Browns, who were off practicing real football. In front of a battery of microphones, Jack Lemmon gave away a free trip to Los Angeles to a hefty, amazed ticketholder. "No——?" he asked Lemmon in an incredulous whisper, after they had stepped away from the microphones.

Then an assistant director stepped up to the microphones and explained that Ernie Green, as "Boom-Boom" Jackson, was going to simulate a punt runback, and the two-section crowd must get on its feet and cheer loudly, being careful not to look at either the camera or Jack Lemmon, who was to be wheeled out the exit on a stretcher.

Wilder told the assistant director to go ahead, the assistant called "OK," the 10,000 fans got to their feet, and one of the Browns threw the football in simulation of a kick. Downfield, Ernie Green took it on the 10 and started running. Upfield he came, 10 yards, 20 yards, twisting caroming off tacklers, knees pumping, while Browns in Vikings uniforms bounced off of him in every direction. The Kent State freshmen along the sidelines were on their feet, yelling "Come on Boom-Boom," and "Go, Boom-Boom. Go!" Green passed midfield, still shedding tacklers, twirling and grinning. And, as he tore toward the enemy goal line on what may have been the most electrifying run of his career, Jack Lemmon was wheeled up the ramp and out of sight past 10,000 cheering fans who resolutely looked the other way.

Leo (trapped in a cave): *"Yesterday there were two thousand people out there."*
Tatum: *"Today there's three thousand."*
Leo: *"Well, who are they? What do they want?"*
Tatum: *"They're your friends."*
Leo: *"I guess everybody's got friends he doesn't even know about."*
—ACE IN THE HOLE

A number of things can happen after a disaster. After *Across the River and Into the Trees,* Hemingway's *The Old Man and the Sea* was hailed as a masterpiece, which was probably more than it deserved. After *Limelight,* Charlie Chaplin made one more film and then let 14 years go by before directing *A Countess From Hong Kong.* It stars Marlon Brando and Sophia Loren, has been hailed as marking the return of a genius, and will be out soon. After *Stromboli* Ingrid Bergman (married Rossellini and) won an Oscar for *Anastasia.* After the game against the Vikings, Frank Ryan helped lead the Browns to a conference championship. Fullback Jimmy Brown, who was allowed to skip the filming of *The Fortune Cookie,* quit football to go into the movies. Leroy Kelly, no bigger than ever, thus got promoted to the first-string backfield, where he has done almost as well as Brown did.

The Fortune Cookie had its first sneak preview in Westwood in June, with Wilder, Diamond, Lemmon, Ron Rich, and Art Modell attending; Walter Matthau, whose heart attack had delayed completion several months, was busy with another picture. The run-back was convincing; it was even shown twice, the second time on stop-action camera. The movie's first big laugh came when Matthau's mother said to a nun in a hospital, "Thank you, Sister," and Matthau said, "Shut up, Mother." Matthau got most of the laughs, but the audience reaction was spotty. Afterward, Wilder said that he was not unhappy. He planned to cut three minutes and change some waltz music at the end to circus music. Lemmon acted cheerful, but he said, "I thought it was a bomb—almost as bad as I thought *Irma La Douce* was at its preview. I thought it died every time Matthau was off-screen."

The Fortune Cookie opened in theaters around the country on October 19, 23 months after *Kiss Me, Stupid,* to generally favorable reviews and good business. Some critics liked it and some didn't, and most liked some of it. Most people said Walter Matthau was marvelous, but some said Jack Lemmon wasn't as good as usual. What it did for Wilder is hard to say.

A few hours before the sneak preview last June, which was his real farewell to the thing, Wilder was asked what the rest of that day would be like for him. "I'm going to go home," he said, pacing up and down his office. "Take a shower. Dinner with Art Modell—you know. Then I'm going to chug down to the theater, wipe my brow, say a few prayers.

"Before a fight, you know you can defend yourself. But I'm just going to get slugged, and there's nothing I can do. If you're a producer, you make eighteen pictures a year. An actor makes three pictures a year. If Al Kaline strikes out, he gets up again two innings later. We get to bat once a year—and the suffering in the dugout is prolonged, believe me, when the people are booing.

"The thing one has to remember is, it's not going to be the greatest—not the greatest hit, not the greatest flop. Do they care—that's the important thing. Are they interested. It's a brand new game. I've invented the rules—do they want to play or not? Because they must do some work. . . ."

Then he stopped pacing. "Look, it's just another picture," he said. "It'll be on the bottom half of a double bill soon." And then he sat down. Anyway, he is now well into the writing of another one, a drama for Walter Matthau. He hopes to start filming this spring.

"If people loved each other more they'd shoot each other less."

"Are you a religious fanatic or something?" —LOVE IN THE AFTERNOON

"Shut up and deal."—Last line of THE APARTMENT

"Kiss me, Stupid."—Last line of KISS ME, STUPID

"Well, nobody's perfect."—Last line of SOME LIKE IT HOT

"Come on, play ball!"—Last line of THE FORTUNE COOKIE

Wilder—"Yes, We Have No Naked Girls"

MARK SHIVAS/1969

IT TOOK SIX WEEKS FOR ME to get to see Billy Wilder. But what the hell? Earl Wilson, they say, came 3,000 miles and only got five minutes. Finally The Call: an endless list of directions telling how to get there. An hour from London. In a graveyard. Where else? And lo, through the yew trees and across the cables is the mordant Mr. Wilder, tweed trilby hat rakishly over one eye, peering down through hornrims at four schoolboys in gray shorts and caps kneeling at two freshly-dug graves. But wait. A close look reveals that they're not schoolboys; they're four wizened midgets. "And please don't give the name of the church," says the publicity man. "After all, it's consecrated ground and we had difficulty getting permission to use it."

"Difficulty? Why?" asks Wilder, craning his head round at an angle, "We have no naked girls here." His accent is a pleasant Viennese-American. "No marijuana. No orgies. Just four midgets praying: you can't get any humbler than that."

Stanley Holloway, Eliza's dad in *My Fair Lady,* stands nearby as a gravedigger. "I'm getting buried in the morning," sings Wilder, half to his collaborator, scriptwriter I. A. L. "Izzy" Diamond, who's sitting quietly in a chair in the long grass behind some tombstones. Diamond smiles a slight and secret smile. "Of course," he says, "Holloway thought we wanted him for the gravedigger in *Hamlet.*"

But Wilder isn't doing *Hamlet.* Not this time anyway. He's in the 19th week

From the *New York Times,* 12 October 1969. © The New York Times Co. Reprinted by permission.

of producing and directing *The Private Life of Sherlock Holmes*. A swirling Victorian copperplate subtitle on the publicity handout calls it "an account of some hitherto suppressed and thoroughly fascinating adventures of the greatest detective of all time as revealed by his friend John H. Watson, late Indian Army." Suppressed, that is, until Wilder and Diamond, the team that produced *Some Like It Hot, The Apartment,* and *The Fortune Cookie,* confected them from several years of head scratching and typewriter pounding. Wilder describes their film as "more *The Odd Couple* than Conan Doyle." If you're unwise enough to ask "Why Sherlock Holmes?" you'll probably get the answer, "Why not?" But it's clear that Holmes occupies a prominent place in Wilder's affections. "To me he's wildly romantic—elegant, all that Baker Street setting, great sharpness, precision and imagination. One of the great minds of the twentieth century. This film isn't camp. It's a valentine to Sherlock."

The sun beats down on the graveyard. It's supposed to be a day of overpowering gloom, but the sky is azure and any welcome clouds quickly disappear. So the crew, the midgets, Diamond and Wilder all wait. Wilder actually sits down, an unusual event in itself. Most of the time he's pacing like a caged cat, puffing on a cigarette, gazing at the ground. If you happen to listen to him talk and you're sitting down yourself, you end up with a bad case of tennis neck. But now he seems relaxed. "We can't work because the shots we did yesterday would not match this Capri sky. You make mistakes like that, they haunt you forever. In this business, we never bury our dead. We bring out the corpses, and show them on television to make a little more money." He is quiet for a moment, pondering the dates on an adjacent tombstone. "The people around here died so old. They can't have had anything to do with the movie industry." The sound man asks if he can record the words of Committal—ashes to ashes, dust to dust. "Be my guest," says Wilder. "Maybe we should all kneel while you take it."

I ask what the scene is all about. A twinkle appears behind the thick glasses. "This is the fourth of four stories discovered in 221B Baker Street in a tin box. The fourth movement of our symphony. But they're not exactly separate movements. You've seen *La Dolce Vita,* well, that's like a lot of separate stories running together." Which is about all you can gather because Wilder believes in keeping the plot a secret, "particularly from United Artists. That way they can't fire you before it's finished." Or he tells portions of it so fast, with such twists, that your head is still spinning when he finishes and smiles, "See? Simple isn't it?"

Robert Stephens, from *The Prime of Miss Jean Brodie* and Olivier's British National Theater, plays Holmes. "I'd never seen Stephens except for 20 minutes in the bar of the Connaught Hotel," says Wilder, "but I thought 'What's good enough for Larry Olivier is good enough for me.' " Colin Blakely, also from the National Theater, is Watson. Neither Stephens nor Blakely knows how the plot ends. "Neither do we," says Diamond quietly. "I'll let you in on a secret," mutters Wilder. "We really do. We just haven't written it down yet."

One or two things are clear, but they tend to provoke more confusion. The plot involves Loch Ness. "Sure we have a monster, but he's not like that Japanese Godzilla fellow." Queen Victoria makes an appearance. Genevieve Page, the madame from *Belle de Jour,* plays a Belgian lady who's seen riding a tandem with Holmes. And Stephens had to learn to stroke for a crew of eight on the Thames at Oxford. "Panavision is very good for rowing scenes," remarks Wilder. "Also for dachshunds. Though not for the Eiffel tower."

The intrepid pair also visit the ballet. A famous ballerina (Tamara Toumanova) suggests to Holmes that with his brains and her body they could make the perfect baby. He declines, saying that his friend Watson wouldn't approve. Word spreads that Holmes and Watson are more than just good friends and the male dancers close in. . . . Later Watson is seen with six ballerinas and a rose behind his ear doing the dance of the little swans from *Swan Lake.* "Colin," Wilder tells Blakely, "I want you to act like Laughton and to dance like Nureyev." Afterward—"Colin, why did you act like Nureyev and dance like Laughton?"

Stephens, who collapsed from physical exhaustion in the middle of the shooting schedule, is unstinting in his praise of Wilder. "Fantastic. He's always good-humored, immensely knowledgeable. He never *ever* seems to get tired and he's 63." Genevieve Page says, "He's the best director any of us has ever worked with. He's always the first on the set, and if everyone is sheltering from the rain, he's the one who'll be first out there waiting for it to stop. We lost our Loch Ness monster, but he didn't seem to worry too much, even though he's the producer as well as the director. He was more concerned to go over and comfort the man who had made it and who was upset about its disappearing. And he knows exactly what he wants. He doesn't over-shoot.

When he's finished cutting, he says there should be nothing left on the cutting room floor but chewing gum wrappers and tears."

Wilder, who's usually noted for his cynicism, this week finds himself among people from all fields of art, science, and politics in the English *Sunday Times* list of "A Thousand Makers of the Twentieth Century," and, to my pleased surprise, the winner of six Oscars confesses himself pleased by it. "The day of the director and the writer is here at last and that's marvelous." But it may have been his normal bleakness of outlook that made his last two pictures, *Kiss Me, Stupid* and *The Fortune Cookie*, unpalatable to many audiences. "I don't know," Wilder says, "with *Kiss Me, Stupid* there was a phenomenal outcry. They said it was the dirtiest movie ever made. Condemned in *Life* magazine. Suggestions that my citizenship papers should be taken away. But pictures have gone much further today. Comparatively, *Kiss Me, Stupid* was nothing. There was just the same kind of outcry when I made *Ace in the Hole* in 1951. I like to mix a little vinegar in the cocktail. I suppose the audience thought they'd come to see another kind of picture and felt they'd been cheated.

"*The Private Life of Sherlock Holmes* is not a comedy and it's not serious," says Wilder. "It should keep audiences in the theater for around three hours."

Isn't there a risk in making such expensive pictures when a low-budget movie like *Easy Rider* can be so successful? "Yes, there's always a risk, but for every one of those low-budget pictures that works, 50 go down the drain. The man with real courage is the one who decides he wants to remake *The Desert Song*. You know, at one time everyone thought that what we call the cinema of mama and papa was dead. Then along came *The Sound of Music*. And *Dr. Zhivago*. Before *Zhivago*, the dissolve had almost disappeared from movies. And then David Lean started dissolving endlessly from snow to daffodils and it was new to a new audience. If you say to your audience, 'Come on, let's play a game,' and you explain it, they'll play, no matter what it is. They're very young now, most of them, but they're also very bright."

The Private Life of Sherlock Holmes is at least a little bit pre-sold by the character of Holmes. "You know the oil is there, if only you can tap it. On the other hand, if you're not sure there's any oil there in the first place, you may only strike you know what. But it's like the thing we have in the picture about 'with your brains and my body we must make a beautiful baby.' It could still turn out to be mongoloid."

Broadcast to Kuala Lumpur

VANESSA BROWN/1970

Q. *Mr. Wilder, your films have outgrossed the works of any other creator in the industry. This is from a book called* The Brighter Side of Billy Wilder *by Tom Wood. If this is so and let's say you had to reshoot your own life, would you do it again the same way?*

A. I certainly wouldn't do it the same way. And I also think that Mr. Wood, who wrote the book, is not quite correct by saying that my particular product has outgrossed the movies made by other picture makers. I must say they are on the black side of the financial ledger. But when it's all said and done I never think of it in terms of financially the most rewarding. This is that American sickness of categorizing everything: Number 1 and Number 2 and Number 3 on the Hit Parade. Bestseller Number 1 for 21 weeks. Some pictures, whether they were very successful or not, give me more the feeling of accomplishment or joy to think about them than others. But not necessarily because they were successes. In fact, quite a few of the pictures which were financial disasters are very close to my heart.

Q. *Would you talk to us about some that are close to your heart, what of your work has had meaning for you?*

A. To begin with, I don't want you to think that I am imbued with my own importance. That I am a very high-browed, *auteur-de-cinema* type. I am a craftsman, I try to do it as well as I simply can. At no time do I put myself in

---

From *Action,* November/December 1970. Reprinted by permission of the Directors Guild of America.

the category of Ingmar Bergman or Jean-Luc Godard; I grew up in an industry and I'm proud of it. I work for a living. Sometimes it's a bit better. Sometimes it has more meaning; sometimes it is just purely commercial, just as long as I don't bore people and just as long as I don't have to be ashamed of what is on the screen and just as long as I can keep my team together and provide work for them, that is enough satisfaction for me. There were certain pictures that have laid an egg at the box office. You always kind of fool yourself by saying, "Well, I was ahead of my time"; "If they re-release the picture now . . ."; "Well, maybe the star was too old for this." The plain fact is that I admit I made the picture, I worked on it hard, took a year out of my life, and people just didn't show any interest. They did not come to see it. And, other pictures which I more or less did with my left hand, where I did not sweat over it, where I just sort of laid back and rode with the waves, they turned out to be great big financial hits.

For instance, pictures like *Ace in the Hole, Love in the Afternoon* and *The Fortune Cookie*—were just failures. They did not work and I don't know why, I could not analyze it. There is no answer. If we knew what makes a hit, if we knew what makes a star, we'd be multi-multi-millionaires. We just never know. So it's the same thing. You always enter a dark room and you can always fall over a piece of furniture and break your neck. Some of us see a little better in the dark than others. But there is no assurance, whatsoever, that it is going to come off.

Q . *Of the three films that have been selected to show in Kuala Lumpur (Malaysia)*—The Apartment, Some Like It Hot, *and* The Fortune Cookie, *what would you say about the making of them?*
A . *Some Like It Hot* was actually the most fun. So I did have a rather rough time with the late—and indeed great and very much missed—Marilyn Monroe. It was fun. We knew we hit on something that was full of entertainment. It was a good era that we chose for the picture—the gangster era, which is very photogenic, like westerns. You know, those are the two great backgrounds for movies. And it was marvelous to work with Tony Curtis and with Jack Lemmon. So much so that right after this picture, I decided to make another one with Jack Lemmon, which turned out to be *The Apartment*. That, of course, was fun, too. *Fortune Cookie* again starred Lemmon. This is actually not the Wilder Festival in Kuala Lumpur; this is a Lemmon Festival as well, because there are three pictures starring Jack. It was fun being surrounded by

truly first rate actors like Lemmon and Walter Matthau. Unfortunately, Matthau had a heart attack during the picture and we had to interrupt the movie for three or four months, and then finish it quite a bit later when he got well. But, you just wait for Matthau, you don't re-cast him. It happens to me so often that actors have heart attacks. Like Sam Goldwyn said, I give heart attacks, I don't get them. I don't know why. I get along with them fine, and I'm kind, I must say. And if I don't say so, who should?

Q. *Where do your stories come from?*
A. As you can detect by my accent, I was born in Austria. I came to America in 1934, and I was not on too safe a ground as far as my language was concerned. Unlike my picture-writing in Germany, I needed a collaborator and I worked a long time with Charles Brackett. We did a great many pictures—*Sunset Boulevard* was one of them. And then I worked with I. A. L. Diamond for twelve to fourteen years. As for source material, it just depends. Sometimes it's a book, like *The Lost Weekend,* sometimes it's a play, like *Witness for the Prosecution* or *Irma La Douce,* or it's an original story like say, *Sunset Boulevard* or *The Apartment.* So sometimes it's existing material which is being shaped with my collaborator into a screen play, and then I direct and produce. And sometimes, if I possibly have something way back in one of the drawers in my desk and if I can cast it at the time, I go to original material. It sort of accumulates, gathers dust, then five years later either you flush it down the toilet or you say, "Well, I think the time has come to make a movie out of this." So it depends.

Q. *People all over the world, including the ones that are going to be seeing your films in Malaysia, want to know how they can make movies. You are a sage. How and where do you learn the technique of film-making? Do you go to a university? How do you try to learn the craft before you get the chance to break in?*
A. I would say that it very much depends as to where you find yourself geographically. I'm very flattered by you calling me a sage. By this time I'm sort of *ancienne vague,* not *nouvelle vague,* not even *moyenne vague* anymore. It very much depends. Now in America, for instance, hundreds of thousands of college students are taking up cinematography—the making of movies, the writing, the cutting, the directing. Eight and 16 millimeter cameras are sort of bursting forth all over the country. I think that so much material is being done, has to be done, because there are so many hours and so many

stations for television. That's a very, very good testing ground for young picture makers. In France, for instance, they have a university, a *cinematheque*; they are very serious about it, they study very seriously. How it would be done in the Asian countries, I don't know. I don't know how they do it in India, although some very good films come out of there. In Poland, in Russia, they have special colleges for cinematography. It just depends on where you find yourself, and what, actually, you want to do. The best, I think, over all this, is if you have a relative. Overall, that is the best shoehorn to get into the industry.

Q. *How did you start? Did you have a relative?*
A. No, I did not have a relative. I kind of started with *avant-garde* group of guys who had never made a picture before the first picture I ever wrote. And the director of that picture was Robert Siodmak, who subsequently became quite a well-known director. And I remember distinctly that second assistant cameraman was Freddie Zinnemann, who certainly has become one of the great directors of our era. And one of the guys just got a camera and got a few thousand marks together and we went out and made a picture with people on the street. We worked, we cut, we improvised, we begged, we stole, and we got it together and somehow it made an impact and we went from there. I started as a newspaperman so I had a certain knowledge of writing. But the longer I live, the more convinced I am that with anybody who has got something on the ball, be it an actor or a director, ultimately 85% make it. For some it takes a little longer, some need a break here and there. Some never make it. But I just think that somebody writing truly first-rate stuff will somehow, someway, somewhere get it into the proper hands and it will be made into a picture and the guy is going to make it.

Q. *What was the greatest influence upon your work—what person, or what visual medium?*
A. When I was a high school kid, those were the heydays of the German picture industry and the old U.F.A. company, the old Jannings pictures and the famous Fritz Lang pictures . . . I knew right then and there that I would like to be able to tell stories on film, be it as a writer or as a director. Subsequently, the chance I had of working with Lubitsch on two pictures was an enormous experience for me and I have drawn on that over and over again. If I look back and if I say, "Well, who would I like to be were I not myself?" I

would have to say, naturally, Lubitsch. He certainly was, as far as my taste
goes, way ahead of his time and still unmatched. This, and then also there
were a couple of experiences I had with Erich von Stroheim, who worked as
an actor in two of my pictures, *Five Graves to Cairo* and *Sunset Boulevard.*
Those were the two men, I guess, that influenced me the most.

Q. *In what capacity did you work with Lubitsch?*
A. As a writer. I was a writer on two of his pictures, *Bluebeard's Eighth Wife*
and *Ninotchka.*

Q. *I wanted to know, aside from making your living in this industry, what is your
main aim? Why do you make pictures? Is it to entertain, to tell a story, or what?*
A. It's just like you sit around a large dinner table and you would like to get
the attention of the people. You tell a good story and build to climaxes and
have them gasp, have them laugh, then bring it to kind of a great big thun-
derous conclusion. It's kind of the passion of the story teller. But, that
unhappily is sort of waning as you get older and it also begins to wane once
you realize that the audiences have changed enormously. It's very, very difficult to keep up with that. I think that we are living in very obtuse times
where everything is murky. Being a man of certain convictions, I cannot
suddenly change my style and do the "now" picture. A self-respecting
painter cannot just suddenly say, "Well, op art is selling now. I am going to
abandon the manner in which I painted and start on op art or pop art or
hard-edge school." I just have to hope that they will still go along with my
manner of telling stories. It's sort of the Scheherezade Complex.

Q. *I don't mean to sound pompous, but there are film makers who are tremen-
dously imbued with a message of the times, religious, metaphysical, or political.
Since these are times of ferment, was any part of that in your make-up as you think
of stories?*
A. Well, to begin with, I have never made a picture which was a lecture. I
try to make pictures for entertainment. I think that after you read the papers,
listen to the radio and watch the news on television, you're sick of it. On the
other hand, I don't want to make pictures absolutely flat and without any
meaning. Whatever meaning you will find in my pictures, it's all put in kind
of contraband, you know—sort of smuggled in a kind of message of, I hope,
decency, of liberal thinking, whatever you want to call it, or something bit-

ing, something satirical, something poking fun at our way of life. But, I never set out just to have them sit down, and then I blast a sermon at them. I just don't believe in it. I think that the primary objective of my kind of picture is entertainment on a certain level, with a little something to talk about after it. If after they leave the movie house they spend half-an-hour just talking as to what they saw, and if it makes any kind of indent within the frame of the entertainment, I think I have achieved something.

Q. *I have one last question. You brought up briefly your uneasiness with the "now" kind of films. What impression does something like* Easy Rider *or other such films make after you see them?*

A. Well, I think *Easy Rider* was really a kind of a work of art, as was indeed *Midnight Cowboy*. I was not talking about those films. I was just talking about *I Am Curious Yellow* and a whole slew of pornographia—gratuitously so in four-letter words and the kind of cheap shock thing that they think is necessary in order to attack the audience. Apparently it is, because those pictures are making money. But, when I see things like *Performance,* I'm totally rattled and, to tell you the truth, also disgusted. I am not a prude, in fact I was accused of making vulgar and shocking and obscene pictures 20 and 25 years ago; they have now been re-rated as G for general consumption on television at six o'clock for kids while they are having their dinner. So, I am not a prude, I just think that we have gone too far but I think that is all for the better because we are beginning to sense that it is a great big bore. It's repetitious and we've had it. We will be very soon like the Danish people, who have totally abandoned any kind of censorship, and the bookstores selling pornographic material are going broke were it not for an occasional tourist who ambles in. That is the one good thing that comes out of that kind of whirlpool of filth and dirt.

Q. *Thank you very, very much, Mr. Wilder. I have many, many other questions but I'll come back another time.*

A. Very good.

Apropos *Avanti!*

MICHEL CIMENT/1972

AVANTI! IS A RARITY THESE DAYS, a romantic film which
deals with contemporary themes, which I worked scrupulously to not make
pretentious. It's based on a play by Samuel Taylor, whose work I had already
adapted in *Sabrina*. That was one of those rare times that a film came out on
screen before the play was staged on Broadway. The two works were different
and both had been successful. This time, I read the play—which was not very
good—and I didn't think that it would work, and it didn't. I didn't use any
of it, except the basic situation: an American man and an English woman
meet in Italy to pick up the bodies of their parents, the boy's father and the
girl's mother, killed in a car accident. The American is straight laced, very
high society and right wing, who begins to see his father and his own life in
a different light. Thirty-six hours later, it's a different man that leaves for
America. It's a sort of education, treated lightly, without pseudo-philosophy;
I always keep in mind that above all, our job is to give the audience two and
a half hours of relaxation, of pleasure, of laughter, with an idea from time to
time, without forcing them to swallow annoying and sententious messages.
All that should be staged, if possible, in an elegant fashion, well played and
well photographed—I hope. At least that's the type of film that I love myself,
not that I don't like films like *Z, Sunday, Bloody Sunday*, or *Clockwork Orange*
by Kubrick, but they go in a completely different direction: you can't compare everything, and only pompous critics say that Lehar is not Beethoven.

A translation of "Apropos d'Avanti!", interview conducted June 18, 1972, published in *Positif*, January 1974. Translated from French by Bridgett Chandler. Reprinted by permission.

There's nothing bad about being bewitched by the *Ninth Symphony* and taking pleasure in the *Merry Widow*. But if you put everything in the same bag, people look over your shoulder and ask you: "Is it important?" I don't want to start asking myself if my film is important, if it'll stand out, if it'll win the Oscar, if they'll discuss it seriously in the *Cahiers du Cinema*. That doesn't interest me; what concerns me is to know if it works, if people want to see it, if they won't be disappointed after the screening, and if they talk about it for a half hour at the neighborhood café, then I'll be happy.

Do you like Italian comedy?

Enormously. Germi is one of my favorite directors and I consider *Seduced and Abandoned* and *Divorce Italian Style* as first class comedies, very Italian yet at the same time universal. I didn't try to make a Germi film; like McCarey or Lubitsch, he has his style, of which one can only make a pale imitation. I simply hope that it will please Italians as much as it will others, but sometimes I wake up at four in the morning and say to myself that I already know the first line of the article Judith Crist or Pauline Kael would devote to the film: "*Avanti!*, or how to sleep with a girl during your parent's funeral." They always find something like that. I mention it although it's not very important to me. What is important is to sit in the theater and hear people laughing at the right moment because it was conceived with that intention. That's more essential for me than to open a newspaper or a magazine that, while praising, throws itself into comparisons, seeing things that I never thought of.

Then don't read what I wrote about you!

I read it. But that's the role of the serious critic, the analyst, to find in the artist's work things about which he is not conscious. Because if I was, I could no longer work the same way. I can't analyze, that's your job! Mine is to make. I'm there with my palette and brush, or piano or camera. I do my best, how I feel about things and how I think things ought to be. But if I become analytical at that point, I would only produce a dead thing. If one motif reappears, if a theme recurs here and there, I'm not aware of it, believe me. Maybe it's because if something intrigued me at one time, it will always intrigue me, but you have the style you're born with, more or less.

Your comedies always pay attention to social background.

The public is much better educated than before, you can speak on a different
level, deepen characters that are no longer two dimensional, and you can
develop the background, without losing the rhythm, without preaching,
without being static, while entertaining. Before, it was black and white, the
hero on the white horse and the bad guy on the black horse, it was all set.
Today, there's gray because we've established rapid communication with the
public. They quickly get what you have to say. One of the problems today is
that the public is more mature than the directors, more intelligent than the
heads of companies. I myself learned that if a story is to be told well, you
have to engage the public. You give them two and two and they make four.
You don't have to do the addition, to hit them on the head with a hammer,
you have to trust their intelligence. It's from that cooperation that good
entertainment is born: you throw the audience the ball and they throw it
back. You don't have to repeat the same thing twice, but at the same time
you can't be obscure and end your film with a nebulous question mark like
a story in the *New Yorker* that the critics have to interpret.

In your film, a man puts certain American values into question.

He starts to have doubts and finally his false beliefs can't hold. It's at its heart
a story of love between a son and his father. He starts to understand a father
about whom he never thought and who was just an employee of a big company. He's closer to his dead father than to his living father. It's a reevaluation of Americans, of their mistakes, of that which matters and that which
doesn't. But, of course, that sounds pompous and it's not how I would pitch
the film to get three million dollars—that's just the side dish. The meat is the
liaison between the American and a girl who is a little too fat but who has a
nice bust; it's the comedy that surrounds it, the Italian music, the schmaltz.
For this film, we were lucky to have found Juliet Mills, a miraculous actress.
It's difficult to find a girl who is twenty pounds too heavy, who is teased for
her weight and who is nonetheless adorable, touching, and in the end,
erotic. That's an enormous risk, and I could have searched fifty years without
finding the actress I needed. All of the action turns around her. And she is
perfect.

How did you find her?

I saw her once in a play in London, *Five Finger Exercise*. She was raised in a
family of actors. Her father is John Mills and her sister is Hayley Mills. She

lived in California where she shot a stupid television series called *Nanny and the Professor,* I believe. In London, I saw an actress who had a nervous depression; on returning to California, I talked with an agent about one of his clients, Hayley Mills, as one of the best English actresses. I asked about her weight, and he said she was skinny as a pole. I explained that the role demanded that she be twenty pounds overweight; about which, you know agents, he told me that she had had a weight problem. Then I thought about her sister, and I was looking at her photo when she entered the office. She was also thin, but she is shorter with a slightly larger build. I gave her the script, and she read it and called me and said, "I want the role, I'll gain twenty pounds, give me eight weeks." She showed such a great desire to play the part, such enthusiasm, that I believed in her. She ate night and day, was very disciplined, and became very chubby, and gave a superb performance.

You considered Nino Manfredi for the role of the hotel manager played by Clive Revill.

And also Alberto Sordi, Romolo Valli, but none of those actors had sufficient mastery of English to play to the rhythm of this film. They would have slowed the action, they wouldn't have hit the ball back fast enough to Lemmon from the other side of the net. I would have had to post-synchronize [the dialogue]. They are marvelous interpreters in their language, but not familiar enough with English, which would have prevented them from concentrating on their roles. That's why I chose an intelligent and skilled actor, Clive Revill, who could play an Italian like he played a Russian ballet master in *The Private Life of Sherlock Holmes.* You also have to consider that I shoot five thousand miles from home, outdoors, with foreign technicians and if something goes wrong, it's a catastrophe. In Hollywood, I can change an actor from one day to the next. Abroad, I can't expose myself to risks, I must be on solid ground. Therefore Clive Revill and Edward Andrews give me the security I need.

Where did you get the idea of the character of Blodgett, the American bureaucrat played by Edward Andrews?

He was part of the Establishment. When he appeared near the end of the film, I stylized him, I painted him like a humorous character, with rapid strokes. Even though I exaggerated a bit, he wasn't very far from the people I knew at the Department of State. The department is full of characters who, when the pilot tells them that Greece is on the left, respond as quickly with "Never, as long as I'm at the Department of State." I also sprinkled the film with satiric notes about the world today, about the dollar crisis, memories of fascism, etc. But it's made without meanness and with a good dose of truth. In *One, Two, Three,* I was without a doubt too caricatured, I opened my mouth too big.

Isn't it also true that you have more affection for Italians than for Germans? When an employee gives the fascist salute in Avanti!, *it doesn't have the same cruel resonance that it does in* One, Two, Three.

The Italians are smiling, open, warm, even if some are corrupt. The Germans, for whom I have affection (I spent years in their country), are stiffer, they have a more natural goose step. If I spoke of Germany today, I would insist more on the economic miracle. You always have to readjust your point of view. Without pretending to pass for a comedy of manners, I wanted to show in *Avanti!* a contemporary portrait of Italy today, of its ambiance, its bureaucracy. Vicenzoni helped me with the Italian dialogue, and I also consulted with him on the morals of the country. He's a very good friend and he was an expert on local color for me.

But I didn't come here to make fun of Italians, and I am harder on us Americans. And if I speak of their faults, I show them nonetheless in a touching way. The Trotta brothers are racketeers, but they help bury the two corpses. As for Clive Revill, I gave him a key: Carlucci is the Toscanini of this place, and he played him with the same precision: that of the Italian hotel directors who only sleep in winter. He, too, is touching: he's a good friend of the father and he's afraid that the son, reactionary and stilted, doesn't understand that his father led a double life that made his existence happier. You never see America, except at the airport at the beginning, but the telephone conversation with Lemmon and his wife gives us an idea of the relationships that exist in their household, of this life made of golf, country club, closed circuit television. I think that this will change in America, even if Nixon is reelected in Autumn, which is likely. I believe in the progress of liberalism. There is on the one hand the horror of Vietnam, and on the other a rapprochement with China and the Soviet Union, which makes me optimistic; and the simple fact that this happened under Nixon is superb because he is beyond suspicion. If McGovern did what Nixon did, there would have been

Barbara Stanwyck and Fred MacMurray, *Double Indemnity*, 1944

Jean Arthur, John Lund, and Marlene Dietrich, *A Foreign Affair*, 1948

Bert Moorhouse, Kirk Douglas, Robert Arthur, and Ray Teal,
Ace in the Hole, 1951

Humphrey Bogart, Audrey Hepburn, and
William Holden, *Sabrina*, 1954

Tom Ewell and Marilyn Monroe, *The Seven Year Itch*, 1955

Audrey Hepburn and Gary Cooper, *Love in the Afternoon*, 1957

Charles Laughton,
Witness for the Prosecution, 1957

James Stewart,
The Spirit of St. Louis, 1957

Tony Curtis,
Jack Lemmon, and
Marilyn Monroe,
Some Like It Hot, 1959

Jack Lemmon and Shirley MacLaine, *The Apartment*, 1960

Hanns Lothar, James Cagney, Horst Buchholz, and Pamela Tiffin,
One, Two, Three, 1961

Ray Walston, Dean Martin, and Kim Novak, *Kiss Me, Stupid*, 1964

Robert Stephens, Colin Blakely, and Geneviève Page, *The Private Life of Sherlock Holmes*, 1970

Juliet Mills and Jack Lemmon, *Avanti!*, 1972

Howard Da Silva and Ray Milland, *The Lost Weekend*, 1945

Gloria Swanson and William Holden, *Sunset Boulevard*, 1950

William Holden, *Stalag 17*, 1953

a revolution in America. But Nixon must have received excellent orders from Kissinger. Progress is necessary and it must come from those who are right-of-center because no one will doubt them.

There's a sequence without dialogue in Avanti! *where Juliet Mills wanders the streets of Ischia. That creates a sort of parenthetical note in the narrative.*

That's a setting where I wanted to evoke the magic of the Italian countryside inundated with sun, the manner in which it touches a young girl who lived her whole life in a damp and cold country. In this way we're preparing for her evolution, but without transforming the sequence into "Debbie Reynolds Goes to Ischia," because it has a certain bite, and that bite—it's the girl who buys four ice creams in front of three small children and eats all four herself, it's the fishermen who want her, it's the coroner who her pinches her bottom. The slightly acidic commentary avoids riding off into the sunset.

In the same fashion, throughout the film I play with cadavers, to remove all the sugary aspects from it. I'm taking a risk, of course. But I remember some years ago, having met an excellent producer—there aren't any more in this genre today—Mr. Selznick, who asked me what I was working on. I told him *Some Like It Hot.* He told me, "Is that a comedy?" I responded, "I hope so." And he said, "What? You're going to have the St. Valentine's Day [Massacre], gangsters, submachine guns, seven dead bodies on the ground. Give it up. You're wasting your time. Mixing gangsters and comedy has already been tried and it doesn't work." In fact, it did work! If I did not have that element in *Avanti!,* I would have had the old story of the romance in Italy. But the fact that he's busy, that he discovers his father's past, etc. gives the story its force and its spice. This balance allows us to have big openly romantic scenes.

You also have the subplot of the valet and the maid that takes place around the death.

That's the left hand playing piano while the right hand plays romantic variations. These are black touches, and if well orchestrated, could give the film its originality. There are also all sorts of counterpoints, of shadow and light, of laughter and moments of tenderness.

You like to shoot clichés, national stereotypes.

First of all, don't forget that the market for films is above all Anglo-Saxon. I try to avoid used-up clichés, what's already been seen, and to shine a new light on them. There's a value in clichés, because you can elaborate on them. It's a common denominator between me and the audience member that allows me to then make additional commentary. I give them orientation lines from which I can then deviate.

More than most American directors, you like subjects that take place in Europe and most of the time you insist on shooting on location.

Once again, it's not conscious. It might come from a deep desire to come back here from time to time, a change of diet, to see the place I came from. Maybe this need is in me, but it's not premeditated.

As for shooting on location, there are many reasons. This film, for example, even though I didn't photograph scenes of Ischia or things like that, tries to mix the dramatic story in a larger context. I couldn't have shot the film anywhere but Italy. There are also financial reasons: it would have cost more in America. What's more, even while filming the interior of a studio, as I am at the moment at Safra Palatino in Rome, the air is Italian. And if I transported the bed, the couch, the vase of flowers to a Hollywood studio, it wouldn't be the same.

How did you come up with the music?

I bought six Italian songs that will be the themes throughout the film. They will act as the base of the score. But the music mustn't be invasive, as much as a certain number of songs naturally belong to the film (the orchestra, the funerals, etc.).

The end stays open, even though one has reason to believe he'll come back.

You can interpret it as you like. Me, I think he'll come back because he said to her, "If you lose one pound, that will be the end of our relationship." And Carlucci announces to him that the suite will always be ready. The play was very different. The second half, for example, was devoted to the dilemma of a man who asks himself if he'll stay in Europe with his mistress or return home to his wife, which raises questions about children, about his membership in society, etc. We've suppressed all of that, all allusions to divorce. That's part of the novelty of *Avanti!*, that's what happens, and that's all. I wanted this to be a romantic film, as popular as possible, without it being banal or insulting. I omitted the type of problem you see in the films of the 40s and 50s, where the hero thinks about writing a letter to his wife, and fearing that she'll commit suicide, decides to go back to her and . . .

I was struck by the quality of Lemmon's acting because he brings something different to each take of the same scene, and of the tight work between you and him.

It's a work of addition, of subtraction, of clarification, of simplification. Lemmon, of course, is a first class professional, gifted with a great talent. That's what it is to make a film: a collaboration with an actor and a director, between a director and a cinematographer, between a director and a set designer. . . . What will the atmosphere be, what color will we use, where will the living room be in relation to the bedroom, how am I going to use this to its advantage, what will allow the best camera movement? You can't separate the functions, all must be integrated, if not, you'll have the terrible botched work that you see on television. It's not like a play where you have eight weeks of rehearsal. In film-making, everything must be minutely prepared because what you do each day is more or less what you're going to keep.

Lemmon plays a very different character from that which he had already interpreted for you.

He's the young vice-president of a company: that's what he would have become had he not been sick of his promotion in *The Apartment.* There are lots of them in America, the young executives who drink a lot, drive Cadillacs, go to the club, play golf. He had to have been like that to go through a transformation. John O'Hara wrote about men of this sort. They have a luxurious life, two telephones in their car, and suddenly, they discover that their existence is empty, that they have no one to talk to and nothing to say on the telephone, and it wouldn't make a big difference if their stocks rose or fell three points. That's the reevaluation of our values that this film talks about.

At the beginning of each take, Lemmon says "magic time."

That's a habit he formed from the theater. Each time he begins to act, he acts like this was a magic moment: "magic time" which is to say: we're going into character, we're going to bring the public to the land of make believe. He also says: "emotional peak"—which is to say, I'm near orgasm, let's shoot right away. These are jokes that we have exchanged for years. We have been neighbors at the seaside for a long time. At first, I was thinking of someone in his thirties, then, as a friend, I gave him the first part of the script to read, and he asked me for the role. I adjusted the character because of his age and I wrote the second part. I love to work with him, we understand each other, and through the thread of years, we have elaborated between us a secret language, and he can read my mind.

How did you choose Luigi Kuveiller?

I looked at the work of a dozen Italian cinematographers, all excellent. Seeing Petri's *Un Tranquillo Posto di Campagna* [*A Quiet Part of the Country*], I'd loved the lucidity, the lightness, the precision of his photography. I like him, and he not only does lighting, but he directs the camera. In Petri's films there are long lenses, effects that I don't use. It wasn't the style of Kuveiller, but the will of the director. I was seduced by his work, and I loved his charm and his personality, which are very positive on the set.

Yesterday, you were shooting a scene and you suddenly decided to divide it in three shots.

If you analyze the scene, you realize that there are lots of knots to unravel in the plot. It has to do with the discussion between Armbruster and Carlucci with respect to the local bureaucracy and the eight or ten obstacles they must overcome before taking possession of the bodies: pay the owners of the vineyard, build a special coffin, have the bodies examined by the doctor, etc. If I had done it in a very long shot, it might have been admired by a few cinephiles, but the conversation would not have been clear. That's why I kept the style of a long shot, but I interrupted it with two close-ups, which allows the audience member to observe and to hear with greater attention than they would have if the characters had been more distant.

You use very little film and edit while shooting.

I leave the editor very little margin and I believe that I am one of the directors who shoots the least amount of footage for each movie.

Your camera movements, your shots, are they described in the technical cutting?

No, nothing is written. We rehearse and I have a visual conception in my head that I verify on the set. Sometimes, it occurs to me, for example, that instead of cutting, I can continue the shot and preserve the fluidity of the action. Or maybe I ask myself if the audience member will see what I want him to see, or if this or that detail risks not being perceived: should I underline this or that, should this man be in the first shot, am I set up well to move to the next shot? I know directors who come with huge books where each shot is designed down to the ashtray on the table. That was never my method. Even though I do lots of work at home, where I prepare and conceive the film beforehand, I need to see things take life, verify on site and sometimes change. But I don't improvise, of course, neither the plot nor the dialogue, even if I add a word or two here and there.

Like all comedic auteurs—Chaplin or Lubitsch—you aim for simplicity on the set, as if it were a requirement of the genre.

Yes, absolute simplicity. That doesn't mean that you shoot without elegance. If you create your effects with the camera, you can destroy the film. I always thought that authors like Flers and Caillavet or Feydeau aren't adaptable to the screen because you always have to see the entire stage with all of the doors that open and shut as people enter or exit. If you start to cut, it's no longer funny. In a comedy, the geography must be clear and precise. It's easy to embellish. And you should not devote everything to style and nothing to content. If you, the audience member, pay attention to the style, if you sense the dolly or a shock effect from editing, that will distance you from the pleasure you take from the totality of the story, it breaks your participation in that which is happening on the screen.

The film is made in a series of repetitions including details like the young girl who, to explain her presence in the room, pretends to be a manicurist, which her mother was.

There are three love stories—that of the parents, that of the children, that of the father and the son. It's also a sort of sentimental therapy, so much that the real cure for his father wasn't the mud baths but the woman he saw again each year. The idea of the manicure makes you think of *Back Street*, the man

believed that she lived at the Savoy, but in fact, she worked as a manicurist
and didn't want to take money from him. And Juliet Mills plays it magnifi-
cently because she's not a whiner, it's interpreted in a direct manner, in the
best English tradition. Like something very sentimental she said about her
mother, you must tell it with a brutal sense of reality, without tears, nothing
but the facts.

Shooting *The Front Page:* Two Damns and One By God

JOSEPH MCBRIDE/1974

IN 1928, BILLY WILDER was an ace reporter in Berlin, known for his crime stories and for such colorful features as his first-person account of life as a gigolo. That same year, in New York, Ben Hecht and Charles Mac-Arthur opened their raucously cynical newspaper play *The Front Page,* the story of a Chicago paper's attempt to scoop the competition by hiding an escaped prisoner in the pressroom of the Cook County Criminal Courts Building.

Forty-six years later, at Stage 24 of Universal Studios, the pressroom has been recreated in all its pristine squalor, complete with pictures of Herbert Hoover and Red Grange, a rack of seven Chicago dailies, and a half-empty mustard jar nestled amidst the ragged playing cards and cigar butts on the long center table. Billy Wilder, true to his newspaper training, still wears his hat while working. He is directing Jack Lemmon and Walter Matthau, as reporter Hildy Johnson and managing editor Walter Burns, in the third screen version of *The Front Page,* and it is hard to escape the feeling that this often-revived play has finally found its perfect cast and director.

A perpetual motion machine, his language as salty and sarcastic as that of the reporters in the story, Wilder spews out a barrage of quips and good-natured insults, his thick Viennese accent filtered through a mouthful of gum. During a brief pause for lighting, I asked Wilder if any of his own newspaper experience will be reflected in the film. His eyebrows arched in mock surprise: "Hardly. It would be very censorable even today."

From *The Real Paper* (Boston), 31 July, 1974. Reprinted by permission of the author.

The $4 million project got rolling in 1972 after Paul Monash, producer of *Butch Cassidy and the Sundance Kid,* saw the Old Vic's energetic mounting of the play. An unexpected hit of the London season, the production was distinguished by flawless comic timing from a uniformly excellent ensemble of players, even if the accents were less than authentic.

Monash then approached Joseph L. Mankiewicz, a master of sophisticated repartee, to direct the film, but Mankiewicz balked, wanting to see a completed screenplay before committing himself; so Monash decided to look elsewhere. Jennings Lang, a Universal vice president who has been one of my heroes since he gave Abraham Polonsky the chance to direct that unheralded masterpiece *Tell Them Willie Boy Is Here,* suggested Wilder. "With Wilder we managed to hook Lemmon and Matthau," Monash said. "After that there was nothing to it."

When Monash hired Wilder, the director and his writing partner I. A. L. Diamond were brainstorming in search of a film subject. Their last two films, *The Private Life of Sherlock Holmes* and *Avanti!,* were bittersweet romantic comedies in the Lubitsch manner, and neither made much impact with audiences or critics. "We felt we should go back to one of the classic farces of the Thirties," said Diamond, a soft-spoken man whose meticulous, professional manner stands in fetching contrast to the ebullience of his raffish partner. "We thought of *Roxie Hart, Libelled Lady,* and we were also considering *Nothing Sacred,* which has a newspaperman as a leading character. It just so happened that those were all newspaper stories. Nobody's made this kind of picture recently." *The Front Page* had also been mentioned in their discussions, so when Monash broached the subject, they eagerly accepted it.

All in the Script

Wilder was once asked how he would define "the Wilder touch," and he said, "It's just all in the writing, in the story." About 60 percent of the dialogue in *The Front Page* is now different, according to Diamond, but he and Wilder regard the script as a faithful "opening up" of the original. The job of adapting the play was "really mechanics, most of it," Diamond explained, with the work basically involving the addition of scenes which occur off-screen in the play, such as a police dragnet for the escaped prisoner, and the straightening out of certain dramatic clumsinesses in the original. The play takes place entirely in the pressroom set, but the film ranges more naturally over Chicago, including scenes in a movie theater where Lemmon's fiancée works as an organist and at the headquarters of a "Red" organization, called "Friends of American Liberty," which is blitzed by the police because they think the convict has sought shelter there.

And happily, the famous ending line of the play—"The son of a bitch stole my watch!"—will be heard on screen for the first time in Wilder's film. The two previous films, Lewis Milestone's 1931 original with Pat O'Brien and Adolphe Menjou and Howard Hawks's 1940 sexually-reversed version *His Girl Friday* with Rosalind Russell as "Hildegarde" Johnson and Cary Grant as Burns, were both "straitjacketed by censorship of dialogue," Wilder thinks. "I've yet to meet a newspaper man who said, 'Oh, heck' or 'Oh, gosh.' " Wilder says he admires both previous film versions but finds them lacking in various ways. Milestone, whom he regards as a master, was handicapped by "the very crude conditions of sound pictures at that time," and Hawks ventured far afield from the play: "It was very well done, naturally, since Hawks is a very good comedy director, but it was not *The Front Page* by Hecht and MacArthur. It was more *The Awful Truth*, where Irene Dunne is going to marry Ralph Bellamy and she used to be married to Cary Grant, that sort of thing."

The Right Tone of Fluster

The day I visited the set, Wilder was shooting scenes of Burns and Hildy goading Sheriff Peter P. Hartman (Vincent Gardenia in cowboy hat and bushy red John L. Lewis eyebrows) into a near frenzy by refusing to reveal the whereabouts of the fugitive; he is, in actuality, quite literally under everyone's noses, curled up inside the roll-top desk. Brisk and efficient, Wilder completed most of the shots in one or two takes, but one difficult scene required a dozen takes because of complicated movements by Gardenia and problems with a prop telephone he was holding. Matthau was supposed to rip out the telephone cord and wiggle it triumphantly under Gardenia's nose while the sheriff fumes and sputters in a paroxysm of helplessness. Getting the right tone of fluster from Gardenia required careful coaching. "Don't be quite that hysterical—we couldn't understand a word," Wilder said at one point. Later, just before calling action, he told Gardenia, "*Tremendous* intensity. And up, *up*, UP!" The actor, obviously charged full of adrenaline by Wilder's contradictory exhortations, declined the offer of a break between takes, wanting to stay in character. A make-up man moved in to wipe the sweat from his face, and Wilder shouted, "No, leave the sweat, a *lot* of sweat." The make-up man, grinning sheepishly, muttered, "*Now* you tell me," as he walked away.

When they did the scene, Gardenia spluttered spit all over Matthau, and Matthau giggled, forcing Wilder to cut the camera. "I would have let it go," said Wilder, looking a bit disappointed. "A little spit is OK." "I'm sorry," Matthau said, "I just knew I'd been hit by a large snot." The set broke up with laughter, and Matthau, who was playing the scene in his stocking feet to minimize his height advantage over Gardenia, turned to the crew and intoned, "Look at me—standing here without shoes, with snot on my feet." Picking up the cue, Wilder stretched out his arms and burst into song. "Snot on my feet,/ You in my arms,/ Nothing but love."

Wilder never tells him anything about the character he is playing, said Matthau in his dressing room. "He will not waste any time at all with intellectual, psychological, and sociopolitical discussion. He'll simply say, 'Too loud,' 'Not enough voice,' things like that. It's almost the antithesis of intellectual discussion about a character, which is fine with me." I asked Matthau if it was true that the character he played in *The Fortune Cookie,* a glibly cynical shyster lawyer, was modelled on Wilder. "I *always* play Wilder," he said. "Wilder sees me as Wilder—a lovable rogue full of razor blades." (In the script for *The Front Page,* Walter Burns is described thus: "He operates in the great tradition of Machiavelli, Rasputin, and Count Dracula. No ethics, no scruples, and no private life. . . .")

Wilder is pleasant to work with, Matthau said, because he doesn't waste time covering a scene from multiple angles. "Most directors don't know what they want, so they have a lot of postcards. Wilder cuts the cloth as he sees it. I think he's probably the best picture maker around. I mean, he knows how to make a movie. The detail is impeccable."

Back on the set, Wilder demonstrated for Matthau the best way to rip out the telephone cord (which was actually fastened on the underside of the table with a piece of tape), suggesting that he do it in two movements, the first one light and the second one abrupt. "Zis is the first one," he said, pantomiming the action, "and the second zis is a ZUMP." Then he told Matthau to wait a moment before showing the sheriff the ripped cord. "Kind of like a trump card—let him hang there for a while and then . . . very quietly . . ."

Turning his attention back to Gardenia, he told him, "Don't shout in the beginning. Please, please, just trying to get it out of him. Very *shrewd*."

Picking up on Wilder's hint, Gardenia kept his voice down at the beginning of the take, as he talked into the phone, then he turned to Matthau with a little cajoling smile, which quickly evaporated as his anger let loose. Slamming the phone onto the desk, he began a frantic tour of the room, at one point pausing next to the roll-top desk. Wilder had told him how to do it: "Don't look at the desk—like you moved there to look into the can . . . *move toward* the desk but don't look *at* the desk." The 12th take worked, but the sound man, Robert Martin, cornered Wilder later and said he was having a hard time with Gardenia's voice level, since his tone was constantly going up and down. Wilder said, "He's having a nervous breakdown," and Martin replied, "*I'm* having a nervous breakdown. He's never the same." "That's the great beauty of it," Wilder insisted. "If it was always the same it would be dull and boring."

Throwing in a 'Big'

Wilder hardly glanced at the script throughout the day's shooting, relying on Diamond, who was sitting attentively near the camera, to listen for aberrations. Gardenia several times said "Goddammit" when he was supposed to say "By God," and Diamond quietly corrected him until the line was delivered correctly. Once, after rehearsing the scene, Wilder paused a moment in thought and turned to Diamond, asking, "Do we have too many damns?" Diamond ran his finger down the page and said, "Yes, three damns. One should be a By God." Diamond told me his function on the set is "mainly to protect the dialogue," but also to be there in case small changes are necessary. Sometimes modifications have to be made in the dialogue "to adjust it to the camera," and occasionally a scene cannot be completely scripted beforehand because it involves several characters doing something complicated, like playing poker.

With Wilder's energies devoted largely to physical business, Diamond also serves as an arbiter on dialogue squabbles. During rehearsals of a scene in which Matthau was to threaten the sheriff with being thrown out of office on his "fat can," Matthau continually changed the phrase to "big fat can," and just before shooting Wilder reminded him to drop the "big." When the scene was shot, Matthau bobbled the phrase, pronouncing it "fayut can."

"*Fayut?*" Wilder said incredulously, and Matthau turned to Diamond, saying almost plaintively, "Can I throw a 'big' in before 'fat'?" Diamond sniffed, "Yes, you have been doing it and I haven't said a word." Matthau, looking a bit bemused, said to himself, "I felt guilty because I didn't say it." The scene was shot a second time, and Wilder asked sardonically, "Are all the words said? I'm going to print it."

His young cinematographer, Jordan Cronenweth, hovered close to Wilder during every rehearsal as the director stalked around with a viewfinder checking out possible shooting angles. Wilder knows "quite specifically" what he wants visually, says Cronenweth, but he always discusses variations before making a decision. The shots are preplanned, Wilder told me; "it just doesn't look that way." He finds it impossible to completely visualize the scene while writing the script, but when the script is finished he knows roughly how it is going to look on film: "I know how many words I need to get them from the bedroom to the bathroom." Working in a relatively small set such as the pressroom is taxing, because it is hard to think of fresh angles to keep the shots from being repetitious. "More into people than he is into the visual," Wilder is instructive to work with, according to Cronenweth, because "he's probably tried every good and bad thing it is possible to do in movies," and as a consequence his camera style is "very straightforward."

Emotional Rapport

Before shooting a crowd scene with Jack Lemmon standing in the midst of a group of reporters, workmen, and policemen as the workmen try to explain why Matthau has summoned them to the pressroom—they have actually come to spirit away the desk, but Matthau tries to make the sheriff think they have come for Lemmon's suitcases—Wilder loosened up the crowd with quips. He told one of the actors, "Go a little closer to Charlie—he's a very fine man," and saying to another, who was partially blocking Lemmon from view, "The gent in the overalls—you will kindly move over to make way for the biggie there." Lemmon, who was patiently waiting for instructions, had told me earlier that the kind of rapport which comes from making six films with a director is invaluable because "it's like shorthand; he doesn't have to get more than one sentence out before I understand what he has in mind."

Wilder asked Lemmon to demonstrate how he intended to lift the two large suitcases for Matthau to see. "Lift them higher," he said, "Look at

Matthau. Be much more assertive, Jack. Come right forward." The simple direction to "look at Matthau," transformed the scene from a mere con-game into something more subtle: Lemmon's gaze, which had been wandering and undirected, was now transfixed as he regarded Matthau with a look of wide-eyed admiration, and the scene became an expression of the characters' grudging emotional rapport. Wilder called out to Lemmon, "Jack, could there be the tiniest little bit of satisfaction there? Tiny, tiny, tiny. . . ."

Cronenweth suggested doing a close-up of Lemmon's reaction to Matthau, but Wilder rejected the idea, saying, "It's too important. Jack is very good in long shots and medium shots." They did the scene in one take, and the camera operator asked, "You want one more just for security?" Wilder consented, "because I hate to work on a set-up for 45 minutes and finish it in three seconds. It's not fair."

The day's work was almost done when I found a chance to ask Wilder what led him to make *The Front Page*. "Money," he replied. "Greed." His earlier disclaimer of the play's relevance to his own experience as a reporter was declared inoperative, however: "I hope to show—until Rex Reed gets at me, that miserable prick—that I have a feeling for the newspaper guys. I understand their problems, their hang-ups. We're dealing with an obsessive occupation."

Wilder's manner turned rueful when I mentioned his mentor, Ernst Lubitsch, and asked if it is possible these days to make successful pictures in the Lubitsch manner. "The time for Lubitsch is past," he said bluntly. "It's just a loss of something marvelous, the loss of a style I aspired to. The subtlest comedy you can get right now is *M*A*S*H*. They don't want to see a picture unless Peter Fonda is running over a dozen people or unless Clint Eastwood has got a machine gun bigger than 140 penises. It gets bigger all the time, you know; it started out as a pistol and now it's a machine gun. There is a different set of values today. Something which is warm and gentle and funny and urbane and civilized hasn't got a chance. There is a lack of patience which is sweeping the nation, or the world, for that matter. Noel Coward would not succeed today. It's all tough guys. It's all Telly Savalas. Today you have to have a dirty jockstrap and a raincoat and be Columbo. They think it's very romantic. I think it's a lot of shit."

In doing *The Front Page*, Wilder said, he is trying to be "as subtle and elegant as possible." Will the time come when the audience will once again be willing to accept the Lubitsch style? "No less a director than Ingmar Bergman plans to do *The Merry Widow*; let's wait and see." But in the meantime what is Wilder to do? Does he simply give up and don the dirty jockstrap? He shrugged. "You are not going to buck audiences at two or three million a clip, or you'll wind up on your keister. What good is it being a marvelous composer of polkas if nobody dances the polka any more?"

"You Used to Be Very Big." "I Am Big. It's the Pictures That Got Small."

JON BRADSHAW/1975

THE OLD MAN HURRIED UP AND DOWN the room, stopping abruptly at either end so he would not walk into the wall. He wore horn-rimmed glasses and a trilby hat. He held a regimental swagger stick which he snapped in the air to emphasize his arguments. "What did you expect to find when you came out here?" he said. "A broken-down director? A wizened, myopic boob in his dotage? Is that what you expected?" He spoke contorted English fluently—with a Viennese accent and a Viennese stutter. "I guess you thought you'd find me playing with my old Oscars? In a wheelchair maybe. Poor old Billy Wilder. The great director. Christ, you should see him now. A wreck. A ruin. A hole in the wall. Is that what they told you?" He snapped his swagger stick again. "Well, they told you wrong. I'm not just functioning in the motion-picture relief home, y'know. I feel just as confident and virile as I did 30 years ago." He paused for a moment and then he said, "I can still hit home runs, y'know." And he continued to move lightly about the room like a dance master.

He looks younger than his 69 years, affecting a kind of opulent casual dress—loafers, slacks, a pullover, an open shirt. He rarely wears a tie to the studio. He has been in this office at Universal Studios for nearly two years. He is not under contract to Universal and sees himself in the role of visiting professor. His office had once been Lucille Ball's dressing room. The walls are cluttered with framed posters of art exhibitions in Berlin, Paris, and New York. Over his desk is an Oriental design of an elongated carp, a Japanese

From *New York,* 24 November, 1975. Reprinted by permission of Carolyn Pfeiffer.

emblem of good luck. The bookshelves, which occupy an entire wall, are filled with books, his six Oscars standing like sentries to one side, the leather-bound collection of his 28 scripts, and signed photographs of Agatha Christie, Noël Coward, Groucho Marx, and Shirley MacLaine. There is a Richard Avedon series of photographs showing Wilder in various poses with Marilyn Monroe. There is a black leather chair designed by his friend, Charles Eames. Everything is in its place, neatly arranged. It is the office of a very fastidious man.

As he walked, he talked. He talked somewhat faster than he walked—a high stuttering monologue, filled with gutteral embellishments, quaint colloquialisms, and oaths. "I am, I trust, only off the hit parade temporarily," he said. "I'm going through a dry spell, that's all. A slump. I've had them before, y'know. You can't figure it. It's element X, I don't know. I did not suddenly become an idiot. I did not suddenly unlearn my craft. It's a dry spell. Occasionally the vineyards produce a bad vintage." He stopped pacing, having reached a wall. Looking over his shoulder, he said, "But there will always be another harvest. I am the youngest of my generation of directors. My generation included Ford, Stevens, Hawks, Wyler, Cukor, and Hitchcock. My immediate contemporaries are Zinnemann, Mankiewicz, and Huston. They had their dry spells too, y'know. They had slumps. They had bad seasons."

Billy Wilder's slump has lasted for more than a single season. He has been in Hollywood since 1934. During that time, he has been nominated for 21 Academy Awards, winning six—three for writing, two for directing, and one for producing. He has both written and directed some 23 films including *Double Indemnity, The Lost Weekend, Sunset Boulevard, Some Like It Hot,* and *The Apartment.* His films grossed something in excess of $150 million. Up until 1964, he had had only two commercial failures—*Ace in the Hole* in 1951 and *The Spirit of St. Louis* in 1957. But during the last eleven years, he has had five successive flops—*Kiss Me, Stupid* (1964), *The Fortune Cookie* (1966), *The Private Life of Sherlock Holmes* (1970), *Avanti!* (1972), and *The Front Page* (1974). *The Front Page* had actually made money, but Wilder considered it one of his lesser efforts.

"Listen," he said, continuing his restless prowl about the office, "every career has its ups and downs. It's just that in our business it goes a little faster. One year you're on the *New York Times* Ten Best Pictures list and the next year you're one of the Hundred Neediest Cases. Sure you notice it when things go sour. When you're in a slump, you go for the fences. You want a home run. You're pressing. Striking out. What's so sad is that Tony Perez comes to bat four times in an afternoon and eight times on Sunday if it's a doubleheader. I come to bat once every eighteen months.

"It's not that I'm not in demand anymore. There are all kinds of propositions. The telephone keeps ringing. Look at all that stuff on my desk. Some stuff. Somebody sent me a script about a rabbi who kicks field goals for the New York Jets. Then I was asked to do a movie of the English play about a scientist who has a formula for blowing up the whole world. The formula is tattooed on his penis and it can only be read when it's erect. Since the scientist is gay, the government has to train heterosexual agents to become homosexuals. How does that grab you?

"It's a bitch to find a project these days that would both interest me and have a chance in today's market. Though, if someone had asked me to do *Fear of Flying*, I'd've jumped at it. Today, we are dealing with an audience that is primarily under 25 and divorced from any literary tradition. They prefer mindless violence to solid plotting, four-letter words to intelligent dialogue, pectoral development to character development. Nobody *listens* anymore. They just sit there, y'know, waiting to be assaulted by a series of shocks and sensations.

"It's not only me, y'know. It's not only the older directors who face this problem. Mike Nichols, Arthur Penn, and other first-class younger directors have had miscarriages lately. It's a difficult time. Ernst Lubitsch, who could do more with a closed door than most of today's directors can do with an open fly, would have had big problems in this market." Adjusting his glasses, he pointed his swagger stick in the general direction of the Universal lot. "Y'hear all those typewriters going out there? What do you think they're up to? I'll tell you. *Jaws II, French Connection III, Airport '77,* and *The Return of the Exorcist.* We used to have cycles. Now everything is recycled."

He continued to pace about the room. At one point, he must have miscalculated, since he walked out of the room and disappeared. A moment later, he returned, laughing loudly. He looked like an elderly leprechaun. "I've often thought I would do a porno-horror movie," he said, "and capitalize on two of the going trends. The plot would have a sloppy hooker who gives all of her innocent customers crabs. The crabs grow into giant octopuses and eat New Orleans. Do you see the beauty in that? You get both nudity and animal horror in the same picture. I might call it *Deep Jaws.*"

He looked round the room and brandished his swagger stick. "It's no wonder they say Wilder is out of touch with the times," he shouted. "Frankly, I regard it as a compliment. Who the hell wants to be in touch with *these* times?"

At noon, Wilder's secretary, Kay Taylor, who has been with him for two years, brought in a tray on which there were two containers of sake—Ozeki sake, Japan's finest in Wilder's view, and served lukewarm the way he likes it. "Hah!" he shouted, "you thought we were all uncivilized out here, didn't you? You thought we all fell off a turnip truck." He looked at his secretary. "Well, some of us are civilized," he said.

Wilder suggested we drive to his apartment in order to see his art collection. Driving down the gaudy sprawl of Ventura Boulevard, he pointed out Art's, one of his favorite hostelries. A large sign ran the length of the restaurant. It said: ART'S DELICATESSEN. EVERY SANDWICH A WORK OF ART. "I forgave Art for that a long time ago," said Wilder.

He wore his trilby at a jaunty angle. He had left his swagger stick behind. During the 30-minute drive in his bullet-gray Mercedes, he talked cryptically of his past. It was a subject which neither amused nor interested him, and he recounted it as though he were recounting the alphabet. He was born in 1906 in the little town of Sucha, then in Austria but now a part of Poland. His given name was Samuel, but his mother, who wanted him to have an American-sounding name, preferred to call him Billy. His was a middle-class bourgeois family. His father, an erratic man with impossible dreams, owned at various stages of his career railroad restaurants, a trout hatchery, coffee houses, and he imported Swiss watches into Austria. Wilder grew up in Vienna and remembers, as a boy, watching Trotsky play chess in the Café Central. He attended the Real Gymnasium and the University of Vienna, but dropped out after three months to become a reporter on the afternoon boulevard paper, *Die Stunde*. His specialties were sports and interviews. During the course of one morning, he remembered, he interviewed Richard Strauss, Alfred Adler, Arthur Schnitzler, and Sigmund Freud, though the doctor, who loathed journalists, showed him the door, but not before he had seen the famous couch with the Turkish rug thrown carelessly over it.

In 1926, Wilder went to Berlin, working as a crime reporter on one of the larger newspapers. When not at work, he liked to hang around the Romanisches Café, a favorite haunt of reporters, artists, actors, and chess-players. They were heady times in those last years before Hitler became chancellor.

Berlin was the most exciting city in Europe. During his seven years in Berlin, Wilder met or became friendly with such artists as Mies van der Rohe, Walter Gropius, Thomas Mann, Bertolt Brecht, George Grosz, Fritz Lang, Peter Lorre, Paul Klee, Hermann Hesse, and Erich Maria Remarque. Remarque, he remembered, was the editor of *Die Dame,* the German *Vogue,* and longed to quit his job in order to write a novel. Wilder tried to talk him out of it. "Erich," he pleaded, "you have a marvelous job, you make a lot of money, you move in the company of beautiful women, don't be a fool, don't give it up." But Remarque quit finally and wrote *All Quiet on the Western Front.* "I almost talked him out of it," said Wilder.

As a journalist he was rather successful, but to make ends meet, he took a part-time job as a tea-time dancer in the Hotel Eden—dancing with unescorted ladies. He had an American girl friend at the time who taught him the Charleston. Because he was the only man in Berlin who knew the Charleston, he was much sought after at the Hotel Eden. During his spare time, he wrote film scripts.

During the next few years Wilder wrote some 75 films, most of them silent, often writing two a week when he was broke. One of them was *People on Sunday,* a minor classic now in the permanent film collection at the Museum of Modern Art in New York. He worked hard. But it was 1933. Wilder was Jewish. Hitler and the Nazi party had come to power in January of that year. A week after the burning of the Reichstag, Wilder fled Berlin. Leaving behind an apartment filled with Mies van der Rohe furniture and carrying some two dozen original Toulouse-Lautrec posters under his arm, he boarded the train for Paris. Before the war was over, Wilder's grandmother, mother, and stepfather were all to die at Auschwitz.

Paris was dull in comparison with Berlin. Wilder fretted. Wilder scrounged, living from hand to mouth with other German expatriates in a shabby Right Bank hotel. Ten months later, he left for Hollywood, where he arrived in 1934. Wilder had little money and less than a hundred words of English and was reduced to living, he recalls, in the ladies' lavatory of the Château Marmont Hotel. Some months later, he moved into an upstairs room, which he shared with Peter Lorre. Lorre, too, was out of work and the two men lived on a can of soup a day. There were many German refugees in Hollywood at the time—Thomas Mann, Kurt Weill, Fritz Lang, Fred Zinnemann, Ernst Lubitsch, and Marlene Dietrich. In order to improve his English, Wilder courted only American girls. He listened to the radio, often for twelve

hours a day, to soap operas, and to baseball games. In the beginning his
rudimentary English consisted almost entirely of baseball terms. But he survived, his English improved, and gradually the writing assignments came in.
In 1938 he teamed up with Charles Brackett to write *Bluebeard's Eighth Wife,*
directed by Ernst Lubitsch. It was a hit and the following year they wrote
Ninotchka, which established their reputation. In 1942 Wilder directed his
first film, *The Major and the Minor.* He and Brackett continued to collaborate
until 1950 when they parted. Given what he continues to feel is an erratic
command of English, Wilder has always worked with collaborators. Since
1957 he has collaborated with I. A. L. Diamond.

Hurrying out of the elevator, Wilder let himself into his twelfth-floor
cooperative apartment and called immediately for his wife. Audrey Wilder, a
trim, attractive woman in her early fifties, was setting the table for a dinner
party that evening. Formerly a Goldwyn girl and a singer with the Tommy
Dorsey band, she and Wilder have been married for 25 years. Wilder never
tires of telling the story of their courtship. When she and Wilder met, Audrey
Young lived in the shabby Pico–La Brea area of Los Angeles, a section she
preferred to call "East Beverly Hills." When Wilder discovered where she
lived, he said to her: "Darling, I'd worship the ground you walked on, if you
lived in a better neighborhood."

They have lived here for twelve years and during that time Wilder has
packed the apartment with paintings. The walls are covered with Mirós,
Picassos, Dufys, Braques, Rouaults, Renoirs, Klees, Chagalls, a Fernando Botero, and innumerable French primitives. There are three Calder mobiles, and
dotted here and there on shelves and pedestals are pre-Columbian figurines,
the Maillols, and the Henry Moores. Beyond the main room, overlooking
Century City, is the large terrace containing Wilder's bonsai trees, the ferns,
the laurel, the ficus, and Ming arelis trees. The apartment has the neat and
polished look of a provincial museum.

Taking off his trilby, Wilder offered a drink, insisting on akvavit. Not your
ordinary run-of-the-mill *Danish* akvavit. No, this was Linie, Norwegian
akvavit, the best there is. Pulling a bottle from the freezer, the bottom of
which was encased in a block of ice, he said, "I'll make an alcoholic gourmet
of you yet." He called for his wife. "Aud, where do you keep the cheese?" His
wife said there was no cheese. "No cheese?" shouted Wilder. "What do you
mean there's no cheese? This man's come all the way from New York and
you tell me there's no cheese. He'll crucify me. He'll think we're all barbar-

ians. He'll think we fell off a turnip truck. What do you mean there's no cheese?" "There's no cheese," said his wife.

We moved to the terrace, Wilder skipping ahead. Looking out over the sprawling city, he shook his head and said, "Hollywood has changed a lot in the last ten years. It's a whole different ball game now. What used to be mah-jongg is now backgammon. The studios used to have more stars than there were in heaven. It's all a darkness now. In the old days, the studio heads were former scrap-iron dealers, butchers, traveling salesmen in ladies' underwear. Now, 80 per cent of our executives are former agents. They used to be dealers and now they want to play. It is they who decide on that ugly word 'bank-able.' It is they who have decreed that Miss Barbra Streisand is irresistible, that Mr. Howard Cosell is a living doll, that Mr. Rod McKuen is a poet." He smiled and, holding his hands up in the air, intoned: "O tempora. O William Morris.

"Even today's critics are not up to the standard of, let us say, James Agee. Y'know? Only a handful of critics really matter. They can't make or break a picture—look at *Mahogany*—but they can sure bolster or dampen your spirits. I mean, the ladies on *The New Yorker* write like angels—with diarrhea. The only thing longer than *Nashville* was Miss Kael's review of *Nashville*. I found it strange that *New York* replaced Crist with Judas. After all those legitimate-theater corpses [John] Simon left strewn around New York, he had to find a new neighborhood for his night of the long knives, so he went into movies. Simon is an irritant, but not deadly. Like hemorrhoids, he's not going to kill you, but he's very unpleasant. The only word I can use to describe him is *ekelhaft* [nauseating, loathsome]. *Time* and *Newsweek* are impish and vine-gary and see things with a jaundiced eye. They review with karate chops, with kung fu and judo, and then they garrote you with a string of puns. They never bring themselves to suppress a particularly nasty witticism, even if they like the movie. And as for Rex Reed, that cultural oracle of the *Daily News,* he's a dilettante. It is fitting, don't you think, that he chose to make his acting debut in that masterpiece *Myra Breckenridge*."

Wilder walked into the study. Here again the walls were covered with paintings, including several of Picasso's early pornographic studies. A table was piled with old copies of *Gourmet,* Wilder's favorite magazine. "It's a curi-ous thing, a loss of reputation," he said. "It hasn't happened to me exactly, but I know that it becomes much more difficult to reach your agent. There is even a difference in the hello you get from the doorman at the studio gate.

Or you're asked to be a judge at the San Sebastian Film Festival, because they know you're not working. When you strike out two or three times, you're not asked to be a pallbearer anymore. That's one of the first signs of decay. I used to be asked all the time. Can you believe I've only been asked *once* in the last two years? You also discover that you weren't the first or even the second directorial choice. But the high point of triumph in this highly competitive community in which we live is not only that *you* must have a smash, but that the director you're competing against must have a failure. Now, that's a great parlay." He grimaced. "There's a canard that the Hollywood community is full of bitterness, dissension, envy, and hostility. It's just not true. I've lived here for 40 years and I can tell you it took one simple event to bring all the factions together—a flop by Peter Bogdanovich. The news swept tinseltown like wildfire. Champagne corks were popping, flags were waving. The guru had laid an egg and Hollywood was united.

"Making pictures," he said, "is a bit like walking into a dark room. Some people stumble across pieces of furniture, others break their legs, but some of us see better in the dark than others. The ultimate trick is to convince, persuade. Every single person out there in that audience is an idiot, but collectively they're a genius. There are moments when I get a little nervous. Am I doing the wrong thing, will it work? But I've not been turned down on a project yet. Not being hot affects an actor or a director much more than it affects a writer. The actor and director have to sit at home and wait for the phone to ring. A writer still functions. Not being hot has affected my ego somewhat, disturbed my confidence. But one hit, and that will change.

"I don't know. I've been doing a lot of bunting lately. I've been getting a lot of scratch hits, nothing very solid. I've not hit a home run in a long time. *Irma La Douce* was a home run, but that was during the 1963 season. *Kiss Me, Stupid* was a strike-out on three straight strikes. After that, Izzy Diamond and I felt like parents who had produced a mongoloid and didn't care to have sexual intercourse anymore. *The Fortune Cookie* was a scratch bunt. I just got on. *Sherlock Holmes* was a strike-out, an expensive error. *Avanti!* was a strike-out too, though it was a double in Europe. My last film, *The Front Page*, was a single. It was a nice hit and drove in a run or two, but that was all. It was solid, but hell, I used to hit the solid stuff over the fences."

He looked around the room and adjusted the angle of his glasses. "Listen, when Mickey Mantle bats .350, that's terrific. But if a director bats .350, he better change professions. He'd better start looking for another job.

"Well," he sighed, "it's hurt my ego, I suppose, but it hasn't hurt me financially. I was never given to mansions and yachts. I never played the market or had race horses or expensive mistresses. My *life* has not been affected. It remains the same.

"It's just possible that I've been designing clothes which by the time the show comes round people are not wearing anymore. But I thrive on reverses. It makes me more determined, more ambitious. It doesn't paralyze me. I've always thought that you are as good as the best you've ever been. In Europe, they recognize that. In Europe, people have some sort of respect for what you have done, as opposed to what you have done lately." He looked around the room again. "That doesn't mean that I look at my old films, y'know. That's like meeting a girl you slept with fifteen years ago. You look at her and you think, 'My God, did I go to bed with that?' "

Wilder got up and began to walk hurriedly around the room, walking nimbly between the tables and the chairs with the confidence of one who had done it many times before. "I'm getting old, I guess," he said. "Anybody who says to you when you reach your sixties, 'Welcome to the golden decade,' as Justice Frankfurter once said, I say to him, 'Bullshit.' It's like finding beauty in arthritis. You lose mobility, flexibility. The steps get steeper, though I myself still feel young and sprightly." And, as if to emphasize the point, he moved even more speedily. The movement was something between a pas de bourrée and the bunny hop. "To paraphrase the guy in *Fiddler on the Roof,*" he continued, "it's no disgrace to be old, but it's no great honor either. In terms of directing, it's a tremendous physical ordeal. I mean, even if the movie's lousy, you still have to get up at 5 A.M. It's not like wine and violins, y'know. You don't get better simply because you get older. But I remain undismayed. It's gratifying to make it, but it's positively thrilling to make a comeback. A comeback is making it in spades.

"I'm working on something completely new now," he said. "Izzy and I have been wrestling with an idea about Hollywood for the past five months. I haven't made one since *Sunset Boulevard,* y'know. But there are too many pictures with a Hollywood background in the works right now. Sixteen or so. So we shelved it temporarily and are now tackling a completely different subject. I can't tell you what it is. It might be in the wastebasket by next Friday. Right now, I'm in a state of flux and indecision."

He was quiet for a time. He stopped pacing, leaned over the table and tidied up the magazines. And then he laughed. "In the old days, I was a good ball player," he said. "What they called an untouchable. No team would have dared to trade me. Not under any circumstances. Today, I guess you could call me a free agent. I'm looking for the big hit. It's going to be a home run and the bases will be loaded. You can bank on it. Next time up," he said, "I'm hitting for the fences."

Billy Wilder

GENE D. PHILLIPS/1976

"Are we rolling?—as we say on the set?" Veteran film director Billy Wilder eyes the tape recorder before him on his desk and the interviewer across from him. It is hard to believe that this energetic, articulate man began his career in films almost half a century ago in Berlin by writing film scripts, most notably for a semi-documentary called People on Sunday *(1929). After he migrated to Hollywood in the 1930's in the wake of the rise of Hitler, Wilder continued his career as a scriptwriter for such major directors of the day as Ernst Lubitsch. When he graduated to film direction with* The Major and the Minor *(1942), he continued to collaborate on the scripts for his films, and finally took over the task of producing the films which he directed in order to insure his artistic independence. He has, therefore, been able to create motion pictures that bear the unmistakable stamp of his own artistic vision and care. He has received six Academy Awards, for co-authoring and directing* The Lost Weekend; *for co-authoring* Sunset Boulevard; *and for co-authoring, producing, and directing* The Apartment, *becoming the first film maker ever to win three Oscars in the same year in three different categories.*

Although Wilder has made comedies as well as dramas, his satirical purpose is always the same in film after film: to expose the foibles and flaws of human nature to the public eye in order to stimulate audiences to serious reflections about the human condition. It has been said that if a satirist like Jonathan Swift were alive today he would be writing screenplays for Billy Wilder!

From *Literature/Film Quarterly*, Winter 1976. Reprinted by permission.

I was a very small fish in the German celluloid pond. After spending some time as a newspaper man, I became a writer of movies, some of which were a little better than others. (I never directed a picture in Germany.) One of the pictures I wrote was a tiny *avant-garde* film called *Menschen am Sonntag* (*People on Sunday*) which was directed by Robert Siodmak with Fred Zinnemann as assistant cameraman. It was a kind of New Wave picture made in 1929, long before the New Wave, about a group of Berliners spending a Sunday afternoon together. The film did make quite a splash at the time but I think that I should put it in a proper perspective.

It was not that a bunch of dilettantes got together and the end result was an *American Graffiti* that made forty million marks; but people talked about it. It was a semi-documentary type film that was very novel for its time. We had a fresh approach to our material because we made the film on our own and we were therefore not caught up in the quagmire of banality of some of the big studio films. We were chiefly concerned with learning our craft and trying from the beginning of our careers to avoid the clichés of the average commercial picture.

After I left Germany because of the change in government to save my skin, I co-directed a film in France called *Mauvaise Graine* (*The Bad Seed*, 1933) which was a comedy about some auto thieves. Then I went on to America.

Basically you would have to divide the influx of German picture makers into the United States into two categories. First there were the ones that were hired by the American studios because they were outstanding geniuses like Murnau and Lubitsch, to mention just the very prominent ones. These were the people who came over in the Twenties who were sought after by studio executives like Thalberg and Zukor because they had made enormously successful films in Europe. That was the first group.

Then in the middle Thirties came an avalanche of refugees who were looking for jobs on the basis of their experience in German pictures such as Zinnemann, Preminger, and myself. We didn't come because we were invited like the first group; we came to save our lives, and from the first we desperately tried to learn English so that we could get work in Hollywood. So you see in my case I was a job seeker, not an accomplished motion picture maker. In addition, Austria, my home country, was no more; so I really had to make good here. It wasn't a question of my saying to myself, "Well, if things don't work out here I can go back to Austria or to Germany." For me it was a question of fighting it out here and surviving or going back and winding up like most of my family in the ovens of Auschwitz.

Since my profession at the time was writing, it was especially important for me to learn English, and here I was knowing only German and French. It was a very tough period for me. I had sold an original story to Columbia while I was still in Paris and I made $150 a week for a short time because of that when I first arrived in Hollywood. But then for months and months I went hungry while I studied English.

I had to make my way here on the basis of my previous work in Germany. So many German artists who claimed to have worked with Max Reinhardt before coming to the U.S.A. really hadn't done so. I thought it was nonsense to make up credentials like that. I was not a "Reinhardt man"; I had worked at the Ufa studios in Berlin but I had been only a tiny wheel in that big machine. I had worked on some pictures there which made something of a name for themselves; but I had never directed, and writers did not have much standing in the picture business in those days, either in Berlin or in Hollywood.

Script writing in Hollywood when I came here was a field for novelists on their way down or for successful novelists and playwrights who came here from the East during the rainy and the snowy seasons in New York in order to steal some money writing for films; and then as quickly as possible they would get back on the Super Chief and get out of town. Screen writers had to build up a place of some standing in the industry over a long period of time, thanks largely to the eventual emergence of a strong Screen Writers' Guild. But in the mid-Thirties I had to entice an agent to handle me because on my list of credits from Germany were films that most people here had not heard of. There was no *Last Laugh* behind me as there was behind Murnau. I had none of the accomplishments of a Lubitsch. It is entirely possible that many of us who came to America on our own initiative without any impressive credentials from Europe could have ended up as a head waiter at the Beverly-Wilshire Hotel or opened a haberdashery store.

William Wyler, for example, when he came to America was just another relative of Carl Laemmle, the head of Universal, who was looking for work. Wyler's father had a man's haberdashery store in his native Alsace Lorraine and he could have wound up in the mail room at Universal's New York exchange for good had he not steadily worked his way up from the bottom of the ladder in the studio as a prop boy.

Future directors like Stroheim and Wyler had no experience in picture making when they came to America and got into the business once they had arrived. So you see, those of us who had little or no background in films when we immigrated to the United States were in an entirely different category from, say, a Frenchman like René Clair who was a master director when he was lured to Hollywood. His stay here, however, did not quite work out because the French are very difficult to transplant and they rightfully are hesitant to leave their own milieu—whereas those of us coming from Germany, as I said, had no choice but to leave home. Although in my case it is also true that even without Hitler I would have dreamed of coming to Hollywood to make pictures.

We who had our roots in the European past, I think, brought with us a fresh attitude towards America, a new eye with which to examine this country on film, as opposed to the eye of native-born movie makers who were accustomed to everything around them. Hence there was some novelty about our approach to the films that we made here from the start.

Once I teamed with Charles Brackett to write screenplays, we wrote a couple of films for Ernst Lubitsch to direct, *Bluebeard's Eighth Wife* (1938) and *Ninotchka* (1939). I have sometimes been called the "heir of Lubitsch." My God, if I could write and direct like Lubitsch I would be a very happy man. There was a uniqueness about him, about the way his mind worked in devising and directing scenes. No one but Lubitsch could make a Lubitsch film.

I remember Pauline Kael writing that *Last Tango in Paris* was going to change the whole course of the film industry the way that Stravinsky's *Firebird* altered the course of ballet. Bertolucci is a very good director, but Ms. Kael's remark was a wild exaggeration. *Last Tango* has come and gone and we still do things pretty much the way that we did. But Lubitsch's *Love Parade*, the first sound musical, did help to initiate a new era of motion pictures, and how seldom that is remembered. So much for critics.

It is true that Lubitsch's kind of comedy is close to my brand of comedy, but I have never specialized in comedy films as he did for the most part. I make serious pictures too. With all my respect for Hitchcock, I can't understand how anybody can always work in the same genre. He does it beautifully, of course, but I get bored and jump around in order to make different types of films.

One of the first pictures I directed was a drama called *Five Graves to Cairo* (1943) which I still remember as one of my better pictures. It was an exciting story about Rommel (Erich Von Stroheim) and his Afrika Korps fighting the British in the desert during World War II, and was made while the fighting was still going on there. Nobody said it was *The Battleship Potemkin* or *Intolerance,* but I thought it was a good, entertaining hunk of celluloid. It worked.

In serious films like *Five Graves, Double Indemnity,* and *The Lost Weekend* I strove for a stronger sense of realism in the settings in order to match the kind of story we were telling. I wanted to get away from what we described in those days as the white satin decor associated with MGM's chief set designer, Cedric Gibbons. Once the set was ready for shooting on *Double Indemnity* (1944), for example, I would go around and overturn a few ashtrays in order to give the house in which Phyllis (Barbara Stanwyck) lived an appropriately grubby look because she was not much of a housekeeper. I worked with the cameraman to get dust into the air to give the house a sort of musty look. We blew illuminum particles into the air and when they floated down into a shaft of light it looked just like dust. Shortly afterwards MGM made another James M. Cain novel into a picture, *The Postman Always Rings Twice,* with Lana Turner as the wife of the proprietor of a hot dog stand. She was made up to look glamorous instead of slightly tarnished the way we made up Barbara Stanwyck for *Double Indemnity* and I think *Postman* was less authentic as a result.

Raymond Chandler worked on the script of *Double Indemnity* and I think that he did the best work on that film that he ever did on a movie. The film has quite a reputation today as an example of *film noir.* I really don't like all of these categories for pictures. For me there are only two types of movies: interesting movies and boring movies. It's as simple as that. Does a film rivet my attention so that I drop my popcorn bag and become part of what is happening on the screen or doesn't it? If the film engages my interest only sporadically, the picture just hasn't got it.

The Lost Weekend (1945) was shot on location partially in New York, just as *Double Indemnity* was filmed in part around Los Angeles. We used P. J. Clarke's bar at the corner of Third Avenue and Fifty-fifth Street in *The Lost Weekend* because that was the bar where Charles Jackson, the author of the novel, did his drinking and that is where his friendly bartender was. I went on location not merely to get away from the Hollywood back lot but because there simply was no other way to reproduce the thirty block trek up Third Avenue that Don Birnam (Ray Milland) made to pawn his typewriter to get money to buy booze. Location shooting wasn't that much of a novelty, even in the Forties. Von Stroheim had shot a lot of *Greed* on the streets of San Francisco back in 1923, so I don't claim to be an innovator in that regard.

I did manage to portray the orderly at Bellevue's alcoholic ward as an homosexual even though homosexuality was a taboo subject in American films in those days. I directed the actor how to play his role as a homosexual. The cognoscenti, those who looked and listened, got the implications of the scene. The censorship office couldn't nail me on it, however, because I had been subtle about it and they couldn't pin anything down to which they could object. Those were different days.

On the other hand, the so-called happy ending of *Lost Weekend* was not something imposed on me by the studio or by the censors or anyone else. When Birnam promises his girl that he is going to stop drinking, this is really not a pat happy ending at all. He says he will *try* not to drink anymore. The film does not imply that he will never drink again because for all we know he may have been drunk again the next day. We end on a note of promise, that he is going to make one more attempt to reform, but that is as far as the picture goes.

I said that *Lost Weekend* was a realistic movie and I think the scene in which we portray the hallucinations that Birnam has while he is suffering from the d.t.'s is part of that realism. An alcoholic in that condition would see bats flying around, etc. By the same token I don't think that there is anything particularly symbolic about my showing the deterioration of the has-been movie actress's estate in *Sunset Boulevard* (1950). I didn't conceive that setting so much as a metaphor for her personal decay but as an authentic depiction of the way a woman like Norma Desmond (Gloria Swanson), living in the past, would allow her property to slide into ruin. Even today there are old Hollywood estates with empty swimming pools with rats running around in them and cracked tennis courts with sagging nets. That's a part of our film community. People are up and then they are down. I used the neglected pool for a dramatic purpose, because later, when the young gigolo (William Holden) enters her life it would be natural that she would have the pool cleaned and filled as an indication of her renewed interest in life.

Sunset Boulevard clearly did not have a happy ending because there was simply no other ending possible. It was inevitable that Norma Desmond would go mad and the picture was designed that way. Of course, in those days, when you dramatized evil your protagonists had to pay for their wrongdoing. Still, no other ending would have worked in the film, and the studio at no point questioned this. So, you see, it is vastly exaggerated that happy endings were expected in Hollywood pictures until recent years.

I directed two other film directors as actors in that film, and I had no problems with either of them. Stroheim played Norma Desmond's former director and ex-husband Max who was now her butler and chauffeur. He was really not an actor but he did have an extraordinary personality which he projected on the screen. And he was enormously helpful with the script. It was he who suggested that Norma be receiving fan letters that were ultimately disclosed as having been written by Max. Stroheim had a very fine celluloid mind. He knew what worked.

Cecil B. DeMille, who played himself and in the story had directed Norma as a young actress, was total perfection. He was disciplined and gave a subtler performance, I thought, than any of the actors in the films that he directed ever gave.

Directors are not difficult to direct because they remember the problems which they have had with their actors when they were directing. As a result they will bend over backwards to be helpful.

I used a clip from *Queen Kelly* in the course of *Sunset Boulevard* but it was not identified since in the film the silent movie being projected starred Norma Desmond and I could not refer to the picture as *Queen Kelly* starring Norma Desmond when it in fact starred Gloria Swanson. It was an interesting tie-in, however, that the clip of Gloria Swanson as a younger silent film star was from the one film in which she was directed by Stroheim, who was playing Norma's former director in *Sunset Boulevard.* And the fact that I could get DeMille to play another of Norma's former directors, when in reality DeMille had directed Gloria Swanson in *Male and Female* in the old days, also gave additional authenticity to the film. So did the cameo appearances of other silent film stars such as H. B. Warner, Buster Keaton, and Anna Q. Nilsson. All of these elements added a more genuine flavor to what I was trying to do.

In the same way Marlene Dietrich's appearance in *A Foreign Affair* (1948) helped give that film a more authentic atmosphere. There was a natural similarity between the café singer that she portrayed in Sternberg's *The Blue Angel* in 1930 and the Berlin nightclub singer she played in my film. And the Lola of *Blue Angel* probably would have still been around in the post-war period in which *Foreign Affair* is set. And by the way, Ms. Dietrich's songs in my film were written by the same composer who wrote the songs for *Blue Angel,* Frederick Hollander, which made the connection between the two roles even closer.

Someone who saw *A Foreign Affair* said that they were surprised to see just how much a GI in post-war Berlin could trade for candy bars and cigarettes. That reflection leads me to recall the theme which often turns up in my pictures: People will do anything for money—except some people, who will do almost anything for money.

I suppose this idea was most clearly expressed in *Ace in the Hole* (1951) in which Kirk Douglas plays a reporter who turns the site of a mine cave-in into a lucrative carnival for the sensation seekers. The film was not successful because I brought the audience into the theater expecting a cocktail and instead I served them a shot of vinegar. In effect I was saying to them, "Look, this is you, you bastards, because there is a man dying in this mine shaft and you are all sensationalists." People rebelled against this image of themselves. Yet, when there is a plane wreck at Kennedy Airport the freeways are clogged with automobiles of people wanting to see the carnage. Meanwhile somebody is going around selling weenies and spun sugar. People are like this but they resent being reminded of the fact. So my film failed in the same way that a very good picture like *Sugarland Express* twenty years later failed for the same reason.

Stalag 17 (1953), which followed *Ace in the Hole*, was much more popular. In it I directed still another director, Otto Preminger, as the commandant of the prisoner of war camp. He had trouble remembering his lines and would get very embarrassed and say that he was rusty because he hadn't acted in so many years. He said he would send me a pound of caviar every time that he had a day when he blew his lines. Well, several pounds of caviar arrived for me in the course of shooting that film, but he gave a fine performance.

We didn't attempt to open up the original play of *Stalag 17* for the screen when we filmed it. Sometimes opening up a play can ruin it, as in the case of *The Diary of Anne Frank*. What worked in *Anne Frank* on the stage was that the audience was confined in that little attic with the family of Jews who were hiding from the Gestapo. When that sense of isolation was lost in the film, the intensity of the story was dissipated to some extent. So, too, in *Stalag 17* I wanted the audience to experience the confinement of the prisoners and therefore shot no scenes outside of the prison compound.

Stalag 17 was well received but frankly I have never been interested in what the critics say of my films. A good review means much less to me than, for instance, a comment Agatha Christie made recently about *Witness for the Prosecution,* which I filmed in 1957 with Marlene Dietrich. She called it the best film that has ever been made from her work. That means a great deal more to me than anything a critic has ever said of one of my films.

Some Like It Hot (1959) seems more and more to be the film that moviegoers remember the best. It's become a kind of posthumous classic. My collaborator, I. A. L. Diamond, and I, got the idea for it from a German picture which played in Bavaria, but it had a contemporary setting and dealt with two guys who joined a girls' band simply because they needed jobs. When we talked about it we decided that they should join the girls' band as an absolute question of life and death. Otherwise it would seem that at any point in the picture they could remove their wigs and skirts and say to the girls that they love, "Look, no problem, we're guys and you're gals and we love you."

So we invented the fact that they had witnessed a gangland killing and had to disguise themselves to protect their lives. Then we set the story in the Twenties in order to make this plot element more believable and brought in the Al Capone background and the St. Valentine's Day Massacre as the killing that they witnessed. So it was not that we sat down and said that we were going to do a satire of the old gangster pictures. Once we set the film in the earlier period for plot reasons we decided to exploit the period by bringing in George Raft and Pat O'Brien, who starred in the early gangster films. I tried to get Edward G. Robinson, too, but he wouldn't do it, so I got his son to play a small part.

By contrast, *One, Two, Three* (1961) was a contemporary comedy set in Berlin. But while we were filming there the Berlin Wall was erected between the Eastern and Western sectors. When refugees were killed trying to cross from East to West in real life, it made it harder for people to accept a comedy that took place in this setting. Film makers are vulnerable to this kind of risk. A situation, a political mood changes in the course of your making a film and things are not the same by the time you finish the picture as they were when you started. If you write a newspaper piece, it appears the next day. If you write a magazine article, it appears a week from Tuesday. But film makers who do a contemporary story have to pray that the situation that they are dealing with in the projected movie will still be valid a year and a half in the future. Otherwise people may say that you are guilty of bad taste in treating a subject that may have been quite different when you began.

This question of bad taste has followed me for years. Mel Brooks is a very talented director, but I wonder what would have been said if Wilder had filmed something like the bean supper around the campfire in *Blazing Saddles*. When I made *Kiss Me, Stupid* (1964) the film was severely criticized. Yet I always thought that it had some tenderness in its treatment, at least in the scenes between the café girl (Kim Novak) and the husband who asks her to masquerade as his wife for an evening. This is the only taste of domesticity that she has ever experienced in her whole life and she is very touched by it. But no one seemed to see this aspect of the story.

In any event the film caused a big scandal and they were going to tear up my citizenship papers! Today *Kiss Me, Stupid* would seem like Disney fare, and I wonder what all the screaming was about. I had some bad luck even when I was making the picture. Peter Sellers was to play the husband but he had to be replaced when he had a heart attack, and there were other things that didn't work out.

Don't misunderstand me. I don't say that for this failure I have this excuse and for that failure I have that excuse, but for this big hit I take all the credit. I have had good luck too, and sometimes I have muffed it when it came my way. But look at the total canon of a supreme dramatist like George Bernard Shaw. He wrote dozens of plays of which you remember six or seven. The rest are never performed. But when you make a bad picture it pursues you the rest of your life. It comes back to haunt you on the Late Show. Directors can't bury their dead. But that's the nature of the business that I have chosen as my profession. It's too late now for me to become a veterinarian.

I don't really like to recall my past films because I get bored with myself and my own work. I don't even have 16mm copies of my pictures, or look at them on TV. The past is forgotten and I am only interested in going onward to my next project. I recently made *The Front Page* (1975), based on the old Hecht-MacArthur play about the newspaper business. We did much more opening out of the story than we did on *Stalag 17*, for instance. As I mentioned above, certain plays call for being opened out more than others. Indeed, the playwright himself might have opened up the play more had he not been straightjacketed by the format of the stage. This was the case with *The Front Page*, which we opened out much more than the 1931 film did: we added a chase scene and some other things, including the printed epilogue that tells what happened to the characters after the end of the story. We took that idea, of course, from the epilogue of *American Graffiti*.

Sometimes a film comes off and sometimes it doesn't and you can't always predict the outcome, which I think is clear from some of the films I've talked about. If I were to sum up my career I would say that I am a competent journeyman who has gotten lucky once in a while. Period. That's all I can tell you about me.

Dialogue on Film: Billy Wilder and
I. A. L. Diamond

THE AMERICAN FILM INSTITUTE/
1976

QUESTION: *You two have collaborated for an unusually long time, considering the high divorce rate of writer-director relationships. To put it simply, how do you two work together?*

WILDER: I imagine the collaboration between a director and writer varies. In the old days, some directors got a script handed to them on Friday and had to start shooting on Monday. But Mr. Diamond and I—and my former collaborators, Charles Brackett and Raymond Chandler—had a special kind of arrangement, since I myself started as a writer and still regard myself as a writer. So, don't take our way of working as something that is normal. In fact, I think it's rather abnormal, because from the day we sit down to start working on the screenplay until the time the picture is reviewed by Vincent Canby in New York, we're always together.

DIAMOND: You obviously have to differentiate among directors who are just directors, directors who are also producers, and directors who are also writers. I think a normal course of events, if you sell a story or are assigned to a story, is to work first with a producer, and only when he was satisfied would the director come in.

WILDER: I'm asked all the time: When there are two names or three names on a screenplay, does one write one scene and the other another scene, and then do you meet every Tuesday and compare? Or does one write the action and the other write the dialogue? I'm already very gratified if anybody asks

Reprinted by permission of The American Film Institute.

that question, because most people think the actors make up the words. But in our case it's very prosaic; it sounds very dull.

We meet at, say, 9:30 in the morning and open shop, like bank tellers, and we sit there in one room. We read *Hollywood Reporter* and *Variety*, exchange the trades, and then we just stare at each other. Sometimes nothing happens. Sometimes it goes on until 12:30, and then I'll ask him, "How about a drink?" And he nods, and then we have a drink and go to lunch. Or sometimes we come full of ideas. This is not the muse coming through the windows and kissing our brows. It's very hard work, and having done both, I tell you that directing is a pleasure and writing is a drag. Directing can become difficult, but it is a pleasure because you have something to work with. You can put the camera here or there; you can interpret the scene this way or that way; the readings can be such or such. But writing is just an empty page. You start with nothing, absolutely nothing, and I think writers are vastly underrated and underpaid. It is totally impossible to make a great picture out of a lousy script. It is impossible, though, for a mediocre director to screw up a great script altogether.

DIAMOND: A writer named Hal Kanter once wrote a monologue for Groucho Marx which had the following line: "Who needs writers? Give me a competent director and two intelligent actors, and at the end of eight weeks I will show you three of the most nervous people you ever saw."

QUESTION: *Could you take one of your original films, say* The Apartment, *and trace its origins—where the idea came from, the problems in writing it?*
WILDER: The genesis of *The Apartment* I remember very, very vividly. I saw David Lean's *Brief Encounter*, which was based on a one-act play by Noel Coward, and in the play Trevor Howard was the leading man. A married man has an affair with a married woman, and he uses the apartment of a chum of his for sexual purposes. I always had it in the back of my mind that the friend of Trevor Howard's, who only appears in one or two tiny scenes, who comes back home and climbs into the warm bed the lovers have just left, would make a very interesting character. I made some notes, and years later, after we had finished *Some Like It Hot*, we wanted to make another picture with Jack Lemmon. I dug out this notion, and we just sat down and started to talk about the character, started the structure, started the three acts, started the other characters, started to elaborate on the theme, and when we had

enough we just suggested it to Mr. Lemmon and to Walter Mirisch and United Artists.

DIAMOND: We had the character and the situation, but we didn't have a plot until there was a local scandal. An agent who was having an affair with a client was shot by the woman's husband. But the interesting thing was that he was using the apartment of one of the underlings at the agency. That was what gave us the relationship—somebody who was using somebody lower than he in a big company, using his apartment.

WILDER: In those days it was a very, very risqué project. Today, of course, it would be considered a Disney picture.

DIAMOND: I also remember some construction problems. There was one point in the second act where Billy kept saying, "The construction is hump-backed." He meant that we were faced with two exposure scenes back to back. In one scene Fred MacMurray's secretary gives away to his wife that he is having an affair. This is immediately followed by a scene in which the guys who had been thrown out of the apartment give away to the girl's brother-in-law that she's staying with Lemmon. Those scenes came back to back, and Billy kept saying, "It's humpbacked. It's humpbacked." But it was the only way we could arrive economically at the third act.

WILDER: But nobody notices any more because neat constructions are out. Third acts are out. Payoffs are out. Jokes don't have toppers. They just have an interesting straight line, and let the audience write its own toppers. We come from a whole different school. A comedy like *Shampoo* I don't think was constructed at all. What makes it successful, I guess, is that it's slapped together with verve and overt language and naked behinds and God knows what. It is a kind of super gusto, sex chutzpah, whatever you want to call it, that makes it come off. It's not constructed in the way we learned. But if you come now with any kind of experience in that direction—I've been at it for forty years—construction is frowned upon, it's not being done, it's old-fashioned. I guess it is, but that's the way we've been doing it, and that's the way we're going to do it until they take the cameras away. The idea that people in a picture can sit around a campfire and break wind and scream for fifteen minutes seems very strange to us.

DIAMOND: Everybody in this room, I am sure, can quote half a dozen good lines from *Casablanca,* from *Ninotchka,* from *The Maltese Falcon,* and any number of other pictures. Now, you know what got the two big laughs in *Shampoo.* . . . I think this is hardly a substitute for wit, except among eleven-year-olds when if you say a dirty line it's considered daring. But it doesn't put very much of a premium on writing clever dialogue.

WILDER: But *Shampoo* had an absolutely marvelous idea, the ambulatory hairdresser with the penis hairdryer under his belt, chugging around Beverly Hills, and it had those couple of dirty lines. "Hey, have you seen *Shampoo?*" "Does she really say that?" "Yeah." "I've got to see that." People wait for that, and then they leave. But it did have a showmanship idea, and it did have Warren Beatty. He was just right for the part, and the movie came at the right time. But I would be embarrassed to write it. I personally would be embarrassed to go to Julie Christie and say, "Here's the dialogue for tomorrow." I would run and hide somewhere.

QUESTION: *Do you tend to have a star in mind when you're writing a script? In* The Apartment *you wanted Lemmon, and I suppose you adapted your dialogue to his personality.*

DIAMOND: I'd say that most of the time we have known pretty early on in the script who was going to be in the picture, which of course makes it much more comfortable for the writer.

WILDER: In *Some Like It Hot* we were way into the script when we found out that Marilyn Monroe was available and wanted to do the picture. I think, as a rule, it's bad to tell the actors, "I'm doing something for you and only you can play it." They don't like that. You just say, "I know that you can do it. You can interpret it because you can play anything." They love to hear that.

DIAMOND: In the old studio days you would start out writing a comedy for Cary Grant, and you would wind up with Robert Hutton.

QUESTION: *You made two films with Monroe. What was your experience working with her?*

WILDER: My God, I think there have been more books on Marilyn Monroe than on World War II, and there's a great similarity. It was not easy. It was hell. But it was well worth it once you got it on the screen. I've forgotten the trouble I had, and the times I thought, this picture will never be finished. It's all forgotten once the picture is done. The beauty of working with actors— not just Monroe—is that you're not married to them. The whole damn thing lasts twelve, fourteen, maybe sixteen weeks. That's why I admire so greatly Fellini, because he lives with actors for three years. Or Bertolucci. My God, to be with the same actor or actress for three years—it's not easy.

DIAMOND: I think that the most interesting trend in movies today is that they are starting to kill actors on the screen—the so-called snuff film. I think it's the greatest development in films. You finish the picture, finish the actor, and that's it!

WILDER: But the way it is here in Hollywood, they're killing the director.

QUESTION: *Do you assume a kind of role with an actor?*

WILDER: It's every kind of role. It depends what the actor or actress will respond to. I can become a masochist. I can become the Marquis de Sade. I can become a midwife. I can become Otto Preminger. I can do all sorts of things. It depends on what will work on actors. They're all very different.

QUESTION: *How do you decide what methods to use?*

WILDER: To begin with, I stay away as far as possible. It never gets too friendly because it's just not good: Other actors sense there's a little clique. I remember that I was once making a picture with Marlene Dietrich and Jean Arthur, *A Foreign Affair.* I had known Marlene from Germany before I ever came to this country, when I was a newspaperman in Berlin, and we were very friendly. In the middle of shooting, one midnight, the doorbell rang, and there was Jean Arthur, absolutely frenzied, with eyes bulging, and in back of her was her husband, Frank Ross. I said, "What is it, Jean?" She said, "What did you do with my close-up?" I said, "What close-up?" She said, "The close-up where I look so beautiful." I said, "What do you mean, what did I do with it?" She said, "You burned it. Marlene told you to burn that close-up. She does not want me to look good." This is typical. It's a little insane asylum, and they are all inmates.

QUESTION: *To get back to your collaboration, how detailed is your treatment before you start writing the dialogue?*

WILDER: The treatment? There is no treatment. We just start right off. There is no outline, no first treatment, which has to be done very often, I imagine, if you need financing. We just start right off with scene one, and since we are on the film set all the time, there is no "Slow fade-in, camera tiptoes"—none of that. Just "day" or "night," not even "morning" or "evening." Just "day" or "night" so that the cameraman knows how to light it, because he can't light "evening" anyway. There's a minimum of those fancy descriptions.

DIAMOND: It's different if you're trying to sell a script. Naturally, you're going to want to try to make it as readable as possible. You will throw in a lot of camera directions. When directors tell interviewers, "The minute I get on the set I throw away the script," what they mean is that they pay no attention to the camera directions, because they're not going to pan when you say so.

WILDER: I find with young writers, and some of them with very, very good ideas, that they get lost, unnecessarily so, in technical descriptions of which they know very little. Nobody will say, "This is a great screenwriter because he always has the camera angles." Just have good characters and good scenes and something that plays. The camera technique, that is secondary. Writers from the theater and directors from the theater who come from New York are very camera-conscious, and the writers will give you minute description, and directors will get on the dolly and they will swish around and up and down. They are afraid that the scene will be too stagy. There's no such thing.

DIAMOND: I think most young directors today, if you offered them the choice between a good script and a zoom lens, would take the zoom lens.

WILDER: Take away the zoom lens. Just don't let them have it.

DIAMOND: Look at an older director like Stanley Kubrick, who is no longer twenty-six years old. *Barry Lyndon* must have twenty scenes in which the camera started close and then zoomed back. If you do it twice in a picture it may be effective, but there it became monotonous. He is a marvelous still photographer, but you have to keep some dynamics of film in mind. There were scenes as beautiful as anything I've ever seen in my life, but any time you're sitting in the theater and saying, "Gee, isn't that a great shot," then you're not involved in the story. I think it was Penelope Gilliatt who said a few years ago, "Movies have now reached the same stage as sex: It's all technique and no feeling."

WILDER: She was speaking for herself, I'm sure.

QUESTION: *How involved do you get, Mr. Diamond, in casting and other matters after the script is done?*

DIAMOND: Oh, I throw out ideas, and sometimes they're listened to and sometimes they're not.

WILDER: He is in my office at all times, except when I cast the starlets who don't wind up with the part. Now tell me, is this a seminar of various specialists? In other words, you're not all going to be cardiac. Some are going to be nose, throat, and ear. If I had a son or daughter who wanted to go into the business, I would say, "The way things are going, go into special effects or become a stunt man." Special effects—with the need for bigger and bigger fish—would be a safe field, I think. No, maybe a lawyer is better.

QUESTION: *Mr. Diamond, have you ever collaborated in any way on the direction?*
WILDER: Oh, he collaborates with me all the time. He just doesn't get the credit for it.
DIAMOND: No. I'll give you an example of two persons who used to direct together: Norman Panama and Melvin Frank. But they had a rule: Only one of them was allowed to talk to the actors. They might consult on the sidelines, but always it was one man in charge. No, we don't co-direct. I may sit on the sidelines, and I may make a suggestion occasionally, but I stay out.

QUESTION: *Do you have any ambition to direct a film yourself?*
DIAMOND: Not really.
WILDER: If they give you a zoom lens? No, he is a very elegant man, and he just does not want to get that close to actors. I have to go into the cage, and he's outside.
DIAMOND: Speaking of zoom lenses, Billy's cutter at Paramount was an associate producer on most of his pictures, and he was once lent out to a young director who was making his first picture. He was a stage director, and he sat on the set every day, and one day he prepared the following scene: Two persons are sitting on a couch talking, and the woman is smoking a cigarette. The idea was to zoom in on the cigarette in her mouth, pan down with it as she put it in an ashtray, and then as she picks her hand up come back and continue the dialogue. The cutter watched this all morning, and finally he went to the director and said, "What is the point of this? Is the cigarette poisoned? Is she a spy and there's a secret message in the filter?" The director could not answer. The point was that he had come from the stage, and he wanted to prove to everybody that he could use a camera. Ultimately, that scene was never in the picture, and the director never talked to the cutter again because he had been caught being completely self-indulgent.
WILDER: Not only didn't it prove anything, but the power of the camera is such that if you have a moment like that audiences get curious, restless. They

think that there must be a reason for it; otherwise he wouldn't show it. They're very, very sharp now. They watch everything.

DIAMOND: In *Alice Doesn't Live Here Anymore,* Martin Scorsese also has a very busy camera. There's one scene where two people are sitting in a booth in a restaurant talking to each other, and the camera goes 180 degrees to the right, then it comes back 135 degrees to the left, then it goes 90 degrees to the right. None of this is for any reason at all, except that he didn't trust the words in the scene. I guess he felt that unless he was engaged in some sort of busywork he wasn't directing. He didn't have the courage to let the camera stay in one place and let the scene play.

WILDER: It's especially the curse of stage directors. They take a play and say, "Now we're going to open it up." They have a very good scene in a living room that has played six hundred times on Broadway. But for the picture they take the people out and put them on the roof garden, then they take them downstairs, then into the drugstore, and it's still the same scene.

One of the best scenes I've ever seen in a picture was between Marlon Brando and Rod Steiger in *On the Waterfront.* They are sitting in a cab, not even a transparency in back to save money. Venetian blinds in a New York cab. The two brothers were talking, especially Brando. The scene was beautiful and very well written, and it lasted seven minutes. No cut, no close-ups, no nothing. One of the great scenes, because you were involved. But I'm not going to like the scene any better if they suddenly got up and walked out somewhere.

DIAMOND: The tip-off is usually in the middle of a scene when somebody says, "Let's get some air."

WILDER: I ran into Scorsese New Year's Eve, and he had just done *Taxi Driver.* We talked about a half hour, and he was talking about simplifying, simplifying. It's like with a young colt: You have to put the blinkers on him. He's going to calm down, and he's going to be fine. He's a very fine talent. There is a whole group of young directors who are just absolutely marvelous.

QUESTION: *For instance?*

WILDER: I'm omitting now the established ones like Arthur Penn or Mike Nichols. But I think Harold Ashby is very, very fine. I think Bertolucci is marvelous. There are twenty I could mention quickly.

DIAMOND: Certainly, Francis Ford Coppola, William Friedkin, Steven Spielberg are as technically accomplished as any director in the business.

WILDER: Coppola is marvelous. I think that Coppola's *Godfather, Part II* is certainly among the five best American pictures ever made. In execution, in perception, I thought it was an absolute masterpiece. On my list of the unforgettable ones, it's way up there.

QUESTION: *What are some others?*
WILDER: Oh, there are many. There's *Grand Illusion, Best Years of Our Lives, Bridge on the River Kwai, Maltese Falcon, The Informer.* And some of the old German pictures, some of the Murnau pictures. But for a man like Coppola, who had made only four or five pictures, it was an outstanding achievement. It was just a very mature work of a very mature man.

QUESTION: *Speaking of a busy camera, Mr. Diamond, what did you think of* Citizen Kane *the first time you saw it?*
DIAMOND: I was very impressed, but that was not a busy camera. That was a very quiet camera. Take *Stagecoach.* I don't think John Ford moved his camera once in the whole picture. There was one pan shot, but what a hell of an effective shot it was. He's shooting down on the stagecoach on the floor of the valley, and suddenly he pans over and there's an Indian watching from a bluff. That's the only time the camera moved. Lots of action, lots of excitement, no camera movement. He made his actors come to the camera.
WILDER: But, you see, in making pictures—I'm not talking now about directing pictures—it's not how you are photographing. It is the juxtaposition of the various shots that you make. It is the scissors that make the picture, the cut. Alfred Hitchcock is certainly a tremendous influence on picturemaking, but, once in a while, he indulged. He said he was going to make a picture called *Rope* and that it would have seven or nine setups in the whole picture. It was absolute, total nonsense. He would wind up on the back of somebody's dark suit, and the next reel would start. They had to rehearse and rehearse. Every ten days they would get one whole reel, and they would collapse in exhaustion. But why not cut? This is writing the Lord's Prayer on the head of a pin. What is he trying to prove? *Battleship Potemkin,* that is movies. It's what follows what. This is where we have it all over the theater.

QUESTION: *After working on a script, have you ever found yourself on a set improvising dialogue or departing from the script when something doesn't work?*

DIAMOND: Never, never, never.

WILDER: We should have, maybe. Totally improvise, no. But sometimes we sense that it does not work, and we withdraw into a corner and rewrite a little or do something during lunchtime. But to sit there for half a day and then kind of slap it together, no, never.

DIAMOND: If you ever listen to actors talk, you will not improvise. When Howard Hawks was making *Man's Favorite Sport?* and *Hatari!,* all the publicity said he was improvising on the set. What was happening was that he would come on the set in the morning and say to the actors, "Now you say something to her, and she says something to you, and then you try to kiss her, and she slaps your face." But in his back pocket he'd have four pages that were written by Charlie Lederer or somebody else. The actors didn't know where the scene was going, but he knew exactly where it was going. During rehearsal he'd gradually work the lines around to what was written in the script. Ingmar Bergman has said, "Before I can improvise, I have to write it." There is no such thing, despite John Cassavetes.

WILDER: The best example is *A Chorus Line* in New York. They were improvising, but they had two writers there, and they were taking the words down, taping it all, and distilling it. I imagine at the first performance, the first time they started improvising, *Chorus Line* was not what it is today.

DIAMOND: The real improviser is the writer. By the time you've gotten to shooting a scene he may have written it fifteen different ways. Now, that's obviously much more economical than waiting until you get on the set with electricians standing around to start to improvise. Then you cannot keep all your options open, because if you shoot one scene two ways you'd have to shoot the following scene four ways and the following scene eight ways. Robert Altman is another man who has no respect for words. The critics rave about the overlapping dialogue, but the fact of the matter is that nobody has anything worth saying in the first place, which is the only time you can afford to overlap dialogue. He may shoot an eight-hour picture like *Nashville* and cut it down to two-and-a-half hours, but this is not the normal way to make pictures, and it's not a very feasible way. Elaine May has now worked over two years on a picture called *Mikey and Nicky.* She's exposed over a million feet of film. The studio finally had to go to court to take it away from her, because she's never going to finish.

WILDER: Maybe they could latch it on to *Casanova.*

DIAMOND: I'll give you another example of improvising on the set. This one happened to me in the old days. A director was shooting, and he didn't like the ending of a scene. But in a later scene in the script there was a tag line he did like, so he simply stole the tag line and put it in the early scene, figuring he'd worry about the later scene when he came to it. What he neglected to notice was that there was a plot point in that line—it's a revelation that required an immediate reaction from the characters. So, what happened on the screen was this: A revelation is made, twenty minutes go by, and nobody pays any attention to it. Then suddenly they react to it. The director had stolen a line from one part of the script and put it in another, and he hadn't stopped to think it all out.

Somebody once asked Dick Brooks, a writer-director, "The night before you shoot a scene, do you sit down with the script and figure out the angles and all that?" He said, "I sit down with the script not to figure out the angles. By now I may have written eight versions of that scene, but I look at it once more just to make sure there isn't a ninth version somewhere that I've overlooked." The stuff that goes into the wastebasket is the improvisation.

WILDER: I remember what made me decide early on that some day I should try to be a director. I had written a picture in Germany for the old UFA company. In one scene something was going on in a nightclub where undesirable elements were to be kept out. A big sign outside said, "Shoes and ties obligatory." There were two doormen looking to see that people had shoes and ties. One of the gags was that a man with a long beard appears, and the doorman stops him and looks under the beard to see if the guy has a tie. Later I went to see the picture, and I found that the director gave that actor a little goatee. There was nothing to lift and look under. But he kept that joke because he thought it was still going to be funny, but it was not.

DIAMOND: I once wrote a scene that took place in the Guggenheim Museum, and at the time I was writing it I had no idea what the exhibit would be when we finally got around to shooting it. I just said, "It's an op art show, and two characters are standing in front of a geometric painting, and one says to the other, 'I bet he cheated and used a ruler.' " Just a throwaway line to get the scene started. The film crew gets to the museum six months later, and now there's a sculpture show. The scene opens and you see somebody standing in front of a piece of round sculpture, saying, "I bet he cheated and used a ruler." It occurred to nobody on the set—the director, the actor, the script girl—that somebody should have said, "Wait a minute. This line is wrong now. We either have to change it or throw it out altogether." But this is what happens when people stick too literally to the script.

WILDER: It is respect for the written word, and you should be very proud.

DIAMOND: But I think today there's probably more respect for writing than any time in the history of the industry.

WILDER: Absolutely.

DIAMOND: Yet I see something happening: Not many people are interested in just writing any more. They see it as a stepping stone toward directing. This is as if every composer said to himself, "It's Bernstein and Previn who get the publicity. If I can just knock off a piece maybe they'll let me conduct it." But writing is a discipline in itself. It may have something to do with directing, and it may not. But today the young are primarily interested in directing, because, let's face it, there's more recognition for the director than for the writer. I hate to see that happen because there are never enough good writers.

QUESTION: *But the writer faces the obstacles of being underrated and under-paid, of not having the kind of ego support that a director has.*

DIAMOND: I think financially the writer is in a very strong position today. In the old days you could not sell an original screenplay unless it was for a Western at Republic. It was all either books or plays or scripts written by contract writers at the studios. A good original screenplay can now command tremendous sums of money. I think it is more wide open than it ever was.

WILDER: This is illustrated by *Lucky Lady,* the follow-up to *American Graffiti.* My suggestion is that you cannot just free-lance and hop around town. You have to latch on to a director with whom you work most of the time or, preferably, continuously. But it's very, very difficult to do that. It's tougher, believe me, to get on in a director-writer relationship than in one's marriage. Somebody asked me one day, "Is it important for a director to know how to write?" It's not important. It's important for a director to know how to read. When you find a director who knows how to read, who asks the proper questions, who is not ashamed to say, "I don't get the meaning of this scene," instead of just going off on location and shooting something contrary to what you wanted to express in that scene, then hold on to him. And if you're good I'm sure he will hold on to you because good writers are rare.

QUESTION: *Mr. Wilder, have you found the dual role of producer and director too much for one man?*

WILDER: It is too much if it's just the two of us. But within a big studio—let's say Universal with the black tower *knesset*—all their executives and executive executives have to contribute, too. I'm not going to go through contracts with actors and conditions. Let them worry about that. That is not producing. There have been some creative producers—I mean a Selznick, a Goldwyn, a Thalberg, and now, I imagine, a Bob Evans. But nowadays a producer is usually a man who knew a second cousin of a reader who got hold of an unfinished book at Random House about a big fish off Martha's Vineyard, and for some reason or other his brother-in-law gave him $10,000, and he put it down, and now suddenly he had the rights for *Jaws,* and owning that he became a producer.

QUESTION: *What was your role as producer in* Some Like It Hot?
WILDER: I had the final say on the making of the picture, the cutting, the casting, and whatever. There was one less nose sticking in my pie. I would be perfectly willing to welcome a producer who added to the picture, but there are very few. Most producers make you feel that if they weren't quite that busy and not quite that involved in six enormous projects which were going to revolutionize the cinema, they could write the movie better, they could direct it better, they could possibly act in it, they could compose. The truth is that if they can't write it, can't direct it, don't know how to write a note of music, can't act, can't do anything, then they become the overseer of it all.
DIAMOND: It's much easier to make six pictures at a time than just to make one picture, because you have no real responsibility. You talk to somebody for an hour and you say, "Go and develop it." Someone is left with the mess to clean up while you're busy with something else.
WILDER: And it's even easier, if you're the head of the studio, to make twenty pictures. It's as if you were standing around the roulette table, and you've got twenty chips. One or two of those chips are going to be winners. Now, *we* have one miserable chip, and we play it and if that doesn't come off we are just out for a year and a half. We are there with egg on our face.

I once talked to a top executive at Columbia, a friend of mine, who said, "You always look at me with a kind of peculiar glance. You always wonder how the hell I deserve $5,000 a week." And I said, "Sam, that's right. It has crossed my mind." He said, "Look, the trick is the following: The studio executives will send down to my office ten projects that they are planning to do.

They're not quite sure whether or not to do those ten projects. And I'll say, 'No,' to every one of them. Always, 'No,' because nine out of ten are going to be stinkers. One will be a big hit, but the executives will be so ecstatic about that one they will forget that I said, 'No,' to it, too. So I just go on and say, 'No,' because how wrong can I be by saying 'No,' when ninety percent of the pictures lose money?"

QUESTION: *You mentioned* Some Like It Hot. *How did the idea of dressing up two men as women develop?*
WILDER: Very early in the structure of that picture my friend Mr. Diamond very rightly said, "We have to find the hammerlock. We have to find the ironclad thing so that these guys trapped in women's clothes cannot just take the wigs off and say, 'Look, I'm a guy.' It has to be a question of life and death." And that's where the idea for the St. Valentine's Day murder came. If they got out of the women's clothes they would be killed by the Al Capone gang. That was the important invention. When we started working on the picture I had a discussion with David O. Selznick, who was a very fine producer, and I very briefly told him the plot. He said, "You mean there's going to be machine guns and shooting and killing and blood?" I said, "Sure." He said, "It's not going to be funny. No comedy can survive that kind of brutal reality." But that's what made the picture. The two men were on the spot, and we kept them on the spot until the very end.

QUESTION: *Did you have problems casting those two roles?*
DIAMOND: The first person we wanted was Jack Lemmon, but he was then under contract to Columbia, and the first actor we actually signed was Tony Curtis because we felt he could play both parts in an emergency. United Artists felt that we needed a big box-office name and that Lemmon wasn't big enough. They suggested that Mr. Wilder see Frank Sinatra. He made a lunch date with him and Sinatra never showed up, which may be one of the luckiest things that could have happened to us. At this point we got Marilyn Monroe, and the studio no longer felt the need for another big name. Then we signed Jack.
WILDER: If you hit on a thing which works, there's that snowball effect of laughter. You get the audience in that rare mood when everything is funny, and you don't need big stars. The best example of a similar picture to *Some Like It Hot* is *M*A*S*H*. There were no big stars in *M*A*S*H* then. It's just one

of those pictures that lends itself to two hours of increasing fun. The audience doesn't have a chance to sober up. The picture just keeps going and going.

QUESTION: *One critic has discussed what he called the underlying homosexual motifs in* Some Like It Hot. *Are there any?*

DIAMOND: The whole trick in the picture is that, while the two were dressed in women's clothes, their thinking processes were at all times a hundred percent male. When there was a slight aberration, like Lemmon getting engaged, it became twice as funny. But they were not camping it up. They never thought of themselves as women. Just for one moment Lemmon forgot himself—that was all. The rest of the time, Curtis was out to seduce Monroe, no matter what clothes he was wearing.

WILDER: But when he forgot himself it was not a homosexual relationship. It was just the idea of being engaged to a millionaire. It's very appealing. You don't have to be a homosexual. It's security.

QUESTION: *This raises a question of the handling of delicate themes. What problems did you have in* The Seven Year Itch?

WILDER: It was a nothing picture, and I'll tell you why. It was a nothing picture because the picture should be done today without censorship. It was an awkward picture to make. Unless the husband, left alone in New York while the wife and kid are away for the summer, has an affair with that girl there's nothing. But you couldn't do that in those days, so I was just straitjacketed. It just didn't come off one bit, and there's nothing I can say about it except I wish I hadn't made it. I wish I had the property now.

QUESTION: *You can be more explicit today, but at what point would you part from very explicit filmmakers?*

WILDER: One can tackle more daring themes, and one can write dialogue without a straitjacket, whereas once if you wanted to call someone a son of a bitch you would have to say, "If he had a mother, she'd bark." But I don't think that we would ever write an out-and-out porno picture. The dialogue, for instance, in *Shampoo*—I don't think that our minds work that way.

DIAMOND: But it's also, especially in comedy, almost gratuitous. I think nudity hurts laughs. If you're watching somebody's boobs, you're not listening to the dialogue. I don't think that any of the Lubitsch pictures or, say,

THE AMERICAN FILM INSTITUTE/1976   125

Philadelphia Story would be any better or funnier if you saw Cary Grant and Katharine Hepburn in the nude.
WILDER: Hepburn? Big laugh.

QUESTION: _What about_ Avanti!_? Was there a straitjacket problem?_
WILDER: Yes. Too mild, too soft, too gentle. We just missed on that. The picture was fifteen years too late, if it should have been done at all.
DIAMOND: I think if Peter Bogdanovich had done it it would have been called "A Tribute to Lubitsch," just like _What's Up, Doc?_ was a tribute to Howard Hawks. But if Howard Hawks had done _What's Up, Doc?_ everyone would have said, "It's old-fashioned and predictable."

QUESTION: _Was_ Ace in the Hole _too late?_
WILDER: Too early. Somebody once said about showmanship: "Showmanship is to know what the audience wants before the audience knows what it wants." You can miscalculate.

QUESTION: _Was there a miscalculation with_ One, Two, Three_?_
DIAMOND: I think it was a flop because it was released after the Berlin Wall incident: I think people suddenly no longer considered that subject very funny. The problem we ran into was that right in the middle of shooting the picture, the border was suddenly closed.
WILDER: The Communists started shooting people who wanted to get in and out of East Berlin, and it all ceased to be funny.

QUESTION: _Was there any consideration of scrapping the picture?_
WILDER: None at all. The studio had to recoup some of the money. There was no such thing as scrapping. Now there is. They ran into trouble with Robert De Niro on _Bogart Slept Here,_ and they just walked away from it.

QUESTION: _You worked for Lubitsch. Were you influenced by his style?_
WILDER: Certainly I was. But he died so young, and I only worked for him on two pictures. I wish I had had more time and that I could have studied under him for a longer period because he was a great director. He took the secret with him to his grave. People keep saying, not about me, but about other directors, "This is just like Lubitsch," but it's not Lubitsch.

QUESTION: *In your visual style, you very often seem to concentrate on one particular object. For example, the filing cabinets in* A Foreign Affair *or the whiskey bottle and the light in* The Lost Weekend. *Is that element there from the very inception?*

WILDER: Sure, sure. When we constructed *The Apartment*, we knew we needed a scene in which Jack Lemmon realizes that Shirley MacLaine is the dame his boss, Fred MacMurray, does it to in his apartment. So, we go back and plant the little makeup mirror that he finds. When he has the promotion and buys himself the young executive black bowler hat, she lets him see himself in the mirror, and he suddenly realizes that's the girl. But surely none of those things are improvised. It's all calculated and planted.

QUESTION: *Is there a source you care to pinpoint for your humor—your families?*

DIAMOND: No. My children are funny. I don't think my parents were particularly funny.

WILDER: And my brother is a dull son of a bitch.

QUESTION: *When you worked in Germany, was the studio arrangement at UFA the same as its American counterparts at the time?*

WILDER: No, it was very different. The studio itself was about ten miles outside of Berlin in what is now the eastern side of Berlin. But they had some smaller studios around town. The big company was UFA, but there were twelve other companies. There was no such thing as writers or directors under contract. There was no such thing as being on the set as a writer while it was happening. It was too far out of town, and you didn't have a car in those days. It was all quite different. It was all in the hands of Erich Pommer, who was the Thalberg of the UFA company, and there were some outstanding directors: Murnau, Fritz Lang, Robert Wiene, and G. W. Pabst. It was a director's medium there.

QUESTION: *Since 1950 not a great deal has been happening with German films. Do you have any explanation?*

WILDER: I understand that they are on their way back, but I haven't seen many of the new films. But before it was just a desert. The decline started in 1933 when Hitler came to power, and later people got out of the habit of seeing movies. There was very little money there except for some big American pictures and some French pictures. Then they got into the porno rut. I understand that one company made millions doing pornographic versions of all the Grimm Brothers fairy tales. You can imagine what the dwarfs were doing to Snow White. But now I understand that there are three or four young directors who do pictures on a much higher level. But no matter what, the German audiences are going to be standing around forty blocks to see *Jaws*. They used to go first to the German pictures, but now they're waiting for the American pictures.

QUESTION: *Closer to home, how did the script of* Sunset Boulevard *come about?*

WILDER: I was working with Mr. Brackett then, and he had an idea of doing a picture with a Hollywood background. I think originally we wanted Pola Negri or Mary Pickford. Once we got hold of a character of the silent picture glamour star who had had it, a kind of female John Gilbert, whose career is finished with the advent of talkies but she still has the oil wells pumping and the house on Sunset Boulevard, then we started rolling. The characters of the writer and the director came after.

Soon we had Gloria Swanson and Erich von Stroheim, and we had a whole slew of the old stars, H. B. Warner and Buster Keaton. The part of the writer, Joe Gillis, who becomes the gigolo there, was written for Montgomery Clift. But about two weeks before we started shooting, he sent his agent in, who said, "Mr. Montgomery Clift, the great New York actor, will not do the picture, because what would his fans think if he had an affair with a woman twice his age?" You would expect that from a Hollywood actor but not a serious actor. We were then confronted with what to do. It was too late to shelve the picture. So we took William Holden, who was playing second lieutenants in comedies at that time. It had also been difficult to find stars to play in *Double Indemnity*—especially to find a leading man who would play a murderer. We went all the way down, actor after actor, until I finally wound up with Fred MacMurray, who told me, "For Christ's sake, you're making the mistake of your life. I'm a saxophone player. I can't do it."

QUESTION: *Were you concerned in* Sunset Boulevard *about having a dead narrator?*

WILDER: Yes, but that was the only way out. I shot a whole prologue, a whole reel—that and another reel of the ending to *Double Indemnity* have never been shown. The prologue was very well shot and quite effective. A corpse is brought into the morgue downtown—and I shot it there, too—and it's the corpse of Holden. There are about six other corpses there under sheets. Through a trick we see through the sheets to the faces, and they are telling each other the events leading to their deaths. Then Holden starts telling his story.

We previewed the picture, with the original first reel, in Evanston, Illinois, right where Northwestern University is. The picture started. The corpse is brought in on a slab, a name tape is put on the big toe of the corpse, and once the tag went on the toe, the audience broke into the biggest laugh I ever heard in my life. I said, "Oh, my God," and the picture just went straight down. It was a disaster. So that whole sequence went out, but we kept the notion of a man telling of the events which led to his demise.

In *Double Indemnity* I had a final scene with the character in the gas chamber. There are pellets dropping and the bucket and the fumes, and outside is Eddie Robinson watching. They are two great friends, and there is something going on between them, an exchange or whatever. It was very good but just unnecessary. The picture is over when he tells him, "You can't even make the elevator," and he tries and collapses. In the distance you hear the siren of the police, and you know what's going to happen. That was the end of it. I added a postscript which was totally unnecessary.

QUESTION: *Have you seen the made-for-TV version of* Double Indemnity?
WILDER: Yes.

QUESTION: *What did you think of it?*
WILDER: I threw up. Universal bought out all the old Paramount pictures, of which this was one. They own *Double Indemnity,* just as they took another picture I directed, *Stalag 17,* and made a whole series, "Hogan's Heroes." They took the script of *Double Indemnity*—and the movie itself represented the height of censorship—and shot exactly that script. The TV picture was terrible. It was miscast. The sets were wrong. Everything was bad.

QUESTION: *Are the blockbuster pictures, the disaster pictures, that are popular now affecting the direction you want to go in?*
WILDER: If you want to make a picture in that direction, but we don't think in that direction. Also, we are old hands at disasters. But those pictures compete with each other.

QUESTION: *Is there an audience for just a good movie, without a $9 or $10 million budget?*

WILDER: Certainly there is. One thing for sure is that you can do a lot of things on the screen that you still cannot do on television. Let us say that somebody were to make *Dog Day Afternoon* for $1 million or $2 million. You couldn't do that on television because the subject is taboo. But you can do it in pictures. *American Graffiti* is another example of a picture that can be done without competing in size. You know, the peculiar thing about movies is that you're going to be charged just as much at a theater to see *American Graffiti* as you would be to see, let us say, *The Poseidon Adventure*. One picture cost $700,000 and the other cost $11 million, but you still pay $2.50 or whatever.

DIAMOND: It is getting tougher now to approach a studio with a project which seems either small or mild. Naturally, everybody is looking for the blockbuster. It's human nature. Before *The Exorcist* opened, William Blatty, the author of the novel, was going around making speeches that this was a picture about the persistence of evil in modern society. But when the picture opened people were not going around saying to each other, "Hey, let's go see that picture about the persistence of evil." They were saying, "Hey, there's a picture where the girl throws up green and masturbates with a crucifix." That's what the picture was about from the audience's point of view, not what Blatty may have thought it was about.

WILDER: And the audience went for the 360-degree turn of the head and the goddamned sound effects. And the osteopaths must have cringed. But it was very effective. People had to see it. It was totally impossible to go to a picnic or a dinner party in Albany without having seen certain pictures: *Exorcist, Jaws*. Now, those pictures are, technically, beautifully done. I think Spielberg's picture was just phenomenal, really beautifully engineered. But as long as we know that this is Grand Guignol, that we know what kind of merchandise we're getting, it's fine. It's just a very effective piece of celluloid, and it keeps you there. You may get up and say, "Well, I didn't like it," but you certainly paid attention to what was happening.

QUESTION: *You think there was a difference in the author's intention and the director's?*

WILDER: I think the direction was rather subtle. The book was just a real smack on the nose—very effective, too, but not a great novel.

DIAMOND: People have forgotten, because the picture was such a big suc-cess, but before it opened Blatty was about to sue Friedkin because Friedkin had thrown him off the set because of disagreements about what was going to be cut out and what was going to be left in. I think Blatty wanted the more significant talk stuff left in, and Friedkin realized what kind of picture he was making. He just cut all that out and stuck to where the money was. Now they're great friends.

WILDER: But I do respect a director such as Friedkin who suddenly is con-fronted with a scene of a party going on and an eight-year-old girl joins the party and pees on the carpet. That's what you have to shoot. That's just a day's work. Where do you put the camera? It is not easy. I can do a chase sequence. I can do any goddamned thing. But an eight-year-old girl peeing during a party, that's a new one. It requires a different technique. It is this kind of never-seen-before that makes for this type of enormous box office. But I think *The Exorcist* is good, riveting picturemaking. I also think that once you make up your mind to make a picture like this you've got to give it both knees, because it is not going to be in great taste or very subtle. If you do it, then do it. That's Sam Peckinpah's technique, the man who gives it three knees.

QUESTION: *What film are you working on now?*
WILDER: We very probably will retire, like Secretariat, to stud. No, we've just come back from a location scouting trip to France and Greece, though we may be shooting in Italy because we didn't find what we wanted else-where. We're doing the first novella in Tom Tyron's new book, *Crowned Heads*. It's called *Fedora*. We had been kicking around Hollywood picture ideas when along came the galleys of this book.
DIAMOND: It's about a retired old film star who lives in Europe, but except for one flashback it has nothing to do with moviemaking.

QUESTION: *What's the schedule for the film?*
WILDER: It's eighty percent plotted and thirty percent in screenplay form. We'll be through in plenty of time to fiddle with it and manicure it. I think we'll start shooting some time at the beginning of next year, and the picture will be out some time in the middle of the year.

QUESTION: *Does the film present any special writing problems?*

DIAMOND: It's a departure for me in that I've never really done a serious picture before. It's a picture with no jokes, or few jokes.

WILDER: It's very Grand Guignol. It's a mystery, but it's not a Hitchcock picture. Actually, it's the first serious picture I've been connected with since *Sunset Boulevard*.

Double Indemnity: A Policy That Paid Off

JOHN ALLYN/1978

B ILLY WILDER' S *Double Indemnity* (1944) has long been recognized as one of the classics of *film noir*. Based on James M. Cain's "hard-boiled" novel about the susceptible insurance salesman, Walter, and the lady, Phyllis, who wants to get rid of her husband, it has been acclaimed for its style by critics everywhere and, I believe, should be equally recognized for the ingenuity of the adaptation by Billy Wilder and Raymond Chandler.

In the original story Walter and Phyllis carry out a murder and stage a phony accident on a train to collect double indemnity on her husband's insurance policy. They might get away with it but fear, inevitably, drives them apart. Each plans to kill the other and Phyllis, who is more than a little pathological, is the first to act. She shoots Walter in a car in the park and he tells all in the hospital to save the neck of Phyllis' step-daughter Lola, who is a suspect in his shooting and with whom he has fallen in love. In exchange for Walter's confession the insurance company allows the murderers to escape, but on the boat to Mexico they feel they have been spotted and decide to jump overboard in a suicide pact reminiscent of some of the plays of Chikamatsu for the classical Japanese puppet theater.

The film version follows the plot of the novel up to a point, but the ending has been drastically changed and several key scenes added in which the characters are more fully developed and portrayed more sympathetically than they are in the original. In particular the part of Keyes, the Claims Manager, who is only one step behind the murderers, has been expanded and his rela-

From *Literature/Film Quarterly,* Spring 1978. Reprinted by permission.

tionship to fellow worker Walter is made much closer. Also added is a
moment in a getaway car that won't start and other scenes in the confinement of the insurance office and elsewhere that serve to heighten the drama.
(In one of these my sharp-eyed students noted that the door to Walter's
apartment unaccountably opens *outward* into the hall so that Phyllis can
hide behind it as Keyes leaves.)

In the film version the ending finds Walter and Phyllis meeting for the
last time in her living room. Phyllis shoots Walter and wounds him in the
shoulder, but she can't fire that second shot and thereby becomes a more
sympathetic, more tragic figure than the cold-blooded Phyllis in the book.
Walter then shoots her to protect Lola and dictates his confession to clear
Lola's boyfriend. Badly hurt, Walter asks Keyes for a head start to make the
border but Keyes tells him he's all washed up.

It should be apparent that the ending is the beginning of all the significant changes in the film story. There is no suicide plan so there is no reason
to establish Phyllis as pathological. This in turn makes her motive for murder
more understandable and makes Walter more acceptable than the sap in the
book who will follow Phyllis anywhere. The change in the ending also eliminated the need to shoot in three additional locations and maintains the
film's claustrophobic atmosphere by "closing down" the action rather than
following the usual pattern in adaptations and "opening it up." By returning
to the living room where Walter and Phyllis first met, as much a cage in the
city as the insurance office, the film is given a satisfying dramatic and visual
unity.

Style, as noted, is beautifully wedded to content. Rain and night and the
device of the dictaphone confession give the film the proper *noir* feel of melancholy and fatalism. Faces are striped by light through venetian blinds to
create shadows like prison bars and many scenes are played out in near total
darkness, with only back or side light defining the action. This extreme low-
key lighting is combined with highly dramatic background music (by Miklós
Rózsa) and what might be called "directorial understatement," evident when
the camera holds close on Phyllis' face as she drives the car while her husband, unseen beside her, is being strangled by Walter. The sleazily realistic
atmosphere even extends to dust in the air in Phyllis' living room when
Walter first sees it. Appropriately, daytime scenes are few: Walter's first
approach to Phyllis' house, his stop for a beer at a drive-in, two establishing
shots of the supermarket where Walter and Phyllis secretly meet, and Walter

and Lola's drive along the beach where, ironically, the view of the ocean is blocked by parked cars.

My comparison of the film to the original novel left me impressed with the magnitude of the changes wrought by Wilder-Chandler, but left me with some questions about their motivations. For example, was the change in the ending made primarily to conform to the Production Code of the day? How did Billy Wilder happen to be teamed with Raymond Chandler on the script and how did they approach this assignment? What influenced the visual style of the film? And lastly, what was James M. Cain's reaction to the adaptation of his novel?

After I had completed the above analysis, I was fortunate enough to obtain an interview with Billy Wilder, conducted in his bungalow at Universal Studio on February 25, 1976.

Any film student knows Mr. Wilder as the writer and director of such outstanding films as *The Lost Weekend, Sunset Boulevard, Some Like It Hot,* and *The Apartment,* just to name a few, but on this occasion our discussion was limited to the adaptation of *Double Indemnity.* Mr. Wilder answered all my questions forthrightly and with vigor (pacing a lot) and I pass along his words as added insight into the art of adaptation by one of its masters.

WILDER: I'm sure that in your research you found out that Mr. Cain, a very, very nice man, and at that time a very sought-after writer, had written that enormously successful *The Postman Always Rings Twice.* And then in the wake of it he wrote *Double Indemnity* in installments for *Liberty* magazine. It was a bit of a copy, or in the same vein of *Postman.* And a producer, he's dead now, by the name of Joe Sistrom, had read the story and had brought it to the attention of the studio and to *my* attention. By the way, he *was* the producer, but they only wanted to give him associate producer credit and he refused it; he didn't want to take any credit at all. I said sure I would do it but for that particular picture Mr. Brackett, my usual collaborator at that time, was working on something else so I sort of took a leave of absence. I wanted Cain himself as a collaborator, but he was busy working at Fox. I think he was doing *Western Union,* a picture that Fritz Lang directed. So Joe Sistrom said there is another writer who is dealing with Southern California and that was the beginning of Chandler. He brought Chandler in and Chandler and I sat down and wrote the script.

ALLYN: *I'm very interested in learning what inspired the radical changes in the ending.*

WILDER: If I remember correctly, the novel was very complex and also there was a slight duplication. He does all that very careful planning to have an alibi when they do away with the husband. . . . Now you would have to go through a similar setup again when he establishes his second alibi. And in this way you would not have the big confrontation scene between him and Mrs. Dietrichson—Phyllis. You needed a scene between the two. Otherwise you would have had the man shot in the park from out of nowhere, we don't know by whom, and then you learn what happened later.

ALLYN: *From the conversation in the hospital, which is undramatic.*

WILDER: Yes, which is undramatic. . . . We also shot, I would like you to know, an epilogue. Where he was being executed in the gas chamber.

ALLYN: *I've heard about that. Was it actually shot?*

WILDER: It was shot—I thought it was very good film. I had the warden come down from San Quentin and the doctor, and it was all done *minutely*, with the stethoscope to the glass and the bucket under the seat and the pellet. And I had a scene between him being gassed and Keyes watching him. I shot that, but then I did the narration thing into the dictaphone and I came to the very end where Keyes says "Where are you going?" and he says "I'm going across the border" and Keyes says "You won't even make the elevator" and in the distance you heard the siren of the police car or ambulance and the two guys looked at each other. That was the ending. I already had the exchange of looks and striking of the match so any more would have been just repeating.

I always find, you know, in writing movies or directing movies, I find that with all the experience you gain, you don't know it but you very often tell the same thing four or five times. The audience is so far ahead of you. Nowadays even farther because their eyes and their ears have been so sharpened by all the television they see. They have become much smarter, so don't spell it out that clearly—let them add two and two together. You have to stimulate their minds and you have to make them work *with* you and once you do that, that's fine. If you make them lazy, if you just do it in the banal way, you don't *involve* the audience in the game you're playing. And if you're not smart enough to make them participate in the game that is going on, you *lose.* They don't want to sit there like animals. They would like to play the game *with* you. . . .

ALLYN: *There's always been the question in my mind as to what was your starting point when you began to adapt it. . . .*
WILDER: The idea was to write a love story between the two men and a sexual involvement with the woman, to see whether we could dramatize it—that even the most normal of men can fall prey to a sexual attraction. And, ultimately, the guy shows an element of decency by confessing so that the innocent boyfriend of Lola won't go to the gas chamber.

ALLYN: *So you were accomplishing two objectives at the same time. You were making it a better story and also making Walter more acceptable.*
WILDER: I hope it's better. I just wanted the audience to go with Walter, to make him a murderer all right, but with redeeming features. The Keyes relationship and ultimately the gesture of letting the innocent man off the hook. If he confesses, then it has to be motivated by him, by his sense of justice. Perhaps he'd done it, but within that murderous act there is still an element of compassion and decency.

ALLYN: *Were there Production Code objections at any stage?*
WILDER: Well, there was Production Code. Naturally, we could not have overt sex, so we did it kind of by innuendo. When she comes to his apartment . . .

ALLYN: *Dissolves. . . .*
WILDER: But we had no problem with the Production Code. This was when it was more fun, you know, because we did this very subtly. We did *not* see a man choking somebody to death. We were on her face as she was driving and we knew that offstage it was happening. Sex was happening offstage. All of those nasty things. And even now I don't do them, *not* because the Code has been relaxed; I'm just not trying to use gratuitously dirty words. But it was a shocker for its time.

ALLYN: *Well, then, that raises a question about style. It seems to me that your style of directing and the style of the acting were deliberately underplayed, whereas the lighting and music are highly dramatic. And* that *is what makes up* film noir, *so called.*

WILDER: Yes, I remember, those things come back to me now. The cameraman was Seitz, with whom I have made many pictures. John Seitz was the original cameraman for Valentino, to show you how far back he goes. And the film was in black and white, which is much more difficult to shoot than color. Black and white is a very difficult medium because you have to create your own values and shadings, whereas in color it's much easier. However, I told him what I would like to get on the screen—you know sometimes when the sun kind of slants through the windows of those old crappy Spanish houses, and the house is not too well kept, you see the dust in the air. And he invented a sort of an aluminum powder which we blew into the air just before we started shooting. . . .

And another tiny episode that may be of some interest. The murder is committed and they put the body on the tracks and now they're waiting. I did the waiting in the car in the studio, everything else I did outside. And we were shooting just before lunch and Walter came into the scene and said "Let's go" and off they drive. And then, lunch. And I'm on my way to get into my car—I had a date with somebody. And my car wouldn't start. And suddenly I said "What is that!" and I rushed back and said "Don't touch a thing! I'm going to do it again—I'm going to do it differently!" And that's when I did that thing with the battery giving out.

ALLYN: *You know what reaction I get in my classroom now to that scene? The girls say you're trying to show the superiority of the man.*
WILDER: Why?

ALLYN: *Because he can start it and she can't.*
WILDER: No, it's got nothing to do with . . . It's just that . . .

ALLYN: *In the script it explains that he pushes the starter and then . . .*
WILDER: Yes, because he is a little smarter than she is, and maybe a better mechanic. But I wanted to get the element of suspense, "Oh, my god, now they're stuck . . ." In other words, since he obviously is older and has been in cars more often, he knows that you have to pump up the gas a little bit and then at the same time you have to switch it on. . . .

ALLYN: *Yes, there were so many fine additions that did build suspense, like the whole scene where Phyllis comes to the insurance office is not in the book at all. The whole scene where Keyes offers Walter the job as assistant claims manager is not in the original story.*
WILDER: Yes, there's a lot of stuff that we actually improved.

ALLYN: *Yes, I think you did.*
WILDER: Then there's another thing. I don't know whether you caught my boo-boo, but I did it deliberately. I knew there was no other way out. And that is when . . .

ALLYN: *The door.*
WILDER: The apartment door opened the wrong way.

ALLYN: *I didn't catch it, some of my students did. . . . You know the big talk now is film noir. I suppose you've read these articles?*
WILDER: Yes, people come around, yes.

ALLYN: *Naturally people making films at that time didn't say "Let's go out and make a film noir." But what were the influences on you at that time. . . .*
WILDER: I don't think there were any pictures in that vein, you know, because that sort of started off with Chandler. . . . But I imagine one influence was subconsciously *M* by Fritz Lang.

ALLYN: *Offscreen murder.*
WILDER: Yes, I don't know, and maybe this will sound very pompous, but possibly a kind of deep-seated influence from having read a lot of Dostoevski when I went to school.

ALLYN: *When you were working with Mr. Chandler, was your system of working with him much like you worked with the others? He was hardly a man of the theater or films.*
WILDER: Yes, it was very tough with him because it was the first time he'd ever been inside a studio. He'd never worked on pictures—he had no idea what a script looked like. As a matter of fact, in a book on him he said that I was a son of a bitch, but all he learned about pictures he learned from me. He was a weird man and he was then in the throes of being on the wagon.

He was a very heavy drinker, but he was on the wagon then. And he was actually a very mean guy, you know, bitter and suspicious, but by god he wrote like an angel. We worked well together, except that being the first picture he ever wrote in his life he was kind of playing in Yankee Stadium. . . . But . . . I was trying to use his descriptive power, you know . . .

ALLYN: *Some of that was used in the dialogue.*
WILDER: And in the narration, yes. But, funnily enough, I got into that rhythm and a lot of the dialogue is mine. You would say "What a Chandler line," but it was my imitation of a Chandler line. Like, for instance, "What's your name?" and she says "Phyllis—you like it?" and he says "Well, let me drive it around the block a couple of times." That sounds like Chandler. But it didn't matter—we worked well together.

And then I got a very high compliment. The picture was previewed at the Fox Theater in Westwood and there standing in the lobby was Cain, and he put his arms around me and he said that this is the first time that somebody did a decent job with any of my . . . and he was very, very happy with it. You know, when Cain says that I did justice to his story, although it was changed a lot, or when somebody sends me an interview with the now deceased Agatha Christie and she says the only good picture ever made out of any of her books was *Witness for the Prosecution,* those are the things that count much more for me than a review in *Esquire* or *Time* magazine. When the original author says "Hey, that's a good job," or "that's the way I visualized it," or "you did it even better than what I had in mind when I wrote it."

Going for Extra Innings

JOSEPH MCBRIDE AND TODD MCCARTHY/1979

IN *FEDORA*, HIS TWENTY-FIFTH FILM as a director, Billy Wilder has created one of his most beautiful works. Like *Heaven Can Wait,* by his mentor, Ernst Lubitsch, it is quintessentially an old man's film, a meditation on mortality, and as such may not find favor with trend-seeking critics and gross-conscious industryites. *Fedora* is based on one of the four novellas in Thomas Tryon's book *Crowned Heads,* and, as usual, Wilder wrote the screenplay with I. A. L. Diamond. The epigraph from Kipling on the first page of the script sets forth the basic theme:

"Youth had been a habit of hers for so long that she could not part with it."

Tryon's *Fedora* is the tale of a Garboesque actress whose retention of her beauty over fifty years is a mystery finally unraveled by a prying writer. Wilder and Diamond heightened the personal undertones of the project by changing the writer to an aging, struggling producer (William Holden) who is desperately trying to convince the reclusive star to return to the screen so he can use tax shelter funding for his own comeback in the film business. Hildegarde Knef plays the great Fedora, Marthe Keller is her beautiful and enigmatic daughter, and Jose Ferrer is a shady doctor with a recipe for the fountain of youth. Wilder explores and amplifies many of his favorite themes—self-delusion, fraud, masquerade, show business mythmaking—and he does so with a grace and elegance that is becoming increasingly rare in world cinema.

From *Film Comment,* January–February 1979. Reprinted by permission.

Last May, Wilder accompanied *Fedora* to Cannes for its first screening, and the reactions were divided: The French almost unanimously acclaimed it; American auteurists (despite qualms about the casting) appreciated it as a deeply felt addition to the late Wilder canon, but Richard Roud and Rex Reed hated it, possibly presaging a negative reaction from other parts of the American critical establishment.

That Wilder sometimes seems unduly defensive about *Fedora* in our interview (conducted over two days last October) undoubtedly stems from that mixed critical reaction and from the entire tangle of events connected with the production. Universal, which originally planned to make the film, eventually turned it down, and Wilder, like Holden's character in the film, had to seek foreign tax shelter production money. Shooting in Europe caused many headaches, and Wilder was frustrated by his inability to find the ideal cast. It was months after Cannes before Allied Artists picked up *Fedora* for February release. The mere fact that AA is the distributor gives the film a certain commercial stigma, since the company is now a relatively minor and indeed financially shaky operation.

Wilder, rebounding from the experience, jokes about being "elderly" (he is seventy-two), but in person he seems less like an old man than anyone else who directed his first film in the early Thirties. He warned us in advance that he wanted to limit our talk to an hour, since he was busy plotting new projects in his elegant but unostentatious Beverly Hills office. Furthermore, Wilder, an avid baseball fan, would not dream of missing the Dodger-Phillies playoffs that were then on TV. But he warmed to the occasion and wound up granting us three hours of interview, an unusually long session for the mercurial Wilder, who tends to be impatient with "film buff" questions about his past work and prefers to discuss the current scene. His attitudes are becoming increasingly, and defiantly, traditional; but Wilder shows a refreshing eagerness to analyze and confront the New Hollywood, despite his scorn for much of what it represents.

Wilder's office, which fronts a noisy thoroughfare in the heart of the Beverly Hills business district, was occupied long ago by Will Rogers. The director has a phony name on the directory to discourage interlopers, as does one of his neighbors, whose door bears a plaque reading "E. Hemingway." Compact, tidy, and decorated with modern artworks, Wilder's office contains a few artifacts from his past, such as his six Oscars and bound leather copies of his scripts, but his lively contemporary interests are reflected in such items as a college football schedule tacked to the bulletin board and copies of new books in several languages. Also, in keeping with his impudent sense of black humor, he has a photo of Adolf Hitler on the board with a newspaper clipping strategically attached by a tack in Der Fuehrer's groin area. The clipping is headed, "European Fare with a Jewish Flavor," and lists kosher restaurants in the Fairfax Avenue area of L.A.

"A writer is always looking for an excuse not to write," Wilder confessed after we began by chatting for a while about sports. "The Dodgers are the best excuse of all. Show me a writer who enjoys writing and I'll show you a lousy writer. That doesn't mean, however, that if you do not enjoy writing, you are necessarily a good writer." With that, we moved on to *Fedora*.

How did you come across Crowned Heads?
I read in *Publisher's Weekly* that a book of Tom Tryon's was coming out and it's got something to do with Hollywood. I felt like a Hollywood picture. I'd been working on a concept of a Hollywood picture at the time, and I grabbed onto *Fedora*, not knowing how I'm going to cast it. That was the big drawback.

Did you ever finish the other Hollywood script?
No, it was just an idea. I wanted to call it *The Foreskin Saga*. It's about the Mayer family. *Roots*.

What appealed to you about The Foreskin Saga?
Well, I know it. And it only takes seven minutes to get to location. I don't have to climb any fucking mountains. I don't have to eat shit food and have diarrhea, you know what I mean? I can go to Chasen's. But just because you know something that well doesn't mean that you can do it right. It's very difficult to do a Hollywood picture. Actually I know very, very few I like. I loved Selznick's version of *A Star Is Born*. I thought that was just marvelous. I loved the original *What Price Hollywood?* And I kind of liked, if I say so myself, *Sunset Boulevard*.

Before I came to Hollywood, I thought Sunset Boulevard *was too cynical a depiction of the film industry. When I moved out here, I realized that it's like a documentary. Everything in it is totally true.*
It's a valentine. But it is not just the picture industry—it is every industry.

You make a picture about Exxon vs. Texaco vs. Shell, every industry has got this kind of slush that is underneath the whole thing. *Network.* The newspaper business. Naturally.

Did the similarities of Fedora *to* Sunset Boulevard *intrigue you or put you off?*
No, I was not as aware of it as people were who read it or who saw it. I did not help creating dissimilarity by taking Holden again. You know, in those days, *Sunset Boulevard* was a unique experiment. And believe me, the town didn't like that picture one little bit. They thought, "The son of a bitch with the accent, Wilder, is biting the hand that helped him out of the water and is feeding him now."

Some of the themes in Fedora *are the same ones in* Sunset Boulevard: *preservation, immortality, fame . . .*
Yes, and the grand exit in *Fedora.* But *Sunset Boulevard,* as I look back at it, was a miraculous series of lucky incidents that helped the picture. I wanted DeMille and I got DeMille. I wanted somebody who at one time had directed a picture with Swanson and I found Stroheim. And I got to use the picture *Queen Kelly.* And I needed the Paramount studio, I got the Paramount studio. Whatever I needed. I was very, very lucky.

Fedora was slightly more difficult. I don't dwell on that. Excuse me, but if I started thinking as to how I would improve things, I would go back to my very first picture. I could rewrite and redirect every single picture I've ever done. Maybe there is five minutes here, a scene there, a little incident there that I think was about as good as I could do. But I cannot kick myself; it becomes obsessive.

I never watch my old films. Never. If you have this kind of temperament . . . Wyler made a picture fifty years ago at Universal called *Three Godfathers* [actually, Wyler's version was *Hell's Heroes*], a very famous Western made before and made afterwards by John Ford. And it was very good. Now he tells me about three or four years ago he wanted to see that picture, so he called Universal and they found it in the vaults. He ran it at his house. And after he saw the picture he took it to a cutting room, he recut the picture, and he sent it back. He couldn't stand it.

I have a wonderful capacity of wiping off the blackboard of my mind old pictures, good or bad, I just wipe it off. All I think is, "What are we gonna do right now? What are we gonna do later like nothing had happened before?"

Never do I dwell in the past. This is like jerking off over a girl that you knew thirty years ago.

At what point did Universal pass on Fedora?
After the screenplay was finished. I don't know who they are, the mysterious people up there: it's Kafka. From what I gather—I didn't even talk to them because I was pissed off, as they say—I gather that they didn't think that it has a chance. What hurts the most is that they may be proven right.

Getting the deal put together took quite a while, didn't it?
I was an ordeal. It just sapped all my strength. Ultimately I wound up making the picture with the Germans. And I had a wonderful little encounter with a group there, Geria, a tax shelter group with a lot of money; they, in conjunction with Bavaria Studios, supplied the money for *Fedora.* I have some kind of a reputation in Germany, why I don't know, because when I left Germany I was just one of the writers at UFA. Since the other ones are dead, suddenly the mantle of Murnau, and of Fritz Lang, and of Erich Pommer, and of Lubitsch falls on my shoulders. I was just a writer of maybe one or two pictures that were of some interest.

But now I come to Germany and they give me a party and, my God, old UFA is going to rise again. And one of the guys at Geria gets up and says, "Herr Wilder, we read the script, it's very interesting. I just would like to ask you a question. The picture plays in Greece, it plays in France, and there's a small scene in Hollywood. Why do you want to shoot it in Munich?"

And I said, "Do you know a man in America by the name of Willie Sutton? He started robbing banks when he was sixteen years old and now, at the age of seventy-eight, he has been in jail for forty-eight years. Now he's caught again and the judge asks him, 'Mr. Sutton, why do you keep robbing banks?' And Willie Sutton says, 'Because that's where the money is.' " And so I told them, "I'm making it in Munich because that's where the money is." The guy very seriously looks at me and said, "You're not going to *rob* us, are you, Herr Wilder?"

It was your agent, Paul Kohner, who set up the deal with the Germans, wasn't it?
Yes, because he's of that origin there and being the—how shall I say this?—Ingmar Bergman man, you know, the Big European Celluloid Connection. It was not difficult to set it up, but I just could not get the money here. Look, I

JOSEPH MCBRIDE AND TODD MCCARTHY/1979   145

can't lose, because if this picture is a big hit, it's my revenge on Hollywood. If it is a total financial disaster, it's my revenge for Auschwitz.

Didn't Kohner actually produce your first screenplay in Germany?
At one time, Paul Kohner was heading Universal Productions in Berlin, when I was a newspaperman there in the late Twenties. And that was the time when he supervised the German version of *All Quiet on the Western Front.* I sold him a screenplay, I don't know, something—

Wasn't it Der Teufelsreporter [The Devil's Reporter, *1929*]?
Oh, it was bullshit, absolute bullshit. The leading man was an old Hungarian-American cowboy actor by the name of Eddie Polo, and he was already, by that time, seventy-five. Then after that, the first picture I really count as having done was *Menschen am Sonntag* [*People on Sunday*, 1929], which was a silent picture, the last of the silents. It came out just about when *The Blue Angel* came out. It was a picture that [Robert] Siodmak directed. It was sort of a Rossellini picture, kind of *cinéma vérité,* for a very good reason: We didn't have the money to have actors, so we had to take the people *vérité.* And we had to shoot in real backgrounds. And the associate of Mr. Siodmak, whose first picture it was as a director, was Edgar Ulmer, who then went on to do kind of early Don Siegel pictures.

Ulmer became kind of a cult figure, too.
Yeah. When you become this kind of a cult thing, they make you a little festival. A *hommage* they give you; in France they are great *hommage* givers. One day some years back I was in Paris and I look at a thing outside a movie house, and kids are lining up, I don't believe it: It was *"Hommage à Betty Hutton."* They're running out of *hommages,* you know. They have a continuous kind of adulation thing going with Jerry Lewis. It's very strange. Who's next, Danny Thomas's daughter?

What did you think of the psychological comments Maurice Zolotow's biography [Billy Wilder in Hollywood] *made about your youth?*
Garbage. Lunacy. Absolute lunacy. It was kind of on the primer level of Freudian analysis. And the conclusion of it is silly. He tried to explain why I hate women. Well, number one, I don't hate women, so there is nothing to be found.

Zolotow says the key incident in your youth was your discovery that a girlfriend you had when you were eighteen, Ilse, was actually a prostitute. Did that happen?
No. Bullshit. Total bullshit. My God, in my youth in Vienna, sex was far less prevalent. I never slept with a hooker in my high school days (a) because I couldn't afford it and (b) because I was scared shitless. In those days, the idea of gonorrhea and the fear which it struck . . . no kid would have.*

Zolotow also makes a big deal of the fact that you dropped out of the University of Vienna at that time—it was 1924—for reasons you've never explained.
No reasons, no nothing. I was to have become a lawyer. You know, in most Jewish families when there are two sons, the mother is pushing the two kids in Central Park, she says, "Hey, I would like you to meet my son the lawyer and this is my son the doctor." So I would have been a lawyer, but the idea of it bored me, so I just dropped out and I became a newspaperman.

Did you do it to rebel against your parents?
No, they were not that rigid. I just felt it would be more fun. And there was not so much affluence at that time. The idea that I would go out and make a few schillings, they were not against that one little bit. To me, the idea of being a newspaperman was a step up. But if you're a lawyer now, you become the head of a studio. Little did I know that I went the wrong route.

You haven't had much luck with the books that have been written about you.
That's absolutely right. As a matter of fact, I don't like reading about myself. It embarrasses me. And it always winds up like a rehash, then it is adorned or watered down, or the names are not proper. Then other people's things are ascribed to me. They did that for years and years and years.

Any joke which is a cynical kind of remark, well, Groucho Marx said that. Anything on the female side, it was always Miss Parker. If it is an idiotic sort of illiteracy and yet it makes some sense, they give it to Goldwyn. These are characters where it fits them. So I got a few of those and that put me really

---

*Wilder's denial of the story is not entirely convincing. Zolotow does not claim that Wilder knowingly slept with a prostitute; the point of the story is Wilder's disillusionment in learning that the girl he loved was moonlighting as a prostitute without his knowledge. Zolotow's book calls it "a betrayal so deep and so wounding that he was never to recover from it." If the story is true, it is easy to see why Wilder, even today, would find it too painful to confirm. —J.McB., T.McC.

in a terrible spot. I know Hal Wallis; I like him, and he likes me. He was married to an old character actress, Louise Fazenda. Somebody wrote a piece about me and said, "Wilder calls him *The Prisoner of Fazenda*." I never said that. So now I have to pick up the phone and say, "Hal, I didn't say it." There's no defense, you know. If it's cruel, I must have said it. And I never said anything cruel. I even have kind words for Hitler. Now how far can I go?

When you were a reporter in Berlin, you did a series of articles about your experiences as a gigolo at the Eden Hotel. Do you still have a copy of the articles?
Somebody sent me one. It was rather well-written reportage, with projections of thoughts, of dreams, it was not all factual. It was serialized in the *B.Z. am Mittag,* which was one of the great German papers—a very classy paper published by a very classy outfit. It was a kudo to be printed in that paper, especially a risqué story, as this was, because it told you about the German bourgeois ladies coming to that hotel for five o'clock tea when people were still dancing there. They still do it in Zurich—between five and seven an orchestra is playing and people are dancing, can you imagine? Ladies are sitting there having their coffee with their *schlag* and their pastry. And the dancers are there, lined up and going up to the ladies, who are almost at their menopause. They get their tips or some basic salary.

I wrote about that series of approaches and dialogues: how to get a better tip, what to do. If you said, "I'm not doing well, actually I'm a writer, but I've got to do anything for a living. Especially—you have no idea—the shoes, the afternoon and the evening shoes, they are very expensive." Then instead of giving you a good tip she'll send you twelve pairs of old shoes from her husband.

You used some of that old-world hotel atmosphere in Avanti!
Avanti! I wiped that off, too. That was fine, but, you see, too soft. It is just too gentle. In other words, the way the picture would have aroused interest or made them talk about it is that the son of the chairman of that enormous corporation goes to claim the body of the father and finds out that the father and a naked bellhop have been found dead in that car. The father was a fag. But it's just a young girl. So who cares? So he got laid. So big fuckin' deal, right? It needs that added element. All of that is gone: Lubitsch, Leisen, *Love in the Afternoon*. It's too soft, you know. Unless there is a man jumping out

of the seventy-sixth floor with his ass afire, unless there is a wreck of sixty-four automobiles hit by a 747, they will not drop the popcorn bag.

It's a miracle any good pictures get made today, under the current system.
As George Axelrod said, very rightly, "Before, you were confronted with an illiterate, finagling, tyrannical guy who was very difficult to converse with, to convince, but once you did that job, that was it, you went ahead. But now there are *twenty* of those guys." You haven't got the strength to weed them out, you know. And then you find out after a year and half that you have been kissing the wrong ass all along.

Now the picturemaker wastes ninety percent of his energy getting the financing. If you are doing a picture, it is kind of like you are the pilot of a plane. You take off and you hope it's going to fly very high and it's going to land very smoothly. But now you have to go out and first of all get the money to buy the plane. Then in the cockpit with you there are twenty people looking over your shoulder saying, "No, wait a minute, you're too high, you're too low, put that rudder up . . ." And ultimately the plane crashes, the picture crashes.

Unless you are riding on an enormous hit, unless you have a deal with Travolta, unless you are willing to do *Damien III*, it is very difficult. You have to go to the money people, the Bank of America, you say, "Hey listen, I've got this great story. I think it would make an absolutely marvelous picture. I need $4,000,000." They say, "Who is in it?"

You say, "Wouldn't you like to hear the story first? Because it's real, kind of brand-new, it's got great scenes, it's got excitement." *"Who is in it?"* "I don't know yet." "Sorry."

Another guy comes and he's got a brown bag. He says, "I want to make a picture out of this. I have Newman and I have Redford and I have Jane Fonda." "How much?" "I need $12,000,000." "Here it is." And on the way out the guy from the bank says, "What is in that brown bag?" He says: "Horseshit!" "It doesn't matter. You have those three people, go and do it." That's the way it goes.

There was a story in the trades when you were preparing Fedora *that you actually asked Garbo and Dietrich to play the role.*
No, never Garbo. I'm not going to make an ass of myself. I did ask Marlene, who was an old friend of mine from Berlin days when she was a small actress,

before *Blue Angel*, and I made two pictures with her [*A Foreign Affair* and *Witness for the Prosecution*]. But she would not, for various reasons. She thought there was some kind of similarity with her own life, which it certainly is not. And she is not well. She played one day on a picture called *Just a Gigolo*, which was being shot in Berlin but they had to move the whole set and everything to Paris, because that's where she lives. She did one day, and she got $250,000.

But if you know the story of *Fedora*, it was almost uncastable and maybe it should never have been done, because there are certain things that read very well but you cannot photograph them. It's extremely difficult. Actually the same person should play both parts; there's no question about it. But if you have Dietrich playing the old countess, from the first shot you know, "Shit, this is Fedora, don't fool around with me." But if I had Dietrich and, say, Faye Dunaway—some similarity, of course—they would say, "That's Dietrich, or that's Gloria Swanson, or that's Bette Davis . . ." Or you fake it and you have it shot from the back or in the shadows, then they get suspicious. Certain things are unphotographable. *Equus:* unphotographable. The moment it's a real horse—even if you had a Secretariat or Seattle Slew—it would not work. It's the mere fact that it's stylized that made it work in a book or on the stage.

Did you consider having a young woman made up to play the old woman as well?
Well, we were considering that with Keller, but Keller is difficult if she is only playing the one part. Naturally, if I had had a young Garbo, it would have been marvelous.

Did you change plans and decide to hire Hildegarde Knef for the countess after you started shooting?
That's right. Keller had been in a very bad automobile accident. Her face was smashed up, and she has a bad cut. It's all fixed up, but the nerve ends are such that when you try heavy makeup, with rubber and stuff like that, she could not tolerate the pain when they took it off.

Why did you decide to add the framing device of the suicide, the Anna Karenina *thing at the train station?*
It's the kind of drop-the-popcorn hook right away. We were trying for something startling.

Also you made major changes in the Holden character. In the book he's a novelist; in the movie he's much closer to you, a producer trying to put together a picture with Fedora using tax shelter financing. Was it easy to decide what the character should be?

I could write *four* pictures about that character. Yeah, sure. That guy that's dragging his ass along Hollywood Boulevard.

Do you wish you had been able to do the film in the United States?

It's difficult to shoot a whole picture outside of Hollywood. Too many worries. Too much playing an executive. The difficulties were enormous. I also am too old to drag around the world. You have to work under the best possible conditions. I'm going to make other pictures—I certainly hope so—and I'm going to try and make them here. I say I hope so, because this is now in the ninth inning. I hope it will go into some extra innings, because I'm gonna tie the game and maybe I can get a few hits.

Have you just finished a screenplay?

Not finished it, no, I'm working on it. By myself right now. Iz [Diamond] is working on something else. Actually I was fooling around with three things and I eliminated one, then it's only last week I decided to do one particular thing.

Could you talk about those ideas?

It's very unwise. But they are in different directions. They are not alike, and they have no similarities to anything I have done before.

Are they original stories?

Two of them.

Do you plan to write them with Diamond?

We don't know yet. If he is available. The project may not appeal to him, but if possible, naturally, I like working with him because we've worked together for so many years and we know each other. And all that bullshit about telling each other our pasts and talking about our families, all of that crap, is eliminated. We can sit down to work right away. I don't have to get to know somebody and he doesn't have to get to know me. It's a waste of time.

When you sit down to think of original ideas these days, do you ever think, "Well, I would like to do this but the twenty-five-year-old audience won't care?"
I never *sit down* to think of an idea. You are either in the toilet or you are at dinner or you are talking to somebody about something entirely different. You sit to *explore* an idea, but the idea comes to you not by just sitting. But then what happens—and I will answer the twenty-five-year-old thing—is that once you have the idea, you have one million, *one million,* variants on how to tackle that idea. And then it becomes more or less a labor of elimination, of dramatization, of putting it into one hat. No, I never think about it, I just kind of think that a great many pictures have been big successes and also they were slightly above the station of the twenty-five-year-old. They have become enormous hits but they had a kind of quality—*Saturday Night Fever* had a quality, it was very good.

But doesn't it distress you—it distresses me—that some of the most successful pictures today are such atrocities? Grease, *for instance? How do you relate to that?*
If you are a decent human being, and if you are, let us say, a composer of dance tunes, and if all you can do are the polka and the waltz, and you keep composing those and the dance floor is empty, they don't come out to dance, then you say, "Well, screw that, if they want rock 'n' roll or disco, I can do that." But *I* can't do it. I cannot even *pretend* that I can do it, because if I did it, that would be real suicide. They still would know that it is a phony, and they would not come out to dance. It just is that they don't want this kind of picture nowadays. I was very much surprised that *Julia,* a very well-made picture by a friend of mine, Zinnemann, was a success. That is very affirmative, something that doesn't have a car chase, doesn't have violence. Mind you, I look at a picture like *Hooper* or even *Smokey and the Bandit* and I have a marvelous time. However, I do see it on the Z Channel. I would not go out and make an evening of it.

But sitting there, I get to see those lunatic kinds of pictures that obviously have been compiled by a computer that says what works, what doesn't work. I saw a thing of Clint Eastwood's called *The Gauntlet.* It is unbelievable. It takes everything that has worked in a picture, kind of piled up and superimposed. The whole thing is like a mad goulash. It's just like when they ran to the computer and asked what would be the most successful picture, and it came out a Biblical Western, called *The Pistol-Packing Apostle.*

One of your stocks in trade used to be a precise social criticism and examination of
contemporary American life—such as in The Apartment—*but you haven't really*
dealt with that in the last ten years. You've gone to Europe, for The Private Life of
Sherlock Holmes, Avanti! *and* Fedora, *or into the past, for* The Front Page. *You*
haven't been dealing with the contemporary American scene.
I always have been all over the place, with an appetite for trying every species
of picture. Maybe I would have been much smarter had I set out on a career
like, say—and I'm mentioning a very good director—like Hitchcock. You
know what a Hitchcock picture is. But it would be very boring for me to
make always the same species. I make pictures of various moods. Sometimes
I'm in the mood for a comedy. Sometimes I do something serious. I cannot
always wear the same suit and the same tie.

Now this is reinforced by trying to find something that is negotiable with
the studios. So I will find myself with samples of three totally different kinds
of things, going in and discussing with them: "Do you think that such-and-
such a project would fit into your program?" But you know, the thing about
a great subject for a picture is not whether I think it's great or you think it's
great, it is whether the reader at Universal or Fox or Paramount thinks that
Mr. Alan Ladd, Jr., Mr. [Sid] Sheinberg, or Mr. [Michael] Eisner will think. It's
not anymore that you write or make a picture hoping that the *audience* will
like it.

And a newspaperman, or somebody who works for weekly or monthly
publications, he knows very well what is of interest right now. But *you* have
to find something that is going to be of interest two years from now, when
the picture is finished. Well, that's why they take a huge amount of money
tying up a hit play. There's no big risk. Or a Sidney Sheldon book—*Bloodline*,
let's say—is on the best-seller list for 40 weeks; they know that there is an
audience interest in that subject.

But if you start with an original subject, they don't know. It's untried.
Nothing to apply their technique of grooving. Everything has to be in a
groove. That was a success, therefore this will be a success. And it's only the
ones that are not in the groove that set the precedent. But then you do a
second one or a third one, it's gonna fail.

Another problem is that for an established director such as yourself or Hitchcock,
the studios don't like to let you try to go out of your image.
In my case, they always say, "Oh, for Chrissake, don't give us that serious

shit. Where are your comedies?" Or, "Why don't you cut out those comedies, they don't mean a goddamned thing. What about another *Sunset Boulevard* or *Double Indemnity?*" There's always something that they are weeping
about.

*Your films in the last ten years have become more openly romantic. There always
was a romantic streak in your work, but it was disguised before under a certain
cynicism. Now you're becoming more willing to have overtly romantic scenes in
your films.*
But if *I'm* cynical, what adjective do you have for Peckinpah pictures?

"Cynical" is another word in Hollywood for "realistic."
I don't know. I think every play by Ibsen was cynical, right? Every play by
Strindberg was cynical.

I don't mean to stigmatize you with that word.
No, that's all right. I'm talking about my efforts, and believe me, I don't
exaggerate the importance of anything like that. They are entertainment for
people to go and spend two hours without their minds being too taxed. On
the other hand, not being insulted either. Now take, for instance, a picture
like *The Apartment*. Did you really think that I went out of my way to dramatize things which did not exist? A society where things like this could not
happen?

Not at all. The Apartment only seemed cynical in the context of movies like Pillow
Talk. *Yours was a breath of realism.*
I thought it was. I was in Berlin, where we were making *One, Two, Three*, and
it was just a week before the Wall went up. We had a party at a building for
the young Communist picture-makers. They had run *The Apartment* before
in the projection room. And then came question-and-answer. They were
very much taken by the picture. They just absolutely loved it, especially the
strong attack on the corrupt capitalist system. And I said, "It's not typical of
New York, it could happen anyplace. Not just in another American town like
Chicago or Los Angeles, it could happen in Sydney, Australia, it could happen in Paris, but the only city where it cannot happen is a Russian city like,
say, Moscow." Well, they just thought that was absolutely terrific. And I said,
"I will tell you why, because if you get a key to an apartment in Moscow so

that you can get laid, there are still seven other families living there that you can't get rid of." *That* they didn't like.

Since Hollywood has gone through the sexual revolution, you don't seem to be trying to shock the audience as much as you used to.
I never shocked unnecessarily. Maybe the subject matter was a little bit more daring. But now, my God, you see everything on soap opera. At nine o'clock in the morning, you see the most shocking things, you know? Tommy Thompson, the guy who wrote *Blood and Money*, wrote an editorial in *Life* magazine after *Kiss Me, Stupid* that I should be deported—absolute lunacy!—for what I had done to the morals of my adopted country.

That was a beautiful picture. I've seen it four or five times.
It was the biggest historic flop in my years of making pictures. They were just absolutely, totally outraged. I don't know, I never quite could understand what the scream was about.

It's actually quite a romantic story.
I thought it was very romantic. I'd like to do it again to show them what the thing was all about. But could you imagine going and telling people that I'm going to make *Kiss Me, Stupid* again?

You could call it Kiss Me Again, Stupid.
Yeah. *Kiss Me, Stupid, Twice, Kiss Me Once and Kiss Me Twice and Kiss Me Once Again.*

Perhaps the change in your work over the last ten years is not so much a change in you as that you have remained true to yourself, whereas most other directors, including some of your generation, have tried to go with the times. You've remained yourself. You've kept your integrity.
Until the last yard of celluloid that they give me! And then comes the obligatory working on the jury of the Teheran Film Festival. That's *Sunset Boulevard*. That's sort of the wind-up, you know. But I refuse to do it.

Once in a while, it's fun to talk to the kids at the universities or at the American Film Institute or at The Museum of Modern Art in New York. I just did one in London and I did one in Paris. Wherever I go. But my fun is talking to the students, not a lecture which I prepare, because that's not my style, but a question-and-answer. I reverse it: *I* ask the questions. What they expect from me, why they are here. And I am always pessimistic. I tell them, "Look, unless you are blessed with extraordinary energy and luck, or an affluent family, there are only two ways to succeed in pictures today: either as a stuntman or as a special effects man. Those are the only two branches of the industry where you know that you're gonna get employment right away."

As a case in point of how things have changed in pictures: Did it ever occur to you that Last Tango in Paris *is a remake of* Love in the Afternoon? *You also had an older American man and a young French girl who met in a Paris hotel every after-noon for an affair. But the tone, of course, is totally different.*
She has to hide from him that she is a virgin. That already is slightly unbelievable nowadays. And that is the whole point of the original, *Ariane,* that she's afraid to tell him. He likes to do it to them and go on, but he would never touch a virgin because it's just too involving. In fact, in *Ariane,* when they do it the first time, there is blood on the sheets and she burns the bed so that he would never find out.

I assume you couldn't have done that in 1957.
I don't know, maybe I could have. But the mistake there was that my beloved friend, Gary Cooper, whom I miss terribly, was the wrong casting, you know? He *was* the guy that I had in the picture, in real life, but he photographed like a decent, tough marshal from *High Noon.* Cary Grant would have been the lover, the sensuous man. Anyway, it's a naive picture, but that's the way we were twenty years ago. I'm filled with nostalgia after watching it. Gary Cooper is dead, Chevalier is dead, John McGiver is dead, and this species of picture is dead. It's erotic in the old Lubitsch manner of eroticism, but today this would be too mild for a sitcom. Today you could use this as one short episode in a 747 underwater.

If you were to make a movie today about a young woman's sex life, how would you do it?
They're doing that all the time. They're doing it quite well. I think that [Richard] Brooks did it quite well in *Looking for Mr. Goodbar.* Look, it has become extraordinarily difficult, because as my collaborator, Mr. Diamond, said, "Nowadays you look at the picture and under the titles, zebras are fucking

women." Now where do you go from there? I mean, how do you top that? It has lost all the cunning of suggestion, of letting the audience guess, all of that behind-the-closed-doors, Lubitschian approach, the innuendo of not showing the night of sex but showing the breakfast after the sex, and you get from the appetite that they're hungry. As Mr. Tony Richardson did in *Tom Jones.*

It's very peculiar today. On the one hand, there is a brand-new generation of film buffs. There is a tremendous increase in the interest in films. There are film students. Universities have picked it up. It's become a very, very smart thing. And they, of course, are on the level. But the other ones—it's flattened out. It's a completely *blasé* big mass of people that have been spoiled by, wrecked by, television. Outguessing it: They've seen every plot, they know every plot. Unless they can dance in the aisles, unless it is one of those strange things that appeal to them which you never quite know what it's gonna be. You can never guess it. Why *Grease* yes and why *Dr. Pepper's Blah-Blah-Blah* not, I don't know. Nobody knows that. The *mezzo*-educated, the *mezzo*-brow audience is falling away. It's the high-brow or it's the lowest. It's very difficult.

And it touches on the problem of casting. What happened to those handsome tall guys? Everybody is Italian. Everybody is under five-foot-four. It's all shrunk. Suddenly it became more realistic—the guy next door. Well, shit, if I want to see the guy next door, I go next door. Mind you, I think that Dreyfuss and those other guys can act rings around the old leading men, the handsome ones. But I'm kind of an old-fashioned romantic, you know. I like handsome people.

Do you have one or two favorite Lubitsch pictures?
Naturally, I would have liked to direct anything by Lubitsch. I would be very happy if I just would have directed the two-minute skit he did with Charles Laughton in *If I Had a Million.* Anything and everything the man did. But all of that, as I've said to you before, is too mild. It is witty. It is beautiful, for me. Any seduction scene in a Lubitsch picture is just so full of charm, it's so erotic, but this is not the age for it.

There was a piece by a columnist that I read someplace, they had a questionnaire on the fifty greatest pictures ever made. And you always wind up with the same goddamn things. It's always *Citizen Kane* and *Battleship Potem-*

kin and *The Bicycle Thief.* But I was outraged, I must say, when I read that of the best fifty pictures, there was not one single Lubitsch picture among them.

Was Howard Hawks one of your models when you started directing?
We [Charles Brackett and Wilder] wrote a picture for him, *Ball of Fire,* and I spent all the time on the set watching him shoot because I wanted to see a picture from beginning to end before I started directing myself. But I would not think he was a model. Maybe Lubitsch much more was, and Stroheim, kind of a strange mixture.

What did you learn from Hawks? Technique?
Yeah, technique. He was a good director. He was an extremely practical, adept, knowing celluloid man.

Robert Stephens' Sherlock Holmes resembles Jack Lemmon in Avanti! *and even Garbo in* Ninotchka *in that he is a closet romantic. His coolness and rigidity, his uptight moralism, is gradually dissolved by his romantic adventures with a European.*
Yeah, that's The Rev. Henderson in *Rain.* It's predictable now, maybe. The Sherlock Holmes thing was premature; after that there came a whole slew of Sherlock Holmes pictures. This was sort of the first one. *That's* the one I would like to redo.

Because of the heavy cuts you had to make in the picture, what we see is about half of the original picture, isn't it?
Well, sixty percent of it. It explained a little bit more about the relations between those two men. It started off with them on a train and he is doing some of his deducing there, and then coming back. There was, subsequently, an episode of Sherlock Holmes in Oxford, the Oxford-Cambridge boat race, and he won the money to go out and pay for a hooker. That's where he finds out that this is the girl he was in love with.

When Avanti! *was recently shown on television, a lot was cut out of that, too.*
I never look at pictures on TV, especially not my own. It just kills me. Usually they cut out the tag line. I think they are looking for unemployed butchers and they let them do it with hatchets.

Do you think there would ever be a chance of reissuing Sherlock Holmes *in the complete version?*

I understand that United Artists has the complete picture in London. I never inquired into that, because I never inquire into old pictures. But if it takes my permission to help restore *Sherlock Holmes,* I'm delighted to, any time they want. If they can get ahold of it, I would not ask for any money, they can show it. I would be absolutely delighted.

How do you feel now about your film of The Front Page?

One should never make a remake of a play that was great. If people would read it now, they would find out that it *was* great but today it is not all that great, because it has been pilfered too much.

When I talked to Diamond on the set, he said the two of you felt the role of the hooker was the weakest element in the play, but that there wasn't much you could do about it since it's so important to the plot. Also, it was my feeling that Carol Burnett was miscast.

It *was* miscast. People expected the television character there. But there was nothing to be done with it. It needed the motivation, some kind of feeling between her and that guy who was in the desk, the protector of the hooker. And then it was the diversion, her suicide, so the guy could escape. Again, don't touch something that is absolutely holy. I had some kind of reverence for Hecht and for MacArthur and we kept that, but it did not work. It could have been written better, too. But that's been wiped off five years ago.

When your pictures made fortunes at the box office, the critics often treated you harshly because they said you were too commercial. Since Sherlock Holmes, *your films have not been blockbusters, and the critics, ironically, have been more enthusiastic.*

No, they have *not* been enthusiastic. The pictures have neither been praised nor have they been financially successful. I made very financially successful pictures, but not what you would call blockbusters in the way they mean now. Even the most successful pictures, like *Irma la Douce* or *Some Like It Hot,* by today's prices they'd just break even, because pictures have become much more expensive.

Yet, in recent years, some critics who used to attack you, such as Andrew Sarris, have made a turnaround and are now praising you.

Sarris, yeah, when he made his Hit Parade, I was in the Less Than Meets The Eye category. It was absolutely silly. I saw him in Cannes and I never even brought up that he knocked me. I never do that. I don't thank them, I don't complain to them, I don't write letters. When I was very successful, they beat me over the head, now maybe some of them are a little gentler because they take pity on me. They commiserate with me. Maybe they are human, at that. They just don't feel like kicking an elderly man in the ass any more.

How do you expect Fedora *to do in the United States?*
I have my grave doubts. I just don't think that it's gonna be properly exploited. They have been sitting on their asses now for nine months. A picture is not like a violin or like wine that increases its quality, you know. It gets to be dusty. This is the last entry on that blackboard which I wiped off. I'll help it as much as I can, but I cannot dedicate my life on a long haul just to that one project. I have to go on. I have other things on my chest that I would like to get rid of.

But Fedora *has quite a good critical reception in Europe.*
The French liked it very much. It got wonderful reviews in France. The Germans were against the picture from the word go. Because their theory was, "What right do Bavaria and Geria have to invest all that money in an American picture when we have those wonderful young picturemakers who cannot get financing?" Fassbinder and all those guys, they somehow scrape the money together. Now Fassbinder is coming over here. This is a rat race. It amuses me.

I remember two years ago, there was such an intra-industry fight with Universal, Warner Bros., and Twentieth Century-Fox. It was the coming of the Second Messiah: "You just get Wertmuller!" Well, she's a very good picturemaker, and Bertolucci, he certainly is a giant, but they are working on themes that are so foreign to us. They think we are deeply interested in the end of fascism as opposed to communism. Look, maybe we have 27,000 Communists in this country, and none of them ever goes to see a movie. But they say, "No, no, no, we must have Wertmuller."

They're also saying, "Oh, for Chrissake, who the hell reads Pauline Kael or Andrew Sarris?" I'll tell you who reads them: those guys read it. They're very pretentious, and they shit in their pants, they're dying for a good review, and they listen to it. They say, "She never sold a ticket." She *doesn't* sell tickets, but she sells a lot of picturemakers and actors.

I admire Fassbinder, too, but I have a completely different attitude about picturemaking. Number one, I go out for some kind of entertainment, some kind of want-see. Something which five minutes after you saw the picture you laugh a lot or it makes you happy. Some kind of elation. *Something.* I don't get it very often, but I'm trying for it.

Now just try to imagine a family in Dusseldorf. The husband is despondent: he comes home and there is a letter from the income tax people. He owes 11,000 marks or he's gonna go to jail. The wife tells the husband, "Look, I'm in love with the dentist and I'm leaving you." The son has been arrested because he's a member of the underground. The daughter is knocked up and has got the syphilis. And now somebody comes to see them and says, "Look, I know you've had a very bad day, but let's cheer ourselves up. Let's go and see Fassbinder's *Despair.*"

A Cynic Ahead of His Time

STEPHEN FARBER/1981

IN AN INDUSTRY WHERE THE WOLVES often wear sheep's clothing, Billy Wilder has survived for 50 years without concealing his fangs. The movies' most colorful and reknowned cynic, Mr. Wilder has never surrendered to sentimentality or sanctimoniousness. Now 75 years old, he continues to needle the studio potentates with his tart, acerbic comments on the follies of the business.

Hollywood has never been entirely comfortable with his cynical sensibility, but Mr. Wilder hung on because his distinctive hard-edged movies managed to achieve popular acceptance. The movies he has written and directed encompass many genres, but most of the best ones—*Double Indemnity, The Lost Weekend, Sunset Boulevard, Ace in the Hole, Witness for the Prosecution, Some Like It Hot, The Apartment, The Fortune Cookie, Fedora*—confronted the darker side of American life with a bracingly sardonic wit.

His latest picture, *Buddy Buddy,* written with his long-time collaborator, I. A. L. Diamond, is a characteristic Wilder movie. For one thing, it stars two of his favorite actors, Jack Lemmon (who has appeared in seven Wilder movies) and Walter Matthau (who won an Academy Award for *The Fortune Cookie*). In addition, it is the blackest of black comedies, about the uneasy friendship that develops between a cold-hearted hit man and a suicidal TV censor whose wife has run off with the head of a sex clinic.

If the subject matter of *Buddy Buddy,* which opens in New York on Friday,

From the *New York Times,* 6 December 1981. © The New York Times Co. Reprinted by permission.

seems typical of Wilder, the movie is atypical in another sense. Most of his
projects have originated with him; they have either been his own ideas or
adapted from plays or novels that he selected. But *Buddy Buddy* was packaged
by an agent at William Morris, who discovered an obscure French film called
A Pain in the A—, brought it to Mr. Lemmon and Mr. Matthau, and then
approached Mr. Wilder to direct.

"Iz Diamond and I were working on another project," Mr. Wilder recalls,
"when William Morris came to us with this one. We looked at the French
movie and saw possibilities in it. I would prefer doing an original story or
screenplay. The most fun is working on a movie like *Sunset Boulevard* or *The
Apartment,* where you start from scratch. Here I found myself with a ready-
made thing, but there are certain advantages to that. I didn't have to audi-
tion for the studios and pass through Checkpoint Charlie before they would
approve the project. We knew we had a starting date, which is rare enough
these days."

Mr. Wilder has had trouble adjusting to contemporary deal-making; he
misses the stability of the old studio system. "In the 30's or 40's," he says,
"you were under contract to a studio and made a picture or two every year.
Paramount had 104 writers under contract, M-G-M 140 writers under contract. No such thing exists today. Studios have lost their personality. In the
past if you walked into a movie after the credits, you knew instantly whether
it was a Warner Bros. picture or an M-G-M picture. Studios had their own
handwriting; you recognized the ensemble players, and the sets of each studio had a distinctive style to them.

"Now studios have become more or less Ramada Inn motels; you move
in, you move out. It is all very gypsy-like. You even have that unheard of
thing, a co-production between two studios like Paramount and Disney. That
could never have happened in the past because the studio heads were sworn
enemies; you had to keep Jack Warner and Louis B. Mayer apart or they
would get into a fist fight. Those were the good old days."

Although Mr. Wilder always had conflicts with the studio executives, he
looks back on the old moguls with affection now. "There was a certain nobil-
ity about them," he admits. "I remember in 1934 when I arrived in Hollywood, there were a lot of German, Austrian and Hungarian refugees who
came here to escape Hitler. They were all taken in by the studios—actors,
composers, writers. Even Brecht got a job."

In those days the moguls prided themselves on doing a few prestige pictures every year. But Mr. Wilder points out, "They could afford an artistic gesture because they made 45 pictures a year, and so if they spent a million and a half on some deep-dish project, that was no big deal. They also had their own theaters where they could play it. But now they don't own the theaters, and it doesn't cost a million and half for a movie. Today the advertising campaign for a middle-priced picture is more than the entire cost of *Gone With the Wind*."

The result is a terror of taking risks; very few people will gamble on untested material. "If Mr. Shaffer had submitted a movie script called *Amadeus*," Mr. Wilder notes, "the executives would not have known what to do with it. They would have said to Shaffer, 'What is this thing? You have a leading character named Amadeus. You have people writing with quills. Get out of here!' But if it is done first as a play and becomes an enormous and well-deserved worldwide hit, suddenly they will go after an *Amadeus*. They would much rather buy *Annie* for $9.5 million than buy an original script for $50,000."

Despite the craziness of today's business—where, Mr. Wilder observes, "A dentist with artistic aspirations" can buy an option on a novel and then nominate himself as producer of the movie version—the director enjoyed working at M-G-M on *Buddy Buddy*. The new M-G-M, he says, is "very eager, very ambitious, very energetic. They want to bring back the roaring lion."

Mr. Wilder recalls the days when the lion was a far more formidable beast. In 1938 he and co-writer Charles Brackett were at M-G-M working with director Ernst Lubitsch on the script of *Ninotchka*. Today his office is right above the office where he was ensconced then. In 1958 he returned to M-G-M to shoot part of *Some Like It Hot* on a stage that no longer exists. "It has become a row of condominiums," Mr. Wilder says. "The stage at Goldwyn Studios where we shot *The Apartment* and *Irma La Douce* is now a parking lot. But you know, if you visit the Parthenon today, it's not quite the way it was in the old days. Everything in this here world changes, with the one exception of Dolores Del Rio."

Some of these changes have been painful to contemplate. "In this Donner Pass expedition known as Hollywood," the director muses, "many fall by the wayside. People eat people. Very few make it. Lately I've been going to more funerals than openings of pictures. Sometimes you have a funeral and an opening on the same day, and you don't feel very good when you see a comedy after you've put somebody to rest or watched the Neptune Society blow his ashes into the Pacific Ocean."

This leads Mr. Wilder to some final thoughts on William Holden, who had been a close friend of his. Mr. Wilder directed Mr. Holden four times, in his Academy Award-winning performance in *Stalag 17*, and also in *Sunset Boulevard, Sabrina,* and *Fedora.* "I really loved Bill," Mr. Wilder reflects, "but it turned out I just didn't know him. If somebody had said to me, 'Holden's dead,' I would have assumed that he had been gored by a water buffalo in Kenya, that he had died in a plane crash approaching Hong Kong, that a crazed jealous woman had shot him and he drowned in a swimming pool. But to be killed by a bottle of vodka and a night table—what a lousy fadeout for a great guy."

Although he has fond memories of a Hollywood that's vanished forever, Mr. Wilder doesn't dwell on the past. He and his partner Mr. Diamond still spend every day working on new scripts, though they sometimes take time away from the typewriter to visit an art gallery or an antiques store or to try a new restaurant. Mr. Wilder knows that his recent movies haven't fared too well at the box office, so he might seem to have a lot riding on the commercial fate of *Buddy Buddy.* Nevertheless, he claims, "I'm not worried about it or brooding about it. I'm concerned with my next project."

He admits some of the battles get harder as he gets older. "Sometimes I feel the way you feel when you find yourself at a dinner party with an uncongenial group of people and you say, 'I've got a great story, but I'm not going to tell it to them tonight. I'm not interested in entertaining them.' A lot of energy goes into it, and sometimes it doesn't seem as if it's worth the trouble. I've been doing it now for over 50 years.

"And some of the younger ones don't even know me. I was talking to a few young people in the commissary the other day and the name Capra came up. One of them said, 'Oh yes, he's running Avco Embassy, isn't he?' I said, 'No, that's Junior.' And he said, 'That's right, there was a senior. Now remind me, what did he do?' "

Whatever he decides to do next, Mr. Wilder refuses to bend his style and personality to fit the current fashions. "I aim a movie at pleasing me and maybe 10 of my friends," he insists. "That's the only way I know how to operate. The audience senses when you're doing something without any conviction. I could never do a picture like *American Graffiti,* good as it was. I don't know those kids, and if I tried to do it they would sense that I'm not one of them.

"To keep your sanity and your self-respect, you must believe that there will be an audience for what you want to do. It may not be the blockbuster of all time, but what is wrong with a modest success? Once you lose the belief that quality will pay off, you are lost. The next thing you know, you're doing a *Tuesday the 11th* horror story. I could do that if I wanted to. After all, there are still about 360 days left in the calendar."

In one sense at least, Mr. Wilder feels that he has an advantage today: the world has caught up with his own cynical vision, which seemed more shocking when he first started working in movies. "Who's not cynical nowadays?" Mr. Wilder wonders. "It's a cold, cruel world. So you can make the downers, but you still have to give people something to hang onto at the end. After watching the news and seeing all the horror and hopelessness of the world, I don't think people are in the mood to go and see *Oedipus*—unless of course it becomes a Belushi-Aykroyd picture with a lot of togas."

The Art of Billy Wilder

MICHAEL BLOWEN/1989

IN THE CRYSTAL ROOM, located just below the Polo Lounge in the Beverly Hills Hotel, Walter Matthau is studying Pablo Picasso's "Classic Head of a Woman," Jack Nicholson is eying Alberto Giacometti's "Standing Woman," and writer-director Billy Wilder, the man who owns these objects, is off in a corner smiling. Amused.

The painting and sculpture are part of the Billy Wilder Collection to be auctioned off by Christie's, the New York auction house, on Nov. 13. The auction, which also includes works by Balthus, Kirchner, Botero and Cornell, is expected to realize $30 million, according to a spokesman for Christie's. "It's more of an accumulation than a collection," said Wilder, the 83-year-old film maker, a few days later in his office just below Sunset Boulevard. "I'm sick of watching all my friends die and their art auctioned off much to the delight of their heirs. This way, my heirs will get the money, but I'll get the laughs."

Laughs have always been important to the writer of such films as *Ninotchka* (1939) and the co-writer and director of such comedies as *The Seven Year Itch* (1955), *Some Like It Hot* (1959), *One, Two, Three* (1961), *Irma La Douce* (1963), *Kiss Me, Stupid* (1964) and *The Fortune Cookie* (1966). "What is not funny about life?" asked Wilder. "I think mostly everything is funny. Especially out here. Especially in Hollywood."

Wilder even thinks his collection of art works has inspired some humor.

From the *Boston Globe*, 22 October 1989. Reprinted by permission of Copyright Clearance Center, Inc.

"I look at the prices the Christie's people expect to get for some of the work and I laugh. My collection is crazy. The Giacometti I had to buy because I knocked it to the floor in an art shop," he said, referring to a bronze piece estimated at being worth between $1 million and $1.5 million. "I never thought about monetary value, I just bought what I liked. But it's nice to know that what I bought some other people are interested in buying as well." He grinned. "I'm just selling it so I can bring the second string out of the basement. It'll give me something different to look at and, at my age, that's essential."

Looking at different things, or looking at things differently, has always appealed to Wilder. Like his movies, his art mixes the contemporary with the historical and the modern with the traditional. His movies range from social commentaries such as *The Lost Weekend* with Ray Milland as the alcoholic New Yorker, and mysteries such as *Double Indemnity,* a film with no heroes, to knockabout comedies in the tradition of *Some Like It Hot* and melodramas such as *Sunset Boulevard.* His art collection mixes 19th-century religious satire with 20th-century examples from Picasso and Miro.

"I have always been interested in many things without ever worrying about consistency," said Wilder, who began his career in Berlin as publicist for band leader Paul Whiteman and a ghost writer on silent films. He immigrated to the United States in 1934 at age 28.

"It was too late for me to lose my accent, but not to appreciate this country," said Wilder, who apologetically described his Austro-American English as a cross between Arnold Schwarzenegger and Bishop Tutu. "What other country would let me make the kinds of films I make?"

Although Wilder has not made a movie since *Buddy Buddy* in 1981, he still goes to his office every weekday to polish a couple of scripts he's working on and a memoir he's planning to publish in both English and German. Appropriately, especially for a filmmaker who only became a director to protect his writing, an Oxford Unabridged Dictionary, on an ornate wooden pedestal, dominates one corner of his small, second-floor office. Along the walls are bookshelves containing leather-bound copies of his scripts, his half-dozen Oscars and an eclectic assortment of novels, art books and historical works. The far wall is dominated by a large sign with the following question emblazoned on it—"How Would Lubitsch Do It?"

"I made that sign," said Wilder, as he lit a cigar. "That way I never allow myself to write one sentence that I would be ashamed to show to my great friend, Ernst Lubitsch." Wilder gazed out the window but continued to talk. "When Lubitsch died, William Wyler and I were leaving the funeral, and we were both a bit teary-eyed. I turned to him and said, 'Too bad, no more Ernst Lubitsch.' 'Worse than that,' said Wyler, without hesitation, 'no more Ernst Lubitsch pictures.' "

Wilder clearly adored Lubitsch, the director of such extraordinary films as *Trouble in Paradise* (1932) and *To Be Or Not To Be* (1942). "Lubitsch made films his way," said Wilder, as he stared at the sign. "Lubitsch pictures were never the biggest hits in the world, but he established a higher level of communication between the picturemaker and the audience. They listened to his pictures. He would never add everything up for his audience. He gave them two and two and let them figure out that it was four. All of that school is gone." Wilder stared out the window, again. "I thought television would kill the picture business," he continued. "But there is more money now in the picture business now, but it's from people going to see fewer and fewer pictures time and time again. The same space ships. The same car crashes."

Wilder's voice was contemptuous.

"Getting a picture done now is ridiculous," he said. "You sit there in the office telling your story. The executive, who can barely stay awake if it's not about car crashes and space ships, can push either a red button or a green button. The green, go ahead; the red, forget it. The young guy who's the head of the studio is like Nero in the Coliseum. It's the thumbs up or it's the thumb down. And while I'm in the middle of the story, I begin to recognize the face of the boy who is supposed to be listening. Sure, that was the boy in the mail room at William Morris. He should be in my office looking for a job. What the hell am I doing here? Do you know what this man has learned between the time he was in the mail room and now that he is the head of the studio? How to shove more cocaine up his nose. That's all?"

Wilder used his cigar to emphasize his points. For a moment, it was the old Hollywood with the master behind the desk. He could have been Louis B. Mayer or Jack Warner or Harry Cohn. He began to rattle off his critique of the movie business as did James Cagney, as the Coca-Cola executive in *One, Two, Three* ordering his employees around.

"There's no more loyalty out here," said Wilder, his hand pointing in the general direction of Rodeo Drive. "We used to feel competition between studios. It was Paramount vs. MGM or Warner Bros. vs. Universal. It's all gone. Now, studios are like the Ramada Inn. You move in, stay the night, pack your bags and check out. The next time it's a Holiday Inn. We used to be loyal. We made hits. We made failures. But each studio made 40 to 50 pictures a year and they did it without a bunch of know-nothings leaning over your shoulder breathing on your neck. They are afraid of strong directors. They are afraid that they might criticize me and be wrong. They are afraid that I might unmask them for the illiterate imbeciles that they are."

Some of these so-called "imbeciles" describe Billy Wilder's work as vulgar. One of his major films, *Kiss Me, Stupid* (1964), was one of the only Hollywood films of the time to ever be condemned by the Roman Catholic Church because it refused to denounce adultery. As expected, the allusion to vulgarity sent Wilder into a rage.

"Vulgar? Vulgar?" he exclaimed. "I'll tell you about vulgar. I'm the last person who believes in censorship in any form, but all these dead bodies piled up and every other word is mother this and mother that. In movies today there's all this nudity. I'm no prude. There's nothing better than a naked woman. But I can't tell what's what in all these movies. Is that her shoulder or his knee? No, no, it's his elbow. I can't stand it. And they call me vulgar because the films have an edge to them. God help us."

Wilder has also been accused of excessive cynicism. His portrait of Hollywood in *Sunset Boulevard* (1950) is a scathing indictment of a system that rewards youthful beauty but, when it fades, shoves the subject out of sight in a symbolic, dusty, old dark mansion off the main drag.

"I'm not really a cynic," said Wilder. "Out here, if you're not grinning from ear to ear all the time and you don't write pictures where the hero is some self-satisfied moron, they call you a cynic."

In his career, spanning six decades, Wilder has directed Greta Garbo, Marlene Dietrich, Marilyn Monroe, James Stewart, Gloria Swanson, Jack Lemmon, Walter Matthau, Kirk Douglas, Shirley MacLaine and Charles Laughton, and he's written scripts with Raymond Chandler, Charles Brackett and I. A. L. Diamond.

"Charles Laughton was great," said Wilder, of one of the stars of *Witness for the Prosecution*, an adaptation of Agatha Christie's mystery. "Give him three days of preparation, and he was set to be perfect throughout the entire picture. None of that Method nonsense. And he was a gentleman."

One of Wilder's least favorite people was his favorite actress, Marilyn Monroe. "I hated her and she hated me," said Wilder, bluntly, of the woman he used in two of his best pictures, *The Seven Year Itch* (1955) and *Some Like It*

Hot (1959). "She was rude, mean, discourteous and completely selfish. She wouldn't show up on time, and she didn't know her lines. She was the most unprofessional person I had ever met. I swore that after *The Seven Year Itch,* I would never work with her again. When we finished the script for *Some Like It Hot,* I knew that I needed her for the key part. I hated her still, but she transformed the movie screen. You swear that when she was on screen that if you reached up and touched it, you'd touch flesh. Nobody else had that. Not even Garbo."

The phone rang. Wilder mumbled a few monosyllabic responses.

It was getting late in the afternoon. "No one calls for months," he said. "Now, everyone calls. In a few months, lots of money and no more calls."

Billy Wilder, who gave us one of the best exit lines in the history of film when Joe E. Brown discovers his bride-to-be in *Some Like It Hot* is really a man and responds, "Nobody's perfect," is about to utter one of his own.

"It's like Sam Goldwyn once told me, 'Billy, sometimes you just have to take the bitter with the sour.' " Then, he put out his cigar.

Saul Bass and Billy Wilder in Conversation

PAT KIRKHAM/1995

L AST A UGUST IN L A I had the pleasure of a leisurely lunch with
Billy Wilder (89) and Saul Bass (75)—both wonderful raconteurs, and both
thought by many to be Hollywood's greatest living director and title-
sequence designer respectively.

Bass—best known to *Sight and Sound* readers for his film-title sequences of
the 50s and 60s, including *The Man with the Golden Arm* (1955), *Anatomy of a
Murder* (1959) and *Psycho* (1960) and for his own film *Quest* (1983)—still runs a
successful design office (last summer he was designing a series of petrol stations in Japan). His work in films was only ever one part of his working life:
when the industry wanted the sort of titles he was not prepared to produce,
he simply returned to what he had done all along, graphic design. In recent
years and, in collaboration with his wife Elaine, he has returned to film work
and some very impressive title sequences, including those for the most
recent Martin Scorsese movies: *Cape Fear* (1991), *The Age of Innocence* (1993)
and *Casino* (forthcoming).

Things were slightly different for Wilder, when the industry wanted the
sort of scripts and films he was not prepared to write or direct. With no other
occupation to fall back on, what might have been hard times were cushioned
by money made from what had been more a hobby: his magnificent art and
design collection. Though he had no financial need to continue writing, he
did—and does so today. Partly I think he continued because there was writ-

From *Sight and Sound,* June 1995. © Sight and Sound/British Film Institute. Reprinted by
permission.

ing in him still to come out, but partly because to stop would perhaps have been to acknowledge that "they" had in some ways won: that what he believed in could not flourish.

SAUL BASS: Billy, your coming over today prompted memories of working on an advertisement for your film *One, Two, Three* (1961) and I'd like to give you this proof of the one we had to withdraw. I should fill you in on this, Pat. Billy ran this as a trade ad, but all hell let loose because I had used the shape of a Coca Cola bottle. It was a striking image but the Coca Cola corporation didn't like it much and that was the end of that.

BILLY WILDER: Boy, was it *not*. Coca Cola made such a fuss that we were forced to withdraw it.

PAT KIRKHAM: *What did you use instead?*

SB: We used a totally different, effective, but less satisfactory approach.

BW: Apart from *your* posters, Saul, I have come to the conclusion that some of the best posters are Polish, especially for movies. I have one of *Sunset Boulevard* (1950). It is simple yet powerful. You look and know it is Gloria Swanson but out of her hair comes film. It is the Medusa. Why can't we do that, I ask myself? The answer is simple: it is because here they insist on the faces of the stars, and then the lawyers of the different stars argue about the size of the images.

SB: That's equally true of the sizes of the names of the stars. It's hard to deal with the typography in a film poster because frequently four names have to be on one line. One name cannot appear ahead of the other. You end up with tall, thin, compressed typography.

BW: And you can never read it—nor do you want to. Then one is obliged to add the names of the seven or so producers—the line producer, the executive producer, the so-and-so producer, a so-and-so picture. It is all ego. Do you think people go to a movie because Joe Smenderink produced something? Nobody knows who these people are.

SB: It was something along these lines that led me into titles. I felt that people certainly wanted (or deserved) more than a long list of names that didn't mean anything at the beginning of a movie.

BW: All you need are the main elements—like you do!—in a poster or in titles. There aren't many people who are good at titles—it is not an easy task. But there is one person I wanted to mention: Maurice Binder who went to England. He did the titles for the *James Bond* series [from 1962]. You remember the gun; it twirls around, it gets bigger and on comes Sean Connery who shoots at you. Actually it was rather silly of them to do all this, because it was the best part of the picture! There is a problem; if you open your mouth too wide with the titles you can only go down. You can't reshoot the picture. Saul, you did your titles almost the best anyone ever did, but even with a good director you can still get a mediocre picture.

SB: True. I had just that happen to me a couple of times.

BW: Is it true that you did that terrific shower montage for *Psycho,* one of the most marvellous moments in it?

SB: That was really an unusual situation. By the time I worked on *Psycho* (1960) I had already worked on *Vertigo* (1958) and *North By Northwest* (1959) for Hitchcock, so we knew each other pretty well. He said there are a few scenes that are very important—fulcrum scenes—and I want to do something special. So he gave me those to work on and think about. But when I came back with the storyboard for the shower scene, Hitch was very uneasy about it. My approach was very different from his. His great forte—his great love—is very long continuous shots, and I'm proposing a staccato-like montage. He was uneasy. So I stayed late one night and used Janet Leigh's stand-in—

BW: —and butchered her.

SB: I just shot a few hundred feet, chopped it up into short cuts, edited it together, and showed it to Hitch. He was reassured. He thought it would work.

BW: And *how* it would work! It is one of those unforgettable things. That reminds me of when I first met him—well, *saw* him, I didn't *meet* him. It was in Germany. I was about 26 or 27 when they started sound pictures at the old UFA company. They did them with three casts, German, French and English. There were three directors on this particular film but the first one was the German one—he decided where the camera would go. Hitchcock was the guy who did the English version. They had not learned how to loop a picture or how to subtitle it (which is something I hate).

I was talking recently to someone about the importance of an insert. People think that inserts are easy to shoot but they are not. Fritz Lang had, say,
a pair of glasses on a surface, and he would take three or four hours deciding
how to shoot it. We were talking about which were the most riveting inserts
in movies. My vote went for Eisenstein's *Battleship Potemkin* (1925).

PK: *Which particular insert?*
BW: The spectacles and the maggots. The sailors are revolting against the
food on the ship and the captain says there is nothing wrong. The sailors say
there are little animals in there eating away at that meat. "OK," says the
captain, "let's get the doctor down." Now in those days we made glasses
where one lens slides over the other one and makes a magnifying glass and,
when you see through the magnifying glass, there are *thousands* of maggots.
The doctor puts the glasses on, turns to the captain and says, "It is perfectly
all right." That's when you wanted to jump out of the seat and right away
become a Communist. Terrific. With Hitchcock it is the man with the missing finger [*The 39 Steps,* 1935].

SB: There was a great edit Hitch did in *The Lady Vanishes* (1938). First cut:
she opens her mouth to scream. Second cut: the train whistle screeches. You
know, your mention of Eisenstein reminded me of Russian cinema and montage and an experience I want to share with you. As I was growing up I
watched Russian films and fell in love with montage. Do you know Slavko
Vorkapich?
BW: Yes, he was here [*i.e. in LA*], and died not so long ago. A special effects
man.

SB: He did all those montages for MGM. You know, the immigrant arrives
in New York. We pick him up digging a ditch. The pick falls, the dirt flies.
Cut: welder's sparks scattering. Factory wheels churn. Pistons pump. Smoke-
stacks belch smoke. Leaves of calendar float off screen. Skyscrapers rise out
of the ground. We pan up the side of a building. Up. Up to the top.
 Through the window to a man at a desk, surrounded by phones and assis-
tants. Answering phones. Barking orders. Zoom in. It's our immigrant. He's
a titan of industry. He rules the world! All in a minute and a half. That was
Vorkapich. Well, I was at an evening with Slavko and I tell him how wonderful and imaginative I thought Russian montage was. He snorts: "Montage!

Let me tell you about montage!" He then tells me that at the time of the Russian Revolution, when he was young, he worked at the German Studios, at UFA. After the revolution the Russians had equipment but no film. So the German comrades in UFA used to collect the short ends and send them to Russia. So Slavko snorts [*and here Bass imitates Borkapich's voice and accent*]: "What could you do with short ends except make montage?" Outrageous but reasonable. Do you believe that?

B W :   Well, it's a good story.

P K :   *How did you two meet?*

B W :   It was through Charles and Ray Eames. I think they suggested I use Saul, whose work they liked.

S B :   Our very first contact was when you asked me to do the titles for *The Seven Year Itch* (1955). It was only the third or fourth title I did. It was after that that I remember meeting you with the Eameses.

B W :   Your reputation was made very very quickly. But with titles the danger is that if you do many pictures, you have to be very inventive or else people say, "Hey, this is the same guy who . . ." You have to change with the picture.

S B :   Absolutely. I did a title for Willie Wyler for *The Big Country* in 1958, and got a call from one of my friends who saw the film and said, "You know, that isn't like a Saul Bass title." I asked, "What the hell is a Saul Bass title?" It's the film that counts, and the title has to be supportive of the film. I tried to have my titles take on a colouration that was appropriate to the film. Eventually titles got out of hand. It got to a point where it seemed that somebody got up there before the film and did a tap dance. Fancy titles became fashionable rather than useful and that's when I got out.

B W :   Pat, his first-rate titles could be hurtful to the director because sometimes his stuff was on a much higher level than the picture. To be first-rate, titles have to be original, help the audience, and put them in the right mood. The most important thing is to get the audience on your side, to work with you, to work for the film.

P K :   *When you hired him for* The Seven Year Itch *did you set a tight brief or did you let this new talent have a fairly free hand?*

BW: I really forget now. But in another area we were absolute idiots not to capitalise on what 30 or 40 years later is the symbol for that film. You know, Marilyn's frock blowing up. We had it there but it didn't occur to us to use it. I forget what the actual advertising campaign was now. Actually *The Seven Year Itch* wasn't a very good picture. Well, it was all right.

SB: What are you talking about? *The Seven Year Itch* was a wonderful film!
BW: I'll tell you what I'm talking about. First of all I went to New York to test, because we knew we had Marilyn Monroe but we didn't have a leading man. And I tested a guy, a very young man who was improvising this scene. He was so funny, I just screamed with laughter. I thought I must have this guy because he's so interesting. The guy was Walter Matthau and he would have been absolutely terrific. But the producers said, "Why do you make it so difficult? Tom Ewell has played that part now 900 times [*i.e. in the original stage version*], he knows all the words, knows where all the laughs are." But I was not powerful enough to get Matthau—and Marilyn Monroe was not Marilyn Monroe back then either.

I said to them, look, this thing is only good in that there is what in German they call a 'straw widower' [*i.e. a husband temporarily separated from his wife*]. The family goes into the country for the summer months and now you go crazy. There are two things we need to plan, and to plan very very well. The one is that the guy who has all those daydreams should not be very attractive at all, and the other that the girl upstairs must be *extremely* sexy and must want something from him so that he thinks she wants him. And that object is an air conditioner. That way she can say, "Can I sleep here tonight?" and he goes crazy. She says, "I can't sleep in that heat. I'll just go upstairs and get my underwear from the refrigidaire." He says, "Wow! From where?"

Censorship was a problem. I argued that at a certain point we *must* say it, see it, feel it: that *he slept with Marilyn Monroe*. "Oh my God, Mary, Mary," the studio said. Censorship, censorship. I remember spending a night wondering what to do. I had to come up with something. I finally said, "There is one thing we can do that will be subtle enough for the censors not to object. Try this: there is a room maid who is making up the bed, and there is a hairpin, which she simply picks up and then throws away." A hairpin, that is all. *That is all I wanted.* But I couldn't get it. I had a tough time. I had a less tough time with *Some Like It Hot* (1959) but that was better material. *The Seven Year Itch* could certainly have been ten times as good.

S B : I remember it very well. For you my title was just one element in a very complex thing—a movie. For me that element was a life. I was doing a piece of film for a man whose work I viewed with awe. I had just done a title for a film called *The Racers* (1955) for Darryl Zanuck. (Actually it was for Julian Blaustein but Zanuck was there behind the scenes.) It was the very first time I had designed something that called for live action. My earlier work had been animation—*The Man with the Golden Arm,* etcetera—and I was very green. I didn't even know I was going to shoot it. All I knew was that they had asked if I was available on Tuesday morning. So I go to stage seven on Tuesday morning thinking it was awfully nice of them to invite me to see what they are going to do with my storyboard. I'm watching them prepare, lay dolly tracks, etcetera. Then some man comes over and says "Are you ready?" Then the Assistant Director yells "Quiet!" and I realise I'm the director! I thought, "Hey, I'm in charge!" I said, "Wait a minute, let me see the move."

B W : What you do is say, "Let me look through the camera." Then you look at a screw in the background and say, "Yes, that looks pretty good."

You know, Pat, in the 1930s—in the days of the big old studios—when I came to Hollywood, we said that MGM had more stars than there are in heaven. The studios were like castles but there was no connection between them. There was a sort of patriotism about which studio you were at: "I'm at Paramount," we would say. "I'm at Warners." I was at Paramount and I didn't know anybody who was at Warner Bros. There was room for the strong man without knowledge but with instinct and ambition. Like Goldwyn. He couldn't spell but he knew what was good and what would work and there was money for the best writers and directors.

Each studio had over 100 writers; Paramount had 105. Eleven pages of script had to be delivered every Thursday and on yellow paper. Why I don't know, but that's what we did. The studio heads simply took scripts from their staff and then asked which of their own stars would be free of filming commitments on such and such a date. "Will Clark be free? No—OK, then we'll have Spencer Tracy for this one instead." The discussions weren't with agents. Today writers work at home, agents make deals and sell scripts to the studios. We move in only for the time it takes to do the final preparations and to shoot. Studios to us now are like the Ramada Inn—you move in and you move out.

P K : *Interest in your work is currently as great as it has ever been. Some of the movies you wrote or directed are currently being remade. What do you think of this?*
B W : Right now I'm King of the remakes. Four of my movies are being remade but I'm not getting a penny. This is because the contracts were made after television.

I tell you, one day I met Jack Warner, who said, "This is the greatest day of my life."

"What has happened?"

"Guess."

"What happened, Jack?"

"I sold the whole shit, the studio, the buildings and all of that crap, for $25 million."

Well, anyone could get $50 million for just *Casablanca* alone, but he was so delighted, because he got rid of it.

P K : *Which films are being remade?*
B W : They have made an opera out of *Sunset Boulevard,* it's in London and here, and they are remaking *Sabrina* (1954), *Love in the Afternoon* (1957), and *The Apartment* (1960, but this will be done in instalments for television). Not one single penny do I get. Only on one picture do I have an option, if somebody wants to redo it—I forget what it is now. Yes, it's *Love in the Afternoon.* They (Columbia, I think) call you to say, "Mr. Wilder, we have good news. You may remember a film called *Love in the Afternoon?*" I say certainly I remember that film. "We may remake it." "How are you going to do it?", I ask: "It will be difficult. There is no Hepburn, Bogart or Holden." They say, "You will get $2,500 now and when we make the picture you will get $25,000." I tell them, "You must be crazy!" They said they would think about it, so I said, "While you are thinking remember that Mr Eszterhas just got $3 million for *Natural Instincts,* I mean *Basic Instinct, three million dollars,* do you hear?" Then I hung up. They called again and I got them up to $100,000. I finally said, "Look, whatever I am going to get, half will go to the widow of I. A. L. Diamond, with whom I worked." We worked together for years, you know.

s b :   What I want to ask you is why you should not be involved in some way in the remaking of 'your' movies. I know why, but it still baffles me because the creator of these works is alive and kicking. All they are buying is a commodity from you.

b w :   It's terrible what they are doing [in the film industry] right now. It's all special effects or mezzo-pornographic and I can't do those things. They are also afraid that I will demand things they don't agree with, afraid I'm going to make a fool of them. But I'd never do that, no matter how ignorant they are. I'm nice and gentle. Straight away, the head of the studio knows that Mr Wilder wants final cut; I tell them this, or my agent does, and then he calls me and says, "I didn't get very far."

But I don't care. I'm not all that eager anymore. There is nobody with whom I'm dying to work. There is just nobody around. Audrey Hepburn was the last one, and she is gone now. If you think of all the people who died—all the way down from Gary Cooper, Clark Gable, Spencer Tracy, blah blah blah blah—and the women too. Now they talk about Harrison Ford like he was a great star. He would have been one of the crowd. Sitting on the bench, in the dugout, were people like Claude Rains, George Raft, Charles Laughton: all of that second string that came in when you were through with the leads. You know, when you need a little pause and you use them. Some great actors—there will never be another Claude Rains or another Charles Laughton.

Today they would each have their own television series: you can imagine *The Claude Rains Show* for 20 weeks. We just did not know what we had. I'm just one of those unfortunate bridges that goes way back—to 1934 when I came to America. I'm looking at what it is like today, at the *cruelty* of it. If you make a picture you work and slave at it—and it's a year and a half if you are a serious picture maker—and if this picture does not make a certain amount of money over the first weekend—say $12 million—they don't advertise it anymore, they don't want to know and you're down in the dumps. But if there is a picture that surprisingly only cost $8 million and is a hit, then come double pages. (I'm so sick of seeing double pages.) "Terrific, never saw a better picture." But if you look below you see it is the *Cucamonga Register* or something. Not great reviewers, but splashed in the double pages. So I'm not all that bothered about making pictures now.

I'm having a very good time. I did a book. I did it in German and now it has come out in French, Italian and Spanish. And I'm going to do an enlarged version of that book. I have my little obsessions. I collect. I got $34 million when I sold half of my art collection in 1989, when prices were at the top. You read all that stuff in the papers about prices but I thought they were bluffing with the estimates so I put in only the little things I bought. But I got $34 million, of which I paid $13 or $14 million in tax. So I don't need to make movies anymore: I don't need the money. As my father used to say, "Kid, you can't eat platinum noodles." I've got enough to keep me interested. As long I have luncheons with good people like you and spend time with some of my friends. As long as I've got the rent money and food money for my daughter, grand-daughter and great grand-daughter (of which I have one).

S B :   I just regret the circumstances don't allow someone of your talent to make a movie.
B W :   I could say I don't regret it.

S B :   You may not regret it, but *I* do.

P K :   *Many others too.*
B W :   You are all so very kind. You English have always been very wonderful to me. I remember the BFI gave me an award. One day I get a page from the London *Observer:* they had been asking directors who is the best director in their eyes. And I (I'm a very modest man, you know), I came out on top. My friend Mr. David Lean ran my 'election' there. Some very good directors were being discussed and someone said, "I would vote for Wilder but he's dead." Mistake. Thank God I was not dead.

S B :   There was a foreign director who got the Academy Award last year and said, "I don't believe in God, I believe in Billy Wilder."
B W :   It was a Spaniard, Fernando Trueba. I was just mixing myself a Martini and I heard it on the television. The bottle of gin falls out of my hand. Some friends were there and I said, "Did you hear that? God? Put me in the class of D. W. Griffith or Murnau, but God?"

S B :   I think it is only proper.
B W :   Pat, my dear, it was absolutely wonderful to meet you. Let's talk again about films and about the Eameses. Saul, it is always wonderful to see you. I

can't thank you enough for this wonderful luncheon and good conversation. It has been delightful talking about movies with people who care about them. It would be lovely to stay longer. There is so much to talk about. I believe that film-makers have not even begun to scratch the surface of what film can do—there are so many possibilities. But I'm late already and I have an appointment before I have to get back to finish a script. You see, I do still enjoy writing the scripts, it's just the producers who won't let me do what I want with them.

An Interview with Billy Wilder

BURT PRELUTSKY/1996

BP: *What sort of home did you grow up in?*

BW: I was born in a small town in the old Austrian-Hungarian empire, and we moved to Vienna when I was four. All I ever wanted to be was a writer, although my middle-class parents wanted me to be a lawyer or a doctor. My father was a businessman and, in his own way, a kind of dreamer. But business did not appeal to me. My family were not theatergoers, and there were very few books or classical records in the house.

BP: *Did you set out to be a screenwriter?*

BW: No, I wanted to work for a newspaper. I had no connections, so I just made the rounds. In those days, in Vienna, there were many papers. One Saturday afternoon I got very lucky. I went up to the third floor of the city's number one tabloid, opened a door and there was the theater critic fucking his secretary. She ran out of the room while he fiddled with his buttons. This was before zippers became popular. He asked me what I wanted, and I told him I was looking for a job. And he said, "You're lucky I was working overtime today."

Newspaper work moved me in the right direction. I went to Berlin to write a piece on Paul Whiteman, who was touring Europe with his band, and I never went back to Vienna. It was in Germany that I began writing scripts. They were silent movies in those days, but I enjoyed writing them even though it was just action.

From *Michigan Quarterly Review*, Winter 1996. Reprinted by permission of Burt Prelutsky.

B P: *I have heard rumors that, during your years in Berlin, you occasionally moon-lighted as a gigolo.*

B W: You could say that. I called myself a dancer. Of course, if I ran into people I knew, I would always say I was doing research for a newspaper story. I wasn't the best dancer, but I had the best dialogue.

The German ladies were usually old and pretty fat, and just wanted someone who'd dance with them at teatime or after dinner.

B P: *And did they give you money?*

B W: Sometimes. Or I'd be dancing with, say, Mrs. Landau, and I'd say, "Mrs. Landau, I think this might be our last dance. My shoes are wearing out." And the next day, I'd receive dozens of her husband's worn shoes.

I was very popular because I had an American girlfriend and she taught me the Charleston. At the time, there were not many of us in Germany who could do it.

B P: *When did you leave Germany?*

B W: The day after the Reichstag fire, I left for Paris. From there, I went to Hollywood. Even without the Nazis, I think I would have wound up in Hollywood. But not so quickly.

B P: *As a reporter in Berlin, did you ever have occasion to interview Hitler?*

B W: No. In fact, I only saw him once. It was at a movie premiere. I looked over and there he was, seated in the loge of honor. I always say I would have shot him, except for two small details—no revolver and no guts.

B P: *Did you come to America fluent in English?*

B W: No. In school, I had to study Latin, but I had the choice between French and English and, like a fool, I took French.

I arrived in Hollywood when I was 28. It took me about two years before I found myself thinking in English. The accent, of course, I was stuck with. If you come after the age of 12, you don't lose it. In the beginning, I wrote my scripts in German, and somebody would translate them.

B P: *How did you come to collaborate with Charles Brackett?*

B W: In 1938, I was under contract at Paramount, earning $150 a week. There were about 140 of us writers delivering 10 or 11 pages every Thursday to a studio executive named Manny Wolf. One day, Wolf called me into his office. It seemed they needed someone to write *Bluebeard's Eighth Wife* for Ernst Lubitsch. For some reason, Wolf decided to team me up with Brackett.

I thought it was a fine idea. I already had great respect for Brackett. He was much older than me and had written several novels and many fine pieces for the *Saturday Evening Post*.

B P : *You wrote with Brackett for a quarter of a century and then another twenty with I. A. L. Diamond. Did you feel you lacked something in your writing or were there other reasons that you always chose to write in tandem?*
B W : I had no confidence when I was first starting out because I only knew English from going to the movies. After Brackett and I split up, I found it too lonely to write by myself.

B P : *How did you work with your partners? Would you each write a different scene?*
B W : No, we always wrote together in the same room. I'd write on a big legal pad and the other one would sit at the typewriter.

B P : *I realize I'm jumping ahead more than a dozen years but why did you and Brackett dissolve what had turned into the most critically-acclaimed, commercially-successful partnership Hollywood had ever seen?*
B W : It was like with a match and matchbook. Something had worn out and the spark was missing. Besides, it was becoming like a bad marriage by then. We had begun squabbling over every little thing.

B P : *There is an old joke about a starlet who was so stupid that she slept with the screenwriter. Did the truth inherent in that joke in any way make you decide to become a director in 1942?*
B W : I didn't become a director to get prettier girls. I have always thought of myself primarily as a writer. The problem was that the directors weren't shooting what Charley and I wrote. Mitchell Leisen, who directed three of ours, would skip lines, even leave out half scenes, and not be the least bit concerned. I'd go on the set and watch Leisen with horror. Then when I'd complain, he'd have me removed bodily from the sound stage. I remember once looking for Leisen to discuss a scene we had written, and I found him in the wardrobe room counting pleats on a dress with Edith Head. You know

you're in big trouble when your director would rather count pleats than discuss characters.

In the theater, when you're a playwright, you sit in the second row at rehearsals and the actors ask your permission to change "usually" to "frequently." But in Hollywood, when you're a writer, you're just a pisher.

When people ask me if it's important that a director can write, I say it's not so important. What's essential is that he can read.

B P : *How did you convince Paramount to take a chance on a fellow who could do both?*

B W : Preston Sturges had just made the transition, so I was able to persuade them to give me a shot. You have to remember, movies weren't such a big deal then. I mean, Paramount would produce 50 a year and, because they owned their own theaters, they could pretty much guarantee that none of them would do too badly. Besides, I was of value to the studio as a writer. So Paramount figured, they'd keep me happy, I'd do something artsy-fartsy and fall on my face. Then I'd go back to my typewriter, keep my mouth shut and that would be that!

B P : *Instead you turned out one of the biggest hits of the year, the comedy smash* The Major and the Minor.

B W : Yes, I was very lucky with the casting on that one. Ginger Rogers had just won her Oscar for *Kitty Foyle.* How often does a director get last year's Academy Award winner for his first movie?

An interesting thing about the movie that most people don't seem to pick up on is that, 20 years before *Lolita* came along, this was the story of a man who gets a hard-on every time he looks at this woman he *thinks* is a 12-year-old.

B P : *You wrote* Double Indemnity *with Raymond Chandler, instead of Brackett. Why was that?*

B W : That was entirely Brackett's decision. He wasn't comfortable with the subject matter. He wasn't the only one. I had a hell of a time getting a male lead. I confess I even sunk so low as to offer the part to George Raft. After I told him he story, he was confused. He said, "I don't get it. Where's the lapel scene?" Then it was my turn to be confused. "What's a lapel scene?" "You know," he said, "that's where I turn over my lapel and there's a badge, and I arrest the dame for knocking off her husband."

When I explained there couldn't be a lapel scene because that character had helped the woman kill her husband, Raft turned around and walked away.

I went over the Paramount contract list and saw Fred MacMurray's name. After he read the script, he also turned me down. He said he couldn't do it because he'd actually have to act. For years, he'd only done very light comedies. But I told him not to worry. I told him he'd play the role just like the saxophone player he used to be. And he did, and he was perfect.

B P : *Didn't you have to work around the censorship codes in* Double Indemnity? *I assume, for example, that when Stanwyck visits MacMurray at his apartment the first time, they have sex.*
B W : Of course, and very good sex, or how could she persuade such a man to kill her husband? I learned from Lubitsch that the scene between the two lovers the next morning tells you much more about their sexual behavior than actually showing them having sex, and pushes the story forward. Now when you see a sex scene, it's usually so hard to figure out what's happening. Is that her elbow? Is that his shoulder?

B P : *The following year you and Brackett swept the major Oscars with* The Lost Weekend. *Were you surprised that such a grim story would do so well?*
B W : I think we did so well partly because they didn't give me any Oscars for *Double Indemnity* in 1944. So, in '45, they made up for it.

It's very gratifying when you win because for maybe three days your agent can get you more money. It's also a validation of the work. Not as good as box office success, but still very nice.

All in all an Oscar is a very good thing. It helps in the business and it also helps in the community.

B P : *How so?*
B W : The dentist looks down. "That's an Oscar-winner in the chair," he says to himself. Maybe he's a little more careful with the drill.

B P : *You mentioned money. Do you feel you were well-paid for your efforts?*

BW: I am very well off but not from the movies. I only made really big money by selling off my art collection and by betting against the Rams.

BP: *All through your career, you've fluctuated between drama and comedy. Obviously you were skilled at both. How did you determine what sort of story to tackle next?*

BW: People see a comedy, and they assume you were in a good mood when you made it. Wrong. With me, when I'm in a good mood, I wrote a drama. In a depression, in order to feel better, I do farce.

BP: *There were two of your movies which I feel were hurt by inappropriate casting. They were* Love in the Afternoon *with Gary Cooper and* Sabrina *with Humphrey Bogart. Am I wrong in thinking that, good as they usually were, Cooper and Bogart were not ideal casting choices?*

BW: We agree. In both cases, I very much wanted Cary Grant. Although he and I were friends, he never wanted to work with me. I don't know why. Maybe it was my accent.

Unfortunately, Bogart knew he was my second choice. All through the shooting of *Sabrina,* he would bring up Cary Grant. He was very mean to me, and I was very annoyed with him. For that role, after all, who wouldn't have wanted Cary Grant? But, when Bogart was dying, I went to visit him at his home. He was very brave and, in the end, I forgave him everything and held him in the highest esteem.

BP: *Have there been other occasions when you had to settle for your second choice? Other times when you had to consider writing in a lapel scene in order to nab George Raft?*

BW: Fortunately, things never got quite that bad. But there were times when we didn't get who we wanted. For instance, we had Montgomery Clift lined up for *Sunset Boulevard* but at the last second, his agent reneged on the deal and we had to sign William Holden, then a young actor under contract to Paramount. I still don't know why Clift backed out that way.

BP: *Wasn't it because of his longtime relationship with the blues singer, Libby Holman, who was twice Clift's age? As I understood it, she had pressured him to turn down the role because she was afraid people would assume that Norma Desmond and Joe Gillis were based on her and Clift.*

B W : Fascinating. I'd never heard that. For *Sunset Boulevard* I thought of Mae West, but I dismissed the notion. The age discrepancy was right, but it would have made it a comedy and we would have lost the tragic overtones. And then I realized that it would be best to have an actress who had never appeared in sound pictures. I thought of Pola Negri, and then of Gloria Swanson.

Now, for *The Apartment* I had signed Paul Douglas to play the head of the insurance company. But, three days before the shooting began, he had a heart attack. So I called Fred MacMurray. He absolutely refused. He said he made movies for Disney and he had his wholesome family image to consider, and he would be ruined if he played this terrible adulterer. But I talked him into it, and it didn't ruin anything.

The next time I had to replace an actor, it was Peter Sellers, who had a heart attack during *Kiss Me, Stupid*. We got Ray Walston, who is a fine actor, but is no Peter Sellers. The movie was a dog. With Sellers it would have been five percent better. So it would only have been 95% of a bomb.

B P : *After* Sunset Boulevard *Charles Brackett went off to write and produce on his own. You teamed up with I. A. L. Diamond. After all those years with one man, what were you looking for in a new collaborator?*
B W : The point of collaboration is that the two guys have to respect each other, but not think alike. If they agree on everything, it's pointless. You have to be conciliatory and respectful, and I had to remember not to throw my weight around just because I was producing and directing. When it came to the writing, there was no fighting. If we didn't agree on a scene or a line, we just went on to find something we were both nuts about.

Of Diamond, my wife Audrey said, "He's the best collaborator there ever was with the possible exception of Quisling."

B P : *Which of your movies do you like the most?*
B W : The big hits mostly, although I'm not too ashamed of *Ace in the Hole*, which didn't do very well. I'd say *The Apartment* was the picture with the least mistakes.

I constantly rewrite my movies in my mind. But with *The Apartment*, not so much as with some of the others.

I also liked *Double Indemnity, Some Like It Hot, Sabrina,* and *Sunset Boulevard.*

B P : *Financially, your greatest success was* Irma la Douce, *but you neglected to mention it.*

B W : Yes, it was a huge hit. But I'm not sure why. It was a very hard movie to do and it didn't come out quite the way I wanted. It's nothing to be ashamed of, but it's not a movie I think about too much.

B P : Irma *was originally a French and Broadway musical but you removed the songs. That's interesting because, on four occasions, you have written movies which were later turned into Broadway musicals.*

B W : Four? I can only think of three. There was *Sunset Boulevard,* of course, and *The Apartment,* which became *Promises, Promises,* and *Some Like It Hot,* which they turned into *Sugar.* What else?

B P : Ninotchka *was the basis for* Silk Stockings.

B W : Oh, yes. That one I never saw.

B P : *You're not a fan of Cole Porter's?*

B W : I'm his biggest fan, but *Ninotchka* was made for Greta Garbo. And there's no way Hildegard Neff [sometimes Knef] could be Garbo.

B P : *You did see* Sunset Boulevard, *though. . . .*

B W : Yes. I don't make any money off it, but Mr. Lloyd Webber, who's a very gracious man, invited me to the openings in London and New York. I think it's a very good show, and would make a hell of a movie.

B P : *One of my favorite movie trivia questions involves you. Six people who have, themselves, directed movies, have appeared in movies you've written.*

B W : Let me think. There's DeMille and von Stroheim in *Sunset Boulevard.* And Mitchell Leisen in *Hold Back the Dawn.* Did you say there are three others?

B P : *Otto Preminger in* Stalag 17, *Jack Lemmon, who directed* Kotch, *and Charles Laughton, who directed* Night of the Hunter.

B W : Very good, I forgot about the two actors. They were very smart. They tried it once and it was enough.

B P : *Do you have any unproduced scripts lying around in your files?*

B W :   No, I'm too practical. I only wrote scripts when people were paying me. What I do have are a lot of ideas jotted down. Once, such a note came in very handy. I had just finished making *Some Like It Hot* and couldn't wait to make another movie with Jack Lemmon. He is wonderful to work with and very talented. So, even before *Hot* was released, I started to figure out what we could do next. I went to my drawer of ideas and on a little piece of paper was written "David Lean's *Brief Encounter*—What about the guy who owned the flat where the lovers met?" Remember? Trevor Howard had a friend who let him use his flat. So, that little note to myself got me thinking. And that's how Izzy Diamond and I came to write *The Apartment*.

B P :   *After 1963, with the possible exception of* The Fortune Cookie, *none of your movies enjoyed either acclaim or box office success. They were* Kiss Me, Stupid, The Private Life of Sherlock Holmes, Avanti!, The Front Page, Fedora *and* Buddy Buddy. *What happened?*
B W :   Maybe I lost the spark. I, myself, liked *Sherlock Holmes* very much. I thought it was a beautiful film, but it was not well received. I think part of the reason is that I had to go to Paris, and while I was away the studio cut out twenty minutes.

I should not have made *The Front Page,* though. That was a big mistake. Never do a remake. People remember the original and, with the passing of time, they remember it as much better than it was. The only movie that was ever improved was *An American Tragedy,* which George Stevens remade brilliantly as *A Place in the Sun. That* was a very fine film.

B P :   *Another exception was* The Maltese Falcon. *They made lousy versions a couple of times before John Huston got it right. Who were your role models?*
B W :   I learned from early Chaplin, from Renoir, from Fellini, from Pietro Germi, from von Stroheim, and, of course, from Lubitsch.

B P :   *Who are the younger directors you admire?*
B W :   Among the best things ever shot were Coppola's first two *Godfather* movies and the first half of Kubrick's *Full Metal Jacket.* Scorsese is marvelous and Jonathan Demme is wonderful.

B P :   *You made two movies with Marilyn Monroe. Are you as astonished as I am that, three decades after her death, there remains this unquenchable fascination with the woman?*

B W :   It boggles the mind. When I was in Vienna, in the '20s, every week in the Sunday supplements there was a new story about what really happened at Mayerling with Prince Rudolf of Hapsburg and his mistress, Marie Vetsera. Did they commit suicide in 1888 or didn't they? And did she really go off with him knowing what was in store, because it's always better to go to a hunting lodge and die with a prince than go to the Riviera with some schmuck? If so, she was the "ultimate social climber."

In any case, it was a lot more interesting than Marilyn Monroe, and even that became too much. I swear, if I see one more theory about her death, I'll scream.

You know all the stories about Marilyn Monroe. How she would keep cast and crew and 300 extras waiting all day and then show up at 3 p.m. or 5 p.m. And yet I would gladly have made another movie with her. The camera loved her, the people loved her. She had It.

B P :   *I think that the biggest laugh of* Some Like It Hot *was the last line.*

B W :   We were set to film that last scene on a Monday, and weren't satisfied how to close it. What could Jack Lemmon say to Joe E. Brown after he gets a proposal, and what on earth would Brown say back to him? When Lemmon finally announces he's not a girl, Brown says . . . "Nobody's perfect." That was Diamond's suggestion, and I said, that's good but maybe we can do better, let's think about it over the weekend. On Monday we didn't have a better line. Who knew it would become so famous?

B P :   *Do you do any writing now that I. A. L. Diamond is gone?*

B W :   A few things, but I don't finish them. I find I miss having a collaborator, a soundingboard, someone whose taste and ideas I respect. Also, having a collaborator makes you come in on time. Now, when I hit an obstacle, I just go on to something else.

I'd still like to make one or two more pictures. It would be a glorious way to go. Actually, making a movie is not so difficult; what's hard is making a deal. How can I go in and pitch an idea to an ex-William Morris mailboy?

B P :   *Which are the movies you wish you'd made?*

B W : Top of the list, *The Battleship Potemkin,* then *The Bicycle Thief, Seduced and Abandoned,* Lubitsch's *The Shop Around the Corner,* Fellini's *La Dolce Vita,* and a couple of Ingmar Bergman's films. But I could not have done what they did. Those directors all had their own handwriting. Particularly Lubitsch.

B P : *Did you and Lubitsch emigrate together?*
B W : No, we were friends, but he came in the '20s which is when the really talented people came over from Europe. I didn't come until '34. My group just wanted to escape the ovens.

But I lived with Lubitsch for a while. He was not only very talented and unique, he was an outstanding man. He had this very sophisticated French humor, but he, himself, was the son of a Russian tailor.

B P : *Has money been important?*
B W : Not very much. I have always lived modestly. I never had a house in Palm Springs or a boat on the Riviera. No excess. What money I spent went into art.

B P : *Most of which you auctioned off in 1989. What made you part with a collection that was regarded as one of the finest in Hollywood?*
B W : It just seemed the right time. I donated some of it to the museum in Jerusalem, and I let Christie's auction off most of the rest. Partly, I was calling their bluff. People kept telling me that prices had never before been so high, and I was a little curious.

B P : *How much did it sell for?*
B W : About $34,000,000.

B P : *Who are the people you wish you'd met?*
B W : I would have liked to have met Proust and Mozart. I have known a lot of people, of course . . . Steinbeck, Stravinsky, Thomas Mann, even Freud, who kicked me out of his apartment. If you have a good constitution and a good doctor, you will eventually get to meet a lot of people.

B P : *What did you say to irritate Freud?*

BW: It wasn't anything personal. He just hated journalists. In 1926, in Vienna, very few people had been analyzed, and the newspapers were always making fun of Freud. So when I went to his apartment to interview him, he tossed me out on general principle. I did get to see the couch though. It was very small.

BP: *Would you advise a loved one to follow in your footsteps?*
BW: No. I'd tell him to go do something else—maybe be a landscape architect. With the movies, you not only have to be talented, you have to be very, very lucky.

INDEX

CONVERSATIONS WITH FILMMAKERS SERIES
PETER BRUNETTE, GENERAL EDITOR

The collected interviews with notable modern directors, including

Robert Altman • Theo Angelopolous • Bernardo Bertolucci • Jane Campion • George Cukor • Clint Eastwood • John Ford • Jean-Luc Godard • Peter Greenaway • John Huston • Jim Jarmusch • Elia Kazan • Stanley Kubrick • Spike Lee • Mike Leigh • George Lucas • John Sayles • Martin Scorsese • Steven Soderbergh • Steven Spielberg • Oliver Stone • Quentin Tarantino • Orson Welles • Zhang Yimou

Lightning Source UK Ltd.
Milton Keynes UK
UKHW02f0208210318
319799UK00001B/112/P